AN ALBUM FOR AMERICANS

AN ALBUM FOR AMERICANS

Edited by
David H. Appel

Foreword by Hon. Walter H. Annenberg
Former U.S. Ambassador to Great Britain

Introduction by Henry Steele Commager

Triangle Publications, Inc.

CROWN PUBLISHERS, INC.   New York

"Bringing Down the Captain's Body," from *Brave Men* by Ernie Pyle.
Reprinted by permission of United Press International.

Copyright © 1983 by Triangle Publications, Inc.
Introduction copyright © 1983 by Henry Steele Commager

Published by Crown Publishers, Inc., One Park
Avenue, New York, New York 10016 and simultaneously in Canada
by General Publishing Company Limited
Manufactured in the United States of America

Library of Congress Cataloging in Publication Data
An Album for Americans.

   1. Patriotism—United States—Addresses, essays, lectures. I. Appel, David H.
JK1759.A36   1983   323.6'5'0973   82-18288
ISBN:0-517-54374-5

Book design by Jacques Chazaud

10 9 8 7 6 5 4 3 2 1

First Edition

Illustrations: Sources and Acknowledgments

We wish to acknowledge the following sources for the use of their illustrations and photographs in this book:
P. ii, frontispiece, Statue of Liberty, United Press International (UPI); p. xviii, The White House, White House Historical Association (WHHA); p. xix, The U.S. Capitol, UPI; p. xx, Supreme Court Building, UPI; p. 1, Liberty Bell, National Park Service (Richard Frear); p. 2, Christopher Columbus, Metropolitan Museum of Art, Gift of J. Pierpont Morgan; 5, Columbian Exposition Stamps, National Philatelic Collections, Smithsonian Institution; p. 6, *lower left*, Pilgrims at Plymouth, from the Collections of The Library of Congress (L.C.); p. 6, *right*, *Signing the Social Compact in the Cabin of the Mayflower* (LC); p. 7, *Landing of Roger Williams*, Museum of Art, Rhode Island School of Design; p. 9, Andrew Hamilton (LC); p. 12, *Boston Massacre* (LC); p. 13, *The Destruction of Tea at Boston Harbor*, Currier & Ives lithograph (LC); p. 15, Patrick Henry (LC); p. 17, *Midnight Ride of Paul Revere*, Metropolitan Museum of Art, Arthur H. Hearn Fund; p. 19, *The Battle of Lexington* (LC); p. 20, statue, *Minute Man of Concord*, National Park Service (Richard Frear); p. 23, George Washington (Charles Willson Peale), Metropolitan Museum of Art, Gift of Collis B. Huntington; p. 24, George Washington at the age of forty (Charles Willson Peale) (LC); p. 26, Martha Washington (Gilbert Stuart), Boston Museum of Fine Arts and National Portrait Gallery, Smithsonian Institution; p. 27, George Washington (Gilbert Stuart), Boston Museum of Fine Arts and National Portrait Gallery, Smithsonian Institution (UPI); p. 29, John Hancock, Boston Museum of Fine Arts, copyright © 1978 all rights reserved; *bottom*, *Signing of The Declaration*, National Archives (NA); p. 32, Abigail Adams (Gilbert Stuart), National Gallery of Art, gift of Mrs. Robert Homans; p. 33, John Adams (J. S. Copley), Fogg Art Museum, Cambridge, Mass.; p. 34, Independence Hall (UPI); p. 35, The Liberty Bell (UPI); p. 37, *The Spirit of '76* (LC); pp. 38–39, *Washington Crossing the Delaware* (Emanuel Leutze), Metropolitan Museum of Art, Gift of John Steward Kennedy; p. 40, *top*, Nathan Hale (LC); p. 40 *bottom*, Molly Pitcher (LC); p. 41, *top to bottom*, Lafayette, Independence National Historical Park Collection; Baron von Steuben, National Archives; Kosciusko (LC); Pulaski, National Archives; p. 42, *The Birth of Our Nations Flag*, Betsy Ross House, Philadelphia, Pa.; p. 43, Washington at Valley Forge (LC); p. 44, Thomas Paine, National Gallery of Art; p. 47, *The Surrender of Cornwallis at Yorktown* (John Trumbull), Architect of the U.S. Capitol; p. 48, Washington resigning his commission, (John Trumbull); p. 49, Declaration of Independence (LC); p. 50, Benjamin Franklin, White House Historical Association; p. 52, Alexander Hamilton (LC); p. 53, *Scene at the Signing of the Constitution* (LC); p. 54, *top*, John Langdon, Independence National Historical Park Collection; p. 54, *middle*, Rufus King, Yale University Art Gallery; p. 54 *bottom*, Roger Sherman, Yale University Art Gallery; p. 55, *top*, Thomas Mifflin, Independence National Historical Park Collection; p. 55, *middle*, Jared Ingersoll, Independence National Historical Park Collection; p. 55, *bottom*, James Wilson, National Museum of American Art, Smithsonian Institution; p. 56, *top to bottom*, John Dickinson, Independence National Historical Park Collection; Richard Bassett, Baltimore Museum of Art, Bequest of Helen Bayard; James McHenry, Independence National Historical Park Collection; James Madison, Thomas Gilcrease Institute of American History and Art, Tulsa, Okla.; p. 57, *top to bottom*, William Blount, Tennessee State Museum, Tennessee Historical Society Collection; Richard Dobbs Spaight, Sr., Independence National Historical Park Collection; Pierce Butler (LC); William Few, Independence National Historical Park Collection; p. 60, George Washington takes the presidential oath, (LC); p. 64, Mount Vernon, Virginia State Travel Service; p. 67, Washington Monument, National Park Service (Jonathan Scott Arms); p.70, Monticello, Virginia State Travel Service; p. 71, statue, Thomas Jefferson, (LC); p. 72, Jefferson Memorial (UPI); p. 74, John Paul Jones (UPI); p. 75, *top*, Stephen Decatur (LC); p. 75, *bottom*, Oliver Hazard Perry (LC); p. 76, USS *Constitution*, The Knickerbocker Club, New York; p. 77, Francis Scott Key (LC); p. 79, Lewis and Clark (Frederick Remington) (LC); pp. 80–81, *Daniel Boone Escorting Settlers through the Cumberland Gap* (Bingham), Washington University Gallery of Art, St. Louis, Mo.; p. 82, *Independence and the Opening of the West* (Thomas Hart Benton), Harry S Truman Library, Independence, Mo.; p. 84, James Monroe (LC); p. 85, Andrew Jackson, National Portrait Gallery, Smithsonian Institution; p. 86, Davy Crockett (LC); Davy Crockett at the Alamo (LC); Sam Houston (Washington Cooper), Tennessee State Museum; p. 88, Daniel Webster, Boston Museum of Fine Arts, copyright © 1982; music cover, "America" or "My Country 'tis of Thee" (LC); p. 89, ship figurehead (LC); *Flying Cloud*, The Bettmann Archives; p. 91, *left*, *The Boy Lincoln* (Eastman Johnson) (LC); p. 91, *right*, young Abraham Lincoln (Jean L. G. Ferris) (LC); p. 93, Lincoln-Douglas Debate (LC); p. 95, Lincoln on Horseback (LC); p. 97, *left*, Lincoln profile (LC); p. 97, *right*, Lincoln portrait (LC); p. 98. Lincoln's inauguration (LC); p. 101, *The Last Moments of John Brown*, Metropolitan Museum of Art, gift of Mr. and Mrs. Carl Stoeckl; p. 102, Barbara Frietchie (LC); p. 104, "Burnt District" of Richmond (LC); p. 105, Lincoln and his generals (Mathew Brady), National Archives; p. 106, *top*, William Techumseh Sherman, National Archives; p. 106, *bottom*, George B. McClellan, National Portrait Gallery, Smithsonian Institution; p. 107, *top*, George Gordon Meade (LC); p. 107, *bottom*, Ulysses S. Grant, National Portrait Gallery, Smithsonian Institution; p. 109, a Beecher family group (LC); p. 110, A sharpshooter of the Army of the Potomac (Winslow Homer), National Collection of Fine Arts, Smithsonian Institution; p. 111, *top*, Julia Ward Howe, National Portrait Gallery, Smithsonian Institution; p. 111, *center, left*, music cover, "Maryland Maryland" (LC); p. 111, *center*, music cover, "Tramp Tramp Tramp" (LC); p. 111, *center right*, music cover, "Battle Hymn of the Republic" (LC); p. 111 *bottom*, George Frederick Root (LC); p. 112, The Emancipation Proclamation (LC); p. 113, President Lincoln reading the first draft of the Emancipation Proclamation to his Cabinet, (John Trumbull), p. 114, Pickett's Charge, The Bettmann Archives; p. 115, Pickett's Charge, The Bettmann Archives; p. 116, Lincoln delivering Gettysburg Address, The Bettmann Archives; p. 119, Lincoln's Second Inaugural (LC); p. 121, Lee surrendering to Grant, National Park Service; p. 122, General Lee, National Archives; p. 124, music cover, "I Wish I Was in Dixie's Land (LC); p. 125, Jefferson Davis, National Portrait Gallery, Smithsonian Institution; p. 126, Lincoln Memorial (Cecil W. Stoughton), National Park Service; Lincoln Statue (Cecil W. Stoughton), National Park Service; p. 128, 129, Lincoln Memorial (Cecil W. Stoughton), National Park Service; p. 130, Walt Whitman (LC); p. 132, Chinese immigrants (LC); p. 133, *top*, Irish immigrants (LC); p. 133, *center*, immigrants registering, Castle Garden (LC); p. 133, *bottom*, immigrants arriving at Castle Garden (LC); p. 134, The National Chorus, *Life* magazine, July 4, 1912; p. 136, music cover, "The Stars and Stripes Forever," Courtesy of Lester Levy; p. 137, *left*, music cover, "El Capitan March," Courtesy of Lester Levy; p. 137, *right*, music cover, "Semper Fidelis March," Courtesy of Lester Levy; pp. 138–139, America's largest flag, Peter B. Kaplan; p. 141, midnight parade in Philadelphia (LC); p. 142, Chicago World's Fair, Culver Pictures, Inc.; p. 144, Corliss Engine (LC); p. 145, 1904 St. Louis Fair, National Archives; p. 146, Statue of Liberty, UPI; p. 148, head of the Statue of Lib-

erty (LC); p. 149, immigrants view Statue of Liberty (LC); p. 150, *Commodore Dewey at the Battle of Manila Bay*, State House, Montpelier, Vt.; p. 152, Teddy Roosevelt San Juan Hill (LC); pp. 154–155, Grand Canyon (Thomas Moran), The Smithsonian Institution; pp. 156–157, Niagara Falls (John Vanderlyn), Boston Museum of Fine Arts; pp. 158–159, *lower left*, wheat fields, U.S. Department of Agriculture; pp. 158–159, *center*, orange groves, National Park Service; p. 159, *right*, Acadia Country (Richard Frear), National Park Service; p. 160, *The Cowpuncher* (Remington) (LC); p. 161, "An Arizona Home" (LC); p. 162, Buffalo Bill Cody (LC); p. 163, Buffalo Bill's Wild West (LC); p. 164, *Grandma Moses Fourth of July*, The White House; p. 165, *top*, *Grandma Moses Going to the Big City*, Grandma Moses Properties Co., copyright © 1979; p. 165, *bottom*, *Thanksgiving Turkey*, Grandma Moses Properties Co., copyright © 1983; p. 168, Woodrow Wilson, National Portrait Gallery, Smithsonian Institution; p. 170, New York City children salute the flag (LC); p. 172, General Pershing, National Portrait Gallery, Smithsonian Institution, Gift of International Business Machines Corporation; p. 173, Sergeant Alvin C. York, National Archives; p. 174, "The Marine's Hymn" (LC); p. 175, "The Yankee Doodle Dandy" (LC); p. 177, Ratification of Nineteenth Amendment (LC); p. 178, *top*, *right*, Big Bill Tilden (LC); p. 178, *bottom*, *right*, Jack Dempsey (LC); p. 178, *center*, *left*, Commander Richard E. Byrd, National Portrait Gallery, Smithsonian Institution; p. 179, Colonel Charles A. Lindbergh (LC); p. 181, Black Thursday (LC); p. 182, Franklin Delano Roosevelt taking the oath of office, Acme Photo; p. 183, President Roosevelt with cigarette holder, Wide World Photos; p. 185, President Roosevelt, National Archives; p. 187, *top*, Federal Theatre *One Third of a Nation*, George Mason University; p. 187, *bottom*, *Composition* (Stuart Davis), National Museum of American Art, Smithsonian Institution; p. 189, Four Freedoms Stamp, U.S. Postal Service; p. 190, *top*, *Freedom of Speech* (Norman Rockwell), Curtis Publishing Company; p. 190, *bottom*, *Freedom of Worship* (Norman Rockwell), Curtis Publishing Company; p. 191, *top*, *Freedom from Fear* (Norman Rockwell), Curtis Publishing Company; p. 191, *bottom*, *Freedom from Want* (Norman Rockwell), Curtis Publishing Company; p. 192, USS *Shaw* (Pearl Harbor), National Archives; p. 193, President Franklin Delano Roosevelt (LC); p. 194, USS *Arizona* Memorial, U.S. Navy Photographic Center; p. 195, General Eisenhower, National Archives; p. 196, *top*, General Douglas MacArthur, National Archives; p. 196, *center*, General Patton, National Archives; p. 196; *bottom*, Admiral Halsey, National Archives; p. 197, *top*, Admiral King, National Archives, p. 197, *center*, Admiral Nimitz, National Archives, p. 197, *bottom*, General Wainwright, National Archives; p. 198, *top*, General Marshall, National Archives, p. 198, *center*, General Omar Nelson Bradley (LC); p. 198, bottom, General "Hap" Arnold (LC); p. 199, USS *Yorktown*, National Archives; p. 200, *top*, USS *Greer*, National Archives; p. 200, *bottom*, U.S. Army crossing the Remagen Bridge, National Archives; p. 201, *top*, U.S. Coast Guard: Normandy, National Archives; p. 201, *bottom*, old German woman—Seventh Army, National Archives, p. 202, The Iwo Jima flag raising (Joe Rosenthal), Wide World Photos; p. 204, *top*, Rosie the Riveter (Norman Rockwell), *Saturday Evening Post*, copyright 1943; p. 204, *bottom*, Women on artillery line, copyright © King Features Syndicate, Inc., World Rights protected; bottom, Schoolchildren in parade, (LC); p. 205, *top* Boyscouts with Flags, (LC); bottom, Schoolchildren in parade, (LC); p. 206, The homecoming GI (Norman Rockwell), *Saturday Evening Post*; p. 207, *left*, "Praise the Lord and Pass the Ammunition" (LC); *right*, The Army Air Corps (LC); p. 208, General MacArthur and troops (LC); p. 210, Cadets marching—West Point, U.S. Army; p. 212, MacArthur statue, U.S. Army photograph; p. 215, Adlai Stevenson, Wide World Photos; p. 217, Dwight D. Eisenhower (LC); p. 219, John F. Kennedy swearing oath of office, U.S. Army photograph; p. 221, John F. Kennedy portrait, National Portrait Gallery, Smithsonian Institution; p. 223, John-John Kennedy saluting, UPI; p. 224, *left*, Operation Oregon (chopper), U.S. Army photograph; p. 224, *right*, Operation Baker—soldier, U.S. Army photograph; p. 225, *top*, The Vietnam War memorial, Smithsonian Institution; p. 225, *bottom*, Operation Sail (bicentennial), Photo Researchers, Inc., copyright © Ray Ellis 1976; p. 226, the moon landing, UPI; p. 227, *top*, Flags at Hermitage, UPI; p. 227, *bottom*, U.S. hockey team, UPI; p. 228, space shuttle blast-off, NASA: p. 229, space shuttle *Columbia* lands, NASA; p. 228, seal of the President, UPI; p. 331, The Oval Office, White House Historical Association (WHHA); p. 232, *top*, George Washington, WHHA; p. 232, *bottom*, John Adams, WHHA; p. 233, *top*, Thomas Jefferson, WHHA; p. 233, *bottom*, James Madison, WHHA; p. 234, *top*, James Monroe, WHHA; p. 234, *bottom*, John Quincy Adams, WHHA; p. 235, *top*, Andrew Jackson, WHHA; p. 235, *bottom*, Martin Van Buren, WHHA; p. 236, *top*, William Henry Harrison, WHHA; p. 236, *bottom*, John Tyler; WHHA; p. 237, *top*, James K. Polk, WHHA; p. 237, *bottom*, Zachary Taylor, WHHA; p. 238, *top*, Millard Fillmore, WHHA; p. 238, *bottom*, Franklin Pierce, WHHA; p. 239, *top*, James Buchanan, WHHA; p. 239, *bottom*, Abraham Lincoln, WHHA; p. 240, *top*, Andrew Johnson, WHHA; p. 240 bottom, Ulysses S. Grant, WHHA; p. 241, *top*, Rutherford B. Hayes, WHHA; p. 241, *bottom*, James A. Garfield, WHHA; p. 242, *top*, Chester A. Arthur, WHHA; p. 242, *bottom*, Grover Cleveland, WHHA; p. 243, *top*, Benjamin Harrison, WHHA; p. 243, *bottom*, William McKinley; p. 244, *top*, Theodore Roosevelt, WHHA; p. 244, *bottom*, William H. Taft, WHHA; p. 245, *top*, Woodrow Wilson, WHHA; p. 245, *bottom*, Warren G. Harding, WHHA; p. 246, *top*, Calvin Coolidge, WHHA, p. 246, *bottom*, Herbert Hoover, WHHA; p. 247, *top*, Franklin D. Roosevelt, WHHA; p. 247, *bottom*, Harry S Truman, WHHA; p. 248, *top*, Dwight D. Eisenhower, WHHA; p. 248, *bottom*, John F. Kennedy, WHHA; p. 249, *top*, Lyndon B. Johnson WHHA; p. 249, *bottom*, Richard M. Nixon, WHHA; p. 250, *top*, Gerald R. Ford, WHHA; p. 250, *bottom*, Jimmy (James Earl) Carter, WHHA; p. 251, Ronald W. Reagan, WHHA; p. 253, Famous Flags in American History, Encyclopedia Britannica; p. 256, Flags of the States, Encyclopedia Britannica; p. 257, Flags of the States, Encyclopedia Britannica; p. 258, The Congressional Medal of Honor, U.S. Army; p. 259, Armed Forces Decorations and Awards, Navy Photographic Center.

Contents

FOREWORD   *ix*

ACKNOWLEDGMENTS   *x*

INTRODUCTION   *xi*

THE THREE BRANCHES OF GOVERNMENT   *xvii*

1. The Great Adventure Begins   *3*
2. Just and Equal Laws   *6*
3. The Roots of Religious Freedom   *7*
4. Free Press: Pillar of Democracy   *8*
5. The Roots of Revolution   *11*
6. 1775: Year of Decision   *14*
7. Call It Macaroni   *21*
8. Washington: Our First Leader   *22*
9. We Hold These Truths to Be Self-evident . . .   *28*
10. The Difficult Road to Independence   *36*
11. Home-grown Heroes and Friends from Overseas   *40*
12. Betsy Ross: A Flag for a New Nation   *42*
13. Valley Forge: The Darkest Hour   *43*
14. "These Are the Times That Try Men's Souls"   *44*
15. A New Nation Victorious   *47*
16. Franklin and Hamilton: Men Who Charted the Course of a Nation   *50*
17. The Constitution: Cornerstone of the Republic   *53*
18. The First President   *60*
19. First in the Hearts of His Countrymen   *63*
20. "Eternal Hostility Toward Every Form of Tyranny": Thomas Jefferson   *69*
21. Sea of Glory   *74*
22. What So Proudly We Hail   *77*
23. The New Nation Spans a Mighty Continent   *78*
24. Two Presidents Who Helped Shape the Nation   *83*
25. "Remember the Alamo"   *86*
26. Daniel Webster: "Liberty and Union, Now and Forever"   *87*
27. Columbia, the Gem of the Ocean   *89*
28. Honest Abe Lincoln   *90*
29. A House Divided   *92*
30. The Union Must Be Preserved   *96*
31. Two American Heroes   *100*
32. A Nation Torn Asunder   *104*
33. Words to Stir a Nation   *108*
34. Songs of War   *110*
35. "Slavery Must Die That the Nation Might Live"   *112*
36. Gettysburg: A Fusion in Blood   *114*
37. A New Birth of Freedom   *116*

38. With Malice Toward None *119*

39. Surrender at Appomattox *121*

40. To Live and Die for Dixie *123*

41. A Leader Is Lost, but the Nation Survives *127*

42. "I Will Bear True Faith to the United States" *131*

43. America Flexes Its Muscles *134*

44. Stars and Stripes Forever *136*

45. "Meet Me at the Fair . . ." *140*

46. "I Lift My Lamp Beside the Golden Door" *147*

47. "A Splendid Little War" *151*

48. "God Shed His Grace on Thee . . ." *153*

49. Cowboy! *161*

50. The Simple Life: This Land Is Our Land *164*

51. Making the World Safe for Democracy *166*

52. A Great Nation in a Great War *170*

53. The General and the Sergeant *172*

54. From the Halls of Montezuma *174*

55. The Yankee Doodle Dandy *175*

56. America Gets Back on Normalcy Track *176*

57. The American Spirit in Crisis: FDR *180*

58. The Struggle for National Regeneration *186*

59. The Growing Shadow of War *188*

60. Remember Pearl Harbor *192*

61. The Nation's Leaders in War *195*

62. The Images of War *199*

63. Patriotism on the Home Front *204*

64. "Praise the Lord and Pass the Ammunition" *207*

65. "Off We Go into the Wild Blue Yonder" *207*

66. "Duty, Honor, Country" *208*

67. Eloquence in the Service of Patriotism: Stevenson *214*

68. How Shall We Use Our Power?: Eisenhower *216*

69. The Thousand Days of JFK *219*

70. From Disillusion to a New Patriotism *224*

71. The Presidents of the United States *231*

72. Long May It Wave *252*

73. Armed Forces Decorations and Awards *258*

74. A Calendar for Americans *260*

INDEX *266*

Foreword

Patriotism, that bright strand of emotion that runs through the entire fabric of American history, is always nobly marked in our prose and poetry, in our song and art. Its quality, whatever the time or place, is unabashed, forceful, unique. Its effect is to provide a common spirit, a unifying sense of pride in our country.

In recent times, especially during demonstrations against the draft and the war in Vietnam, patriotism came to be criticized as a refuge for hypocrites. It became fashionable in some circles to look with scorn upon those who publicly professed love of country, who spoke with respect of our national institutions and goals. Indeed, for a time, disenchantment with government, with politics, with business, and with our educational system became the norm among certain intellectual and political groups. This disenchantment soon waned with our bicentennial celebrations, with the spontaneous surge of national pride in the American hockey team's defeat of the Soviet team at the Lake Placid Olympic Games, and with the release of fifty-two hostages held for 444 days under disgraceful conditions in Iran.

It was inevitable that after years of neglect there would come a resurgence of patriotism, for throughout our history America has always found its way back from periods of dissension to assert its place in the minds and hearts of its citizens.

When we express the nature of our affection, when we sing "The Star Spangled Banner," our emotions may be no different from those a citizen of Britain may feel when he or she sings "Rule, Britannia," or when a citizen of France sings "La Marseillaise." But we believe we have a special heritage of patriotism. And we do. For ours is a heritage that comes entirely from the people, from ourselves, with no legendary, medieval, or aristocratic sources to lend a historic depth.

We are a comparatively new folk. We have generated our own flags and our own heroes. We may split on a thousand issues, engage in violent political debate at certain times, even listen to doubts about our country's goals. But we know how to close ranks. We find new heroes. We find strength in our own history, short though it may be.

My associates at Triangle Publications, Inc., and I believe—fervently—that a volume of patriotic readings belongs in every citizen's home. It has long been our aim to provide such a volume to support and encourage the much needed resurgence in patriotism we are now enjoying and which we hope will continue to gain momentum. In selecting an editor I felt that David Appel, a writer, editor, and critic with whom I worked for many years on the *Philadelphia Inquirer*, would be eminently qualified and that the distinguished American historian Henry Steele Commager would be the appropriate scholar to act as our consultant.

This book, *An Album for Americans*, reaches into many areas of patriotic expression. It may not be as comprehensive as some would prefer, but I believe it reflects the ways we have found to celebrate our patriotism, to place it in historical perspective, to thrill to it once more.

Wynnewood, Pennsylvania
February 1982

Walter H. Annenberg

Acknowledgments

The following individuals contributed to the development of this book:

Honorable Walter H. Annenberg, who sparked the original idea and supported it with enthusiasm;

Merrill Panitt, who brought his editorial acumen and historical knowledge to focus on this project;

Nahum Waxman, who fashioned the pattern of this book and who capably assumed the role of publishing editor on the death of Herbert Michelman whose early response lifted the idea off the launching pad; James O. Wade who steered it into final orbit;

Joan R. Appel, who assisted me over the rough spots;

Grace E. Evans and John H. Moore, who tracked the illustrations;

Irene H. Leibig, Sue Brook, and Marjorie Kelley who attended to the 1,001 details that demanded attention;

Judy Organ, who helped to assemble key documents;

Suzan Richmond, who provided specific research;

Mary Jane Reed, who assisted with the early mechanics;

Leslie Webb, who was on hand to help with the closing questions.

Introduction

Just a century after the Founding Fathers had created the American Republic, Andrew Carnegie published a song—nay, a very symphony of praise—to the United States, which he called *Triumphant Democracy.*

"The old nations of the earth," he said in his opening sentence, "creep on at a snail's pace; the Republic thunders past with the rush of the express. The United States, the growth of a single century, has already reached the foremost rank among nations, and is destined soon to out distance all others in the race."

Every page breathed an almost religious exultation in the achievements of the United States. And no wonder. Carnegie himself had contributed not a little to that triumph which he celebrated. He had come to the United States from Scotland at the age of thirteen and found work as a bobbin boy at the wage of a dollar and twenty cents a week. Within thirty years, he was the "Steelmaster of America"; another quarter of a century and he controlled the largest corporation in the Western world and had launched upon that career of enlightened philanthropy which, in the end, distributed his fortune of almost 400 hundred million dollars to libraries, endowments, universities, and the advancement of science and of peace. It was America, he boasted, that had given him the opportunity—America, with its democracy, its equality, its freedom, its welcome to the poor of all lands.

Carnegie and his *Triumphant Democracy* give us an insight into the special character of patriotism in America. In America—and, until very recently, only in America—it was something that could be acquired, rather than inherited. It was not confined to those who had deep roots in their native soil; those roots could be put down in fertile soil in a single generation. It was inspired by, and vindicated by, political and social institutions, by the grandeur and the generosity of nature, by the opportunities offered every man and woman and child, not by history or tradition, not by military prowess, not by religious establishments. It was, above all, something to which every American could contribute.

The special nature of American patriotism was never better put than by an early "immigrant," the Frenchman who called himself J. Hector St. Jean de Crèvecoeur. His famous *Letters from an American Farmer,* published at the very beginning of our history as a nation, achieved the status of a classic not only in American literature but in the history of patriotism. Listen to him as he answers his own question: What is an American?

> What then is the American, this new man? ... He is an American who, leaving behind him all his ancient prejudices and manners, receives new ones from the new mode of life which he has embraced, the new government he obeys, and the new rank he holds. He becomes an American by being received in the broad lap of our great Alma Mater.

Crèvecoeur sounded a note that was to prove prophetic: "The American," he said, "is a new man who acts upon new principles; he must therefore entertain new ideas."

He did, indeed, and both the new principles and the new ideas found expression in his conceptions of patriotism, loyalty, and nationalism.

Let us begin with an emphasis on what Crèvecoeur had to say: that the new United States presented not only a new but a unique situation in the history of nationalism itself. Where, heretofore, all other nations had been the products of centuries of history and tradition, the American nation was deliberately made. Just what Lincoln said: "Our fathers brought forth . . . a new nation."

But how could they do this? If nationalism was everywhere else the product of centuries of history, how could a people without any history expect to create a nation? How would it command loyalty, how would it inspire patriotism?

We take for granted the existence of American nationalism but should not. The history of nationalism in modern times has been, on the whole, not one of growing centralization, but of fragmentation, and that process is still going on. Almost everywhere else in the world—in Latin America, in Africa, in the Middle East, in much of Europe—nationalism has gone from the general to the particular.

In the United States, it went from the particular to the general. But even that, we should remember, was for a long time touch and go. After all, there had been threats of secession by New England in the early years of the nineteenth century, threats of unrest in the trans-Appalachia States before the United States acquired firm control of the Mississippi, and the schemes hatched in the fevered brain of Aaron Burr. And under the pressure of slavery, particularism triumphed in the South and, in 1860, erupted into secession and civil war.

All this is not surprising. For consider the drawbacks to, and the dangers to, nationalism in the new station.

First, the new nation, in lacking a history, lacked that most essential of all ingredients of nationalism—a usable Past. Patriotism elsewhere was rooted in and nourished by common memories, common language, common faith, shared glories and triumphs, shared tragedies and crises; it relied on a common body of heroes and heroines, on familiar songs and stories and legends and myths; on deep attachment to a familiar land, watered by streams that had flowed through familiar valleys for a thousand years, villages that had witnessed the passing of a hundred generations, cathedrals and palaces, battlegrounds and cemeteries—in short, History.

The new United States had little of this, and what it had was by no means a common possession.

Americans overcame this handicap with astonishing ease and speed and, we might add, with astonishing versatility and ingenuity. Indeed, before too long, that very handicap became a source or pride. Americans agreed with an early Virginia poet when he wrote, "We have no ancestors, we ourselves are ancestors."

Not content with this, however, the Americans provided themselves with a past in record time—history, legends, stories, symbols, paintings, monuments, shrines, "holy days," ballads, patriotic songs, and heroes. By 1800, they had provided themselves with a flag which had its own mythology and which had the added advantage of being a continuous key to geography as well. They had not one but many national songs; they had not only a Declaration of Independence which everyone could understand, but a Liberty Bell to toll its fame. They had no fewer than three national mottoes—all equally valid: *E pluribus unum* (Many out of One); *Novus Ordo Saeclorum* (A New Order of the Ages); and *Annuit coeptis* (Heaven has favored our enterprise). And when it came to heroes, what other nation could match a Washington, a Jefferson, a Hamilton, an Adams, a Franklin, a Tom Paine—all in a single generation!

A second potential drawback to nationalism commands our attention: the lack of that homogeneous population which almost all other nations could take for granted. The new American population was made up of English, Scots, Irish, Welsh, French, Swedish, German, Dutch—and even Spanish and Indian—ingredients. The Africans were there too, but, alas, as slaves, not as free men; in time, they, too, were to be blended with the rest of the American population, though that intermixture was not, for a long time, voluntary. In other countries, heterogeneous populations nursed hostilities over periods of centuries: the Irish versus the English, the Finns versus the Swedes and Russians, the Germans of northern Italy versus the Italians, the Basques versus the Spaniards.

But no other modern nation had so varied a people as the American, yet in America the ingredients in the "melting pot" did for the most part, blend.

Most of those who came from the Old World to the New were more anxious to throw off their Old World allegiances, loyalties, even languages, than to retain them. Within a single generation, the pressures—or the potentialities—of American life (public schools, political parties to which all were welcome, labor unions) spurred by the deep instinct to belong to something which is common, had operated to erode ancient loyalties and create new ones.

There was, from the beginning, a third danger to patriotism; the absence of an Established Church, however, proved to be more of an advantage than a disadvantage. We in the United States take separation of Church and State for granted, but no one else could in the eighteenth century, or for that matter the nineteenth. Everywhere in the Old World, Church and State were one, and everywhere, too, the Sovereign was head of both.

An important element of nationalism in the Old World, such religious conformity meant religious intolerance, a religious persecution, religious wars. It had meant, too, the imposition of a single body of religious beliefs and practices on the entire population.

By adopting from the beginning a policy not only of toleration but of complete religious freedom, and almost complete religious equality, the new United States escaped all this without sacrificing national cohesion. This enlightened American policy was dictated by philosophy; it was also dictated by necessity or, we might say, the common sense of the matter, for, after all, if twenty or forty or one hundred different religious faiths flourished, it was essential that all be accepted. The alternative was chaos.

What this signified was that in America patriotism meant that scores of different religious elements in the population could unite on a common religion—a "civil religion" of loyalty to America. Loyalty to America became, itself, a kind of religion, but one which united rather than divided.

A fourth threat to the integrity and the endurance of the new nation was inherent in what was otherwise an immense asset: its size. How interesting that the United States was born the largest nation in the Western world! Even more interesting, that within the lifetime of a single man, it extended its boundaries from the Atlantic to the Pacific! Young John Quincy Adams was a boy of sixteen when he was with his father, John Adams, in Paris, witnessing the Treaty of 1783, which recognized the independence of the new United States; he was in the halls of Congress, an old man, when California knocked on the door asking for admission as a state. There is nothing comparable to that in the whole of history.

But vast size carried its own dangers. One of them was obvious: how to hold together a vast territory that embraced a dozen regions; each with its own character, its own interests, and, in time, its own loyalties? A second was that against which the great philosopher Montesquieu had warned: immense nations required a despotic government to hold them together; moderately sized nations can be governed by a king; republics alone must be small. Would the United States, born so large, disintegrate into a dozen separate nations as South America had disintegrated into a dozen nations? Would it abandon Republicanism and embrace Despotism and Empire?

Here again the new United States was fortunate. It was born in the age of the Industrial Revolution, and it was the Industrial Revolution that enabled it to overcome the threat of disintegration. Even as the Constitutional Convention was meeting in Philadelphia, in 1787, John Fitch was piloting his steamboat down the Schuylkill River; within another half century the country was crisscrossed with roads, canals, and even railroads. All this meant that industry and invention had conquered space, and that the threats of an immense size had evaporated.

Yet regionalism did develop, and with it regional and sectional loyalties. In the end, these erupted in the secession of eleven Southern states and the formation of a Confederate States of America. It took four years of war to overcome that threat—four years of war and the statesmanship and vision of Abraham Lincoln. Out of it came, if anything, a deeper and richer loyalty: a loyalty that associated "union" with freedom.

More than with most other countries, American patriotism is associated with the whole of the American territory rather than with particular places— towns, streams, mountains, valleys, sections. While in the Old World it is the locality that inspires loyalty and patriotism, in the New it is the whole country, "from sea to shining sea." Immigrant newcomers who could not find much to rejoice in in the slums of New York or the coal mines of Pennsylvania or the steel mills of Indiana might more readily delight in the Great Lakes, the Father of Waters—the Mississippi River—the Rocky Mountains, or the Yosemite Valley. How interesting that in this country songs celebrating Nature, on the whole, are the most familiar; songs such as "Dixie Land," "Ol' Kentucky Home," "Swanee River," "Oklahoma," "Ol' Man River," "Home on the Range," and, best of all, "America the Beautiful," which exulted in "spacious skies and amber waves of grain," and "purple mountain majesties above the fruited plain."

Nor did it prove a handicap that what the new United States lacked was taken for granted in all other Western countries—objects of personal loyalty such as kings, queens, princes, feudal lords, an aristocracy of both State and Church. From the beginning, Americans had rejected all this: the Declaration of Independence was, after all, a full-throated repudiation of the British king. Instead, Americans turned to their institutions. "Where," asked Tom Paine, "is the King of America? I will tell you, Friend . . . in America the Law is King." If the objects of American loyalty came to be the Declaration of Independence, the Constitution, the Bill of Rights, or, better yet, freedom and justice and equality (the French were to imitate this in their Revolution), the objects of their veneration tended to be historical monuments such as Plymouth Rock, Monticello, the White House.

Eventually—indeed very rapidly—Americans did conjure up also a gallery of heroes: Washington, who was incomparable; Franklin; Jefferson; and later, Lincoln and Robert E. Lee, and Franklin Roosevelt—all men who inspired veneration by their character, not by their family or position.

At the beginning and throughout the nineteenth century and most of the twentieth, American patriotism flourished without a military. Not only was the military rigorously subordinated to the civilian authority, it was all but eliminated. As late as 1860, when the population of the nation was over 30 million, the American Army consisted of some sixteen thousand officers and men! Though the Civil War did much to militarize patriotism, and to create a galaxy of military heroes, and provide national monuments and national songs—above all, the noble "Battle Hymn of the Republic"—it did not in any respect create a Military Establishment, an officer class, or a military psychology. All that came in our own time.

By far the most serious threat to American nationalism and thus to American patriotism, came from slavery and the persistence of racial animosities. "I tremble for my country," wrote Thomas Jefferson late in life, "when I reflect that God is just; that His justice cannot sleep forever, and that, when we come before His justice seat, the Almighty has no attribute which can take side with us in such a contest."

A decade or so later the great French philosopher Alexis de Tocqueville reached the same conclusion. *Democracy in America* was, on the whole, a tribute to American democracy as the wave of the future, but it contained one sober warning.

The American Union, for all its virtues and advantages, could not endure, he concluded: it would be torn apart by slavery! And that is indeed what happened. The defenders of slavery, to be sure, suffered defeat and the Union endured, but racial hostilities and racial injustices lingered on for another century, eroding many of the claims of democracy and of liberty, and threatening the nation with continuous social unrest.

That, notwithstanding two centuries of slavery, and another century of social and economic and political injustice, the great majority of blacks have remained loyal to this country is something of a miracle. Now that equality at last appears to be generally accepted, the memories of centuries of inequality may fade away, and the nation may achieve a degree of unity and of common patriotism it never knew before.

It has, after all, surmounted all the other potential limitations on nationalism and patriotism: an imperial territory, a heterogeneous population, limitless religious differences, the absence of a historical past, and the threat from hereditary enemies. Thus, Americans had been able to do what none had done before—and few since—to create a nation, a state, a people, and to provide its people with the opportunity to realize the great objectives of union—justice, domestic tranquility, common defense, general welfare, and with these the opportunity to "pursue happiness."

Much of this was achieved by avoiding hazards and dangers that might have imperiled the experiment. Much too was achieved by capitalizing on the immense advantages that the new nation did indeed enjoy in this "brave new world." What is significant here is that the Founding Fathers—and their successors, too—realized from the beginning what those advantages were, and harmonized their social and political experiment with both Nature and history.

The advantages, not so clear as the disadvantages at the beginning of our history, have become increasingly clear with the passing of time. They are by now familiar enough, and it is sufficient to restate them briefly.

First, the new United States ushered in modern nationalism, and this under the most auspicious of circumstances. It was free from history, and free from the tyrannies of the past—the tyranny of kings, of aristocracies, of a class society, of an Established Church, of militarism and wars, of the heavy weight of ignorance and poverty; it was free to write upon a clean page of history, and this its leaders proceeded to do.

Second, for the first time in history, the nation and its institutions was to be made by the people themselves, not by kings or warriors or religious leaders. It was the people who declared and won independence, the people who fought the war, the people who drafted state and federal constitutions, the people who took over the land and dictated the terms on which it should be distributed. Because the nation was theirs, their loyalty and their patriotism was direct and obvious, for most people are more deeply devoted to what they themselves make than to what they inherit. This process was not just something that happened in 1776 or 1789; it was a continuous process, one that still goes on.

Third, even at the time of the writing of state and national constitutions, Americans had the longest experience in self-government of any people. That experience had begun in the hold of the *Mayflower*, off Provincetown; was repeated in a hundred New England town meetings, a hundred county courts in the South, on a hundred frontiers where all adult men came together and drew up a rough constitution that would establish law, clarify land grants, open and maintain schools; it was to be found just as much in the mining camps of California and Montana in the 1850s and 1860s, as in Plymouth and Boston in the 1620s and 1630s.

Fourth—as we have already seen, the material circumstances were favorable beyond the dreams of men. "Land enough," said Jefferson in his first Inaugural Address, "for our descendants to the thousandth and thousandth generation"; a soil of unparalled fertility, riches under the soil beyond the avarice of men, a system of lakes and rivers such as no other nation ever enjoyed, a climate at once equable and sufficiently varied to permit every conceivable kind of agriculture and industry. "What more," said Jefferson, "is necessary to close the circle of our felicities." What indeed?

Fifth, as America was born in the age of Enlightenment, it was the first nation to democratize the Enlightenment. In the Old World, Enlightenment was something that concerned the aristocracy, or a handful of geniuses; in the New it meant quite simply education for all—education not only in the schoolroom and the college, but in politics, in farming, in the conduct of social life, in the homely household arts as well as in the higher arts.

Sixth, relative immunity from foreign wars, and the ability to develop all the resources and talents of the nation without dependence on a vast military establishment. Where other nations dissipated their manpower and their resources on great armies and navies, Americans could concentrate their energies on the pursuit of peace.

Seventh, the new Republic enjoyed an increase in population more rapid than any that had been known in the whole of history. Much of this—through immigration—came at the expense, as it were, of other nations and societies. Altogether, over the centuries, some 50 million people voluntarily sought American shores; an astonishing tribute to the new nation, for very few ever went the other way.

The leaders of the new nation were wise enough—or shrewd enough—to see all this and to accommodate American institutions to American realities. They knew that they were embarked upon an experiment unique in history. They knew that loyalty and patriotism must be won not just by history and tradition but by character. They were aware of the advantages, the benefits, even the blessings the new nation enjoyed, and they knew, too, that these blessings carried with them practical and moral obligations. They even translated all this into a kind of historical philosophy, that History was Prospective not Retrospective, and they concluded that America had been selected by a benign and all-wise Providence to preside over that Future.

Listen to George Washington as, after eight years as commander in chief of the Continental Armies, he made this final appeal to the states, and to the American people, to vindicate and justify the long struggle for freedom:

> The foundation of our Empire was not laid in the gloomy age of Ignorance and Superstition, but at an Epoch when the rights of Mankind were better understood and more clearly defined than at any former period, the researches of the human mind after social happiness have been carried to a great extent, the treasures of Knowledge, acquired by the labours of Philosophers, Sages, and Legislatures through a long succession of years, are open for our use, and their collected wisdom may be happily applied in the establishment of our forms of Government. . . . At this auspicious period the United States came into existence as a Nation, and if their citizens should not be completely free and happy then the fault will be entirely their own.

Turn, then, to those special features of patriotism and nationalism in America and to that vast literature of patriotism that this book explores and displays.

Henry Steele Commager

The Three Branches of Government

George Washington described the durable document we call our Constitution as a miracle. It sets up a framework of government of, by, and for the people, and it is as alive and pertinent today as it was when it was finally ratified and went into effect on March 4, 1789.

The Constitution provided three major pillars of government to form its "more perfect union": a legislature of two houses to make the laws; an executive branch, headed by a President, to carry out the laws; and a judiciary to interpret the laws. The three were interrelated by a system of checks and balances to make each responsible to the other two. The three branches are the essence of the way our nation is governed. The buildings they occupy are the seats of our power.

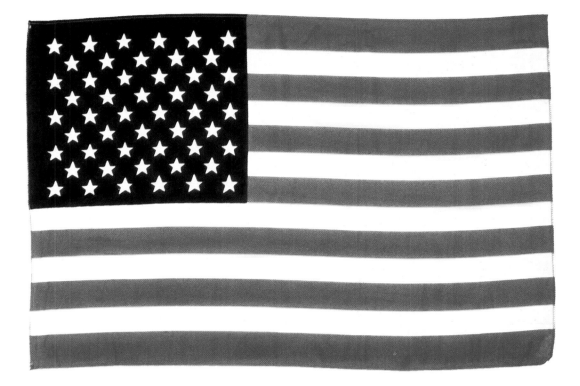

I pledge allegiance to the flag of the United States of America,
and to the republic for which it stands, one nation, under God,
indivisible with liberty and justice for all.

The Executive

The White House, standing on its plot of eighteen acres at 1600 Pennsylvania Avenue, is the official residence of the President. It is the oldest public building in Washington, D.C.

George Washington chose the site, but he never lived there. The design originated in a competition that was won by an architect-carpenter named James W. Hoban, who received an award of five hundred dollars, plus a city lot in Washington, for his effort. Thomas Jefferson also submitted a design, under a pseudonym, but he did not win.

The cornerstone for the building was laid on October 13, 1792, and at an early date the structure came to be called the "White House" because the sandstone building material was painted white during construction. Porticos and terraces were added later.

In 1814 the British invaders burned the White House, and Hoban supervised the rebuilding. In 1948 the structure was judged to be in dangerous condition and was substantially rebuilt with new underpinning.

The White House

The Legislative

All legislative powers herein granted shall be vested in a Congress of the United States, which shall consist of a Senate and House of Representatives.

That majestic 135-foot dome on the U.S. Capitol has become the major architectural symbol of the federal government. It is in this building that both the House of Representatives and the Senate meet. In daytime or at night, it is an imposing sight, which never fails to arouse an emotional response.

Nine architects have been involved with the Capitol building as we know it today. The first of these was Dr. William Thornton, under whose supervision the cornerstone for the structure was laid in 1793.

The Capitol dome, with the female figure sometimes called "Armed Freedom," was originally planned with a type of French bonnet on the lady's head. But that seemed too suggestive of slave revolt to President Pierce's secretary of war, Jefferson Davis, and the idea was discarded. Instead, she wears a headdress topped by ten lightning rods.

By the time of the Civil War some rebuilding was necessary, and President Lincoln urged that the needed work be completed as quickly as possible to convince any of those who doubted that the Union would survive the Secession crisis.

The rotunda, decorated in later years, offers a huge fresco by Constantino Brumidi, *Apotheosis of Washington*, fitting into the "eye" of the dome. An encircling fresco depicts great national events from Columbus to the Wright brothers.

The Capitol's Statuary Hall, formerly the meeting place of the House of Representatives, is now graced with images of great state heroes, while the old Senate chamber still seems to echo with the voices of the great orators of the American past.

The U.S. Capitol

The Judiciary

It was not until 1935 that the Supreme Court of the United States was finally installed in its own quarters, the largest marble building in the world. This structure, located at the corner of Capitol and Maryland avenues, housing the least familiar of the federal branches, is a stirring example of architectural classicism. It cannot boast grand vistas, such as those leading to the Capitol, or the gemlike setting of the White House, but it has, even on the gloomiest days, its own special grandeur, its own luminous dignity.

It is here that the nation's highest tribunal proclaims its function as the temple of law and justice and lends its prestige to the other two branches of government.

This was not always so. There was a time when the Court met in a spare room of the Capitol basement and its sessions were held in a local tavern building. The Justices had to do their work at home. But President Taft, who later became a Chief Justice of the Court, took the initiative and saw to it that the Supreme Court had its own home.

The Court has had a varying number of Justices. It started with six in 1789, headed by John Jay, who held the post of Chief Justice in 1795. In 1807 there were seven Justices, in 1837 there were nine, in 1863 ten, in 1866 back to eight, and in 1869 up to nine again, where it has remained.

The Court, with its credo "Equal Justice Under Law," is regarded as far above the political arena. Americans see it as sacrosanct—the final bastion of a government ruled by laws.

The U.S. Supreme Court Building

AN ALBUM FOR
AMERICANS

Christopher Columbus
in a portrait completed in 1519,
six years after his death.
The artist was Sebastiano del Piombo,
an Italian painter of the Venetian
school. This painting of the
Admiral of the Ocean Sea hangs
in the Metropolitan Museum
in New York.

1. The Great Adventure Begins

He was an Italian sailor, son of a Genoese weaver, who charted new sea routes under the flag of Spain. He was daring and persistent, self-confident, and definitely made of the stuff of heroes. Our young nation has always appreciated such qualities. Although he never set foot on the North American continent, Christopher Columbus became the first American hero.

Columbus was absolutely convinced that by sailing westward, over the farthest horizon, he would reach, after perhaps 2,500 miles, the fabled Orient with all its riches. It was not idle speculation, but there were problems. The sailor from Genoa simply did not grasp the great distances involved (not 2,500 miles but about 10,600), and he did not know there was a mighty continent that blocked his way to the Orient.

Columbus approached the king of Portugal to sponsor a voyage and was turned down. Then he went to Spain, where, after eight years, he managed to gain the ear of Queen Isabella. She listened to the "Enterprise of the Indies" project. Eventually, the royal Spanish treasury came up with the funds he needed, about $14,000.

In late summer of 1492, brash master mariner Christopher Columbus was ready, at the age of forty-one, for his great gamble. On August 3, at the Spanish port of Palos, the anchors of Columbus's three ships—the *Nina*, *Pinta*, and *Santa Maria*—were raised, and Christopher Columbus, with his crew of ninety, departed into the unknown.

A refitting stop was made at the Canary Islands, and on September 6 the tiny expedition set off westward. After more than six weeks under sail, Columbus's crew sensed that their leader had taken them farther into the unknown than anyone had ever ventured before. There was restlessness and a growing fear; there was even talk of mutiny, of forcing the expedition to turn back. Columbus had to use all of his determination to hold the course he had set.

Early on Friday, October 12, 1492, the lookout, Rodrigo de Triana, cried out the news: "Land! land, ho!" It was an island in the Bahamas, and de Triana would win a prize for his eager shout. Columbus was convinced he had reached an outpost of Japan. He carried ashore the royal banner of Spain and called the island San Salvador.

Before the turn of the century, a Florentine navigator, Amerigo Vespucci, sailing to South America with more precise navigation, lent his name to the mapmakers of that time, and the New World became America instead of Columbia.

Christopher Columbus made four voyages to the new lands he had discovered. But it was the initial voyage that counted. It was the first great adventure in the making of our history. Although he died in obscurity and poverty, Columbus's persistence and his faith assured him a niche as an American hero.

COLUMBUS

Behind him lay the grey Azores,
Behind the Gates of Hercules;
Before him not the ghost of shores,
Before him only shoreless seas.
The good mate said: "Now must we pray,
For lo! the very stars are gone.
Brave Admiral, speak; what shall I say?"
"Why, say: 'Sail on! sail on! and on!' "

"My men grow mutinous day by day;
My men grow ghastly wan and weak."
The stout mate thought of home; a spray
Of salt wave washed his swarthy cheek.
"What shall I say, brave Admiral, say,
If we sight naught but seas at dawn?"
"Why, you shall say at break of day:
'Sail on! sail on! sail on! and on!' "

They sailed and sailed, as winds might blow,
Until at last the blanched mate said:
"Why, now not even God would know
Should I and all my men fall dead.
These very winds forget their way,
For God from these dread seas is gone.
Now speak, brave Admiral, speak and say—"
He said: "Sail on! sail on! and on!"

They sailed. They sailed. Then spake the mate:
"This mad sea shows his teeth to-night.
He curls his lip, he lies in wait,
Brave Admiral, say but one good word:
What shall we do when hope is gone?"
The words leapt like a leaping sword:
"Sail on! sail on! sail on! and on!"

Then, pale and worn, he kept his deck,
And thro' the darkness peered that night.
Ah, darkest night! and then a speck
A light! a light! a light! a light!
It grew—a star-lit flag unfurled!
It grew to be Time's burst of dawn.
He gained a world! he gave that world
Its watch-word: "On! and on!"

Joaquin Miller (1839–1913)
wrote mainly of the West,
but his poem "Columbus,"
celebrating the Discoverer,
caught the imagination,
found a niche in the
repertory of patriotic
expression, and became a
standard item of school
recitations.

JOAQUIN MILLER

A Celebration of Columbus

In 1893, a bit late by the calendar, a giant international fair was held in Chicago to mark the four hundredth anniversary of Columbus's discovery of America.

The great Chicago Columbia Exposition, as it was known, surely calls for superlatives. Generally regarded as the grandest spectacle of modern times, the exposition was opened to the public on May 1, 1893. This staggering collection of lagoons, canals, and gushing fountains on Chicago's South Side envisioned a world of the future when all the marvels of science would join to create a wonder world for everyone. Its exhibition halls, huge white palaces, bulged with dynamos, steam engines, and other fruits of contemporary technology. Its mile-long Midway outdid any pleasure dome of antiquity. In six euphoric months a total of 25 million visitors visited this Utopia on Lake Michigan.

On January 2, 1892, the Post Office issued a series of Columbia Exposition commemorative stamps to mark the quadricentennial. They depicted a variety of episodes in the life of Columbus and proved to be somewhat controversial, since in some scenes Columbus is cleanshaven while in others, supposedly the following day, he has a full-grown beard. The stamps were heavily purchased as souvenirs at the Exposition and became collectors' items.

The Columbia Exposition Issue of Postage Stamps. 1¢—Columbus Sights Land. 2¢—The Landing of Columbus. 4¢—The Fleet of Columbus. 5¢—Columbus Seeking Aid from Isabella. 6¢—Columbus Presenting Indians. 15¢—Columbus Announcing His Discovery. 30¢—Columbus at La Rabida. 50¢—Recall of Columbus. $1—Isabella Pledging Her Jewels. $2—Columbus in Chains. $3—Columbus Describing His Third Voyage. $4—Isabella and Columbus. $5—Columbus.

2. Just and Equal Laws

The Signers of the Mayflower Compact

Mr. Edward Winslow
Mr. William Brewster
Isaac Allerton
Miles Standish
John Alden
John Turner
Francis Eaton
James Chilton
John Craxton
John Billington
Joses Fletcher
John Goodman
Mr. Samuel Fuller
Mr. Christopher Martin
Mr. William Mullins
Mr. William White
Mr. Richard Warren
John Howland
Thomas Williams
Gilbert Winslow
Edmund Margesson
Peter Brown
Richard Bitteridge
George Soule
Edward Tilly
John Tilly
Francis Cooke
Thomas Rogers
Thomas Tinker
John Ridgate
Edward Fuller
Richard Clark
Richard Gardiner
Mr. John Allerton
Thomas English
Edward Doten
Edward Liester

Our sense of Union, our national dedication to a common cause, had its misty beginnings with a document written in the cabin of the 180-ton sailing ship the *Mayflower,* which set sail from Plymouth, England, about 360 years ago.

Bound for the Virginia settlements with 102 passengers, the ninety-foot former wine ship was tossed far north off its course by heavy weather, during which a sailor and a servant boy were lost and two babies were born. There was some talk of mutiny. On November 11, 1620, forty-one of the passengers gathered for a significant meeting. The purpose was to discuss and sign an agreement, a compact, sanctioning a preliminary plan of government for "just and equal" laws based on a religious structure.

The document signed that November day, known now as the Mayflower Compact, was to become an important part of our heritage. Even though our country would not come into being for more than another century and a half, the "just and equal" credo was established as one of the key tenets of life in the New World.

Mayflower Compact (1620)

In the name of God, Amen. We whose names are under-writen, the loyall subjects of our dread soveraigne Lord, King James, by the grace of God, of Great Britaine, France, and Ireland king, defender of the faith, etc., haveing undertaken, for the glorie of God, advancemente of the Christian faith, and honour of our king and countrie, a voyage to plant the first colonie in the Northerne parts of Virginia, doe by these presents solemnly and mutualy in the presence of God, and one of another, covenant and combine our selves togeather into a civill body politick, for our better ordering and preservation and furtherance of the ends aforesaid; and by vertue hearof to enacte, constitute, and frame such just and equall lawes, ordinances, acts, constitutions, and offices, from time to time, as shall be thought most meete and convenient for the generall good of the Colonie unto which we promise all due submission and obedience. In witness whereof we have hereunder subscribed our names at Cap-Codd the 11. of November, in the year of the raigne of our soveraigne Lord, King James, of England, France, and Ireland the eighteenth, and of Scotland the fiftie fourth. An⁰: Dom. 1620.

Pilgrims at Plymouth, by Clyde O. DeLand (1872–1947)

Signing the Social Compact in the Cabin of the Mayflower (1853), by American genre artist Tompkins Harrison Matteson (1813–84)

3. The Roots of Religious Freedom

The Puritan oligarchy ruled its members with an iron hand, but there were those who dared to raise their voices in dissent. One who believed in the basic sanctity of the human conscience and expressed democratic and humanitarian ideals was Roger Williams (1603–83), a teacher and minister of great personal charm and a persuasive manner.

Williams took Anglican orders in 1627 and emigrated to Massachusetts in 1631. He quickly became impatient with the Puritan rigidity, questioning the validity of the Massachusetts charter and denying that civil authorities had power over matters of personal conscience. In religion, he felt, man was answerable to God alone.

Because he was generally a nuisance to the Puritan authorities, even championing Indian rights, Williams was banished from the colony in 1635. He thereafter went out and founded his own colony in Rhode Island. Williams bought the land from the Indians, and called the colony Providence. It was to be a refuge for those who were distressed in conscience and wanted to avoid religious persecution.

Roger Williams, himself a target of persecution, effectively established religious freedom as a credo of the American way.

Above:
Landing of Roger Williams,
by Alonzo Chappel

7

4. The Free Press: Pillar of Democracy

"Freedom of the press" is a vital ingredient of our democratic identity. It is a right so fundamental that we have come to regard it as an accomplished fact, without remembering that this was not always so.

In New York City around the year 1730, a group of concerned citizens persuaded a German-born printer, one John Peter Zenger, to establish a newspaper called the *New-York Weekly Journal*, which they would use to expose New York's Governor William Cosby, who they claimed was dealing harshly with certain religious groups and accumulating personal gain from land grants.

Zenger, a printer by trade, was initially reluctant. But in November 1733 Zenger's accusations, clearly written by knowing hands, began to appear, much to the fury of Governor Cosby. Readers of the *Weekly Journal* were amazed, and the governor was quick to react. Zenger was charged with seditious libel. A prohibitively high bail was set, and when two lawyers came forward to assume the defense, they were both disbarred

Zenger spent nine months in jail. Then his supporters made a master move, calling in Andrew Hamilton, the most distinguished lawyer in the Colonies at that time. Zenger's trial began on August 4, 1735, and in that trial Hamilton argued that truth is not libelous and sounded a powerful warning on the arbitrary uses of power. This was quite contrary to precedent and, the presiding judge notwithstanding, the jury found John Peter Zenger not guilty of seditious libel. A burst of cheering greeted the verdict.

The Zenger case, an early salvo in the rising barrage of Colonial opposition to the British crown, was a landmark. Even before we had achieved our independence, a brave printer, with the help of a courageous lawyer, dared a confrontation with arbitrary power. He helped to establish a key principle of our democratic system.

A Defense by Andrew Hamilton in the Case of John Peter Zenger (August 4, 1735)

May it please your honors, I agree with Mr. Attorney [Richard Bradley] that government is a sacred thing, but I differ very widely from him when he would insinuate that the just complaints of a number of men, who suffer under a bad administration, is libeling that administration. Had I believed that to be law, I should not have given the court the trouble of hearing anything that I could say in this cause. . . .

There is heresy in law as well as in religion, and both have changed very much; and we well know that it is not two centuries ago that a man would have been burned as a heretic for owning such opinions in matters of religion as are publicly written and printed at this day. They were fallible men, it seems, and we take the liberty, not only to differ from them in religious opinion, but to comdemn them and their opinions too; and I must presume that in taking these freedoms in thinking and speaking about matters of faith or religion, we are in the right; for, though it is said there are very great liberties of this kind taken in New York, yet I have heard of no information preferred by Mr. Attorney for any offenses of this sort. From which I think it is pretty clear that in New York a man may make very free with his God, but he must take special care what he says of his Governor. It is agreed upon by all men that this is a reign of liberty, and while men keep within the bounds of truth, I hope they may with safety both speak and write their sentiments of the conduct of men of power; I mean of that part of their conduct only which affects the liberty or property of the

people under their administration; were this to be denied, then the next step may make them slaves. . . .

It is said, and insisted upon by Mr. Attorney, that government is a sacred thing; that it is to be supported and reverenced; it is government that protects our persons and estates; that prevents treasons, murders, robberies, riots, and all the train of evils that overturn kingdoms and states and ruin particular persons; and if those in the administration, especially the supreme magistrates, must have all their conduct censured by private men, government cannot subsist. This is called a licentiousness not to be tolerated. It is said that it brings the rulers of the people into contempt so that their authority is not regarded, and so that in the end the laws cannot be put in execution. These, I say, and such as these, are the general topics insisted upon by men in power and their advocates. But I wish it might be considered at the same time how often it has happened that the abuse of power has been the primary cause of these evils, and that it was the injustice and oppression of these great men which has commonly brought them into contempt with the people. The craft and art of such men are great, and who that is the least acquainted with history or with law can be ignorant of the specious pretenses which have often been made use of by men in power to introduce arbitrary rule and destroy the liberties of a free people. . . .

This is the second information for libeling of a governor that I have known in America. And the first, though it may look like a romance, yet as it is true, I will beg leave to mention it. Governor Nicholson, who happened to be offended with one of his clergy, met him one day upon the road; and, as it was usual with him (under the protection of his commission), used the poor parson with the worst of language, threatened to cut off his ears, slit his nose, and, at last, to shoot him through the head. The parson, being a reverend man, continued all this time uncovered in the heat of the sun until he found an opportunity to fly for it; and coming to a neighbor's house felt himself very ill of a fever, and immediately wrote for a doctor; and that his physician might be the better judge of his distemper, he acquainted him with the usage he had received, concluding that the Governor was certainly mad, for that no man in his senses would have behaved in that manner. The doctor, unhappily, showed the parson's letter; the Governor came to hear of it, and so an information was preferred against the poor man for saying he believed the Governor was mad; and it was laid in the information to be false, scandalous, and wicked, and written with intent to move sedition among the people and bring his Excellency into contempt. But, by an order from the late Queen Anne, there was a stop put to the prosecution, with sundry others set on foot by the same Governor against Gentlemen of the greatest worth and honor in that government. . . .

Gentlemen, the danger is great in proportion to the mischief that may happen through our too-great credulity. A proper confidence in a court is commendable, but as the verdict (whatever it is) will be yours, you ought to refer no part of your duty to the discretion of other persons. If you should be of opinion that there is no falsehood in Mr. Zenger's papers, you will, nay (pardon me for the expression), you ought to say; because you do not know whether others (I mean the court) may be of that opinion. It is your right to do so, and there is much depending upon your resolution, as well as upon your integrity.

The loss of liberty to a generous mind is worse than death; and yet we know there have been those in all ages who, for the sake of preferment or some imaginary honor, have freely lent a helping hand to oppress, nay, to destroy, their country.

This brings to my mind that saying of the immortal Brutus, when he looked upon the creatures of Caesar, who were very great men, but by no means good men: "You Romans," said Brutus, "if yet I may call you so, consider what you are doing; remember that you are assisting Caesar to forge those very chains which one day he will make yourselves wear." This is what every man that values freedom ought to consider; he should act by judgment and not by affection or self-interest; for where those prevail, no ties of either country or kindred are regarded; as, upon the other hand, the man who loves his country prefers its liberty to all other considerations, well knowing that without liberty life is a misery. . . .

Power may justly be compared to a great river; while kept within its bounds, it is both beautiful and useful, but when it overflows its banks, it is then too impetuous to be stemmed. . . .

I hope to be pardoned, sir, for my zeal upon this occasion. It is an old and wise caution that "when our neighbor's house is on fire, we ought to take care of our own." For though, blessed be God, I live in a government where liberty is well understood and freely enjoyed, yet experience has shown us all (I am sure it has to me) that a bad precedent in one government is soon set up for an authority in another; and therefore I cannot but think it mine and every honest man's duty that, while we pay all due obedience to men in authority, we ought, at the same time, to be upon our guard against power wherever we apprehend that it may affect ourselves or our fellow subjects.

I am truly very unequal to such an undertaking, on many accounts. And you see I labor under the weight of many years and am borne down with great infirmities of body; yet old and weak as I am, I should think it my duty, if required, to go to the utmost part of the land, where my service could be of any use in assisting to quench the flame of prosecutions upon informations, set on foot by the government to deprive a people of the right of remonstrating, and complaining too, of the arbitrary attempts of men in power. . . . But, to conclude, the question before the court, and you, gentlemen of the jury, is not of small nor private concern; it is not the cause of a poor printer, nor of New York alone, which you are now trying. No! It may, in its consequence, affect every free man that lives under a British government on the main continent of America. It is the best cause; it is the cause of liberty; and I make no doubt but your upright conduct, this day, will not only entitle you to the love and esteem of your fellow citizen, but every man who prefers freedom to a life of slavery will bless and honor you as men who have baffled the attempt of tyranny, and, by an impartial and uncorrupt verdict, have laid a noble foundation for securing to ourselves, our posterity, and our neighbors that to which nature and the laws of our country have given us a right—the liberty of both exposing and opposing arbitrary power (in these parts of the world at least) by speaking and writing the truth.

5. Roots of Revolution

The ties of the Colonies to the mother country were deep and binding. There was the common language, of course, a lifestyle and a code of law that were basic. There was a blood kinship and there was tradition.

But there was also a growing wish to be free. In the course of a century and a half Great Britain's American colonials had come to regard themselves as quite capable of managing their own affairs. Many of them had been born and nurtured in this new land with its invigorating spirit of liberty and earthy self-reliance. Ties with England, which had begun to seem remote and even burdensome, were fading.

A host of onerous levies, prohibitions, and regulations were being announced by a faraway monarch, many of them designed to keep the restless Colonies in line. These taxes and rules intruded on everyday life and grew progressively into coercive irritants that generated growing resistance. Some of the more vocal colonists, who called themselves "Sons of Liberty," saw independence as the only way out. These first patriots were still a considerable minority.

From London's point of view, the Colonies were increasingly a burden and an expense. The French and Indian War, conducted at a great distance and under difficult circumstances, had shackled the British government with a huge national debt. More money was needed for the army and navy to protect a sprawling empire, and the taxes at home were already too heavy. And since the French and Indian War had been fought chiefly on behalf of the Colonies, the British reasoned they should bear the cost. It was time to tighten the reins.

Thus, for example, the enforcement of the Navigation Acts, which had been on the books for more than a century. These had provided simply that goods be carried to and from the Colonies only in British ships manned by British sailors. There was a loophole here, since the Colonies might be viewed as British and the Colonial sailors as British seamen. Now London insisted on strict interpretation of the law, and the profitable and widespread occupation of smuggling became more risky.

Also on the books was the irritating Sugar Act of 1733, which placed a prohibitive duty on molasses entering the Colonies from the French and British islands. Americans needed molasses for their rum distilleries. But the act, which also covered wines, silks, and linens, was tightened in 1760. The main result was a flourishing trade in false papers.

The Stamp Act of 1765 marked a new departure: the first direct tax ever imposed on America. There was a funereal air in the streets when the regulations went into effect on Black Friday, November 1, 1765. The new taxes were levied on newspapers, on real estate documents, on all popular almanacs, on insurance policies, on licenses to practice law and to sell liquor, and even on playing cards. It was a deliberately punitive tax, and it aroused anger in every corner of the Colonies. The levies were seen, angrily, as taxation without representation.

Earlier that year, in March 1765, the Quartering Act had called upon civil authorities in the American colonies to provide barracks and supplies for British troops. Later under the act, inns, alehouses, and unoccupied buildings were commandeered for army use. The British saw trouble ahead—the Redcoats versus Sons of Liberty—and were overplaying their hand in this effort to bring the Colonies to heel. The fuse was lit, but the explosion was not yet ready.

In the spring of 1767 there were rumblings in New York, where British troops had demolished a Liberty Pole, a symbol of tax resistance. They advanced on the crowds with loaded muskets, but the authorities intervened in time to avert bloodshed.

Taxation without representation is tyranny.

Attributed to
JAMES OTIS (1763)

Boston, however, was the cockpit of Revolutionary activity. A tax collector was hanged in effigy by the Sons of Liberty. In 1768 the British brought in fresh troops, and in 1769 there was a clash, but no bloodshed. Then came two decisive events that blew the lid off the Revolutionary pot. Debates ended. It was time for action.

The Boston Massacre

Boston was under a cover of snow that March day in 1770. On King Street, near the State House, a group of laborers stopped to taunt some British soldiers on the street. There had been a number of such confrontations in recent months, but all had been defused. This particular clash appeared to have serious overtones from the start. It began as a fistfight and developed rapidly into a general snowballing, with some of the snowballs concealing chunks of ice. The tension built as the snowballs flew with increasing speed. The Redcoats felt the pressure and called for reinforcements, who soon arrived with loaded rifles.

Suddenly the nervous Redcoats opened fire. Three laborers fell dead into the snow. Two more were wounded. One of the dead was Crispus Attucks, a mulatto from Nantucket, who had tried to grab one of the British rifles.

News of the incident spread rapidly in the Boston tinderbox. The governor pulled the British troops out of the city in an attempt to prevent any further confrontation. Six of the Redcoats were put under arrest and were defended by John Adams, who managed to obtain acquittals for four of the soldiers; the other two were convicted of manslaughter.

The clash on King Street that March day became known as the "Boston Massacre," and the drawing by Paul Revere, reproduced in handbills, became a patriotic symbol.

The "Boston Massacre," March 5, 1770, an engraving attributed to Paul Revere

12

The Boston Tea Party

The Destruction of Tea at Boston Harbor, December 16, 1773. Lithograph by N. Currier, 1846

A three-pence-a-pound tax on tea, passed by Parliament in 1767, was to the colonists another infuriating example of taxation with representation. Gradually the Americans gave up drinking tea.

To save the East India Company, floundering under a surplus of 17 million pounds of tea, Parliament came up with a diversion. Upon payment of the tea tax, the East India Company could bypass the Colonial tea merchants and sell directly, at a much lower price, to the American consumer through its own agents.

The maneuver served only to solidify Colonial resentment. Not only was there no rush to buy, but colonists kept the tea ships from unloading.

There had been tea incidents before, based on a general refusal to knuckle down to the law, in New York, Annapolis, and Greenwich, New Jersey. But now, in December 1773, three ships loaded with tea were sitting in Boston harbor. The city was in a nervous stew. The governor, whose family was involved in the tea arrangements, refused to order the three ships to leave. A town meeting was called for December 16. From that meeting, a group of men, disguised as Mohawk Indians, ran down to the harbor, boarded the tea ships, and, using their tomahawks to open the cases, dumped 342 chests of tea into the harbor.

When news of the Boston "tea party" reached London, the reaction was swift and decisive. Boston harbor was shut down to everything except military supplies. Even food and fuel called for special permits. Trials for certain capital offenses stemming from riots were transferred to England from Massachusetts. Public meetings had to be officially sanctioned. Certain Colonial government officials were to be appointed by the king or the governor, and damages had to be paid for all that soggy tea. King George remarked to his prime minister: "The die is cast. The Colonies must either submit or triumph."

A call went out for a Continental Congress to meet in Philadelphia. The die was indeed cast.

This is the most magnificent movement of all! There is a dignity, a majesty, a sublimity, in this last effort of the patriots that I greatly admire. The people should never rise without doing something to be remembered—something notable and striking.

JOHN ADAMS,
on the Boston Tea Party, from his diary
(December 17, 1773)

13

6. 1775: Year of Decision

There is a time to talk ... and, sometimes, a time to fight. Early in 1775 the time to talk had ended.

Attempts at reconciliation were fruitless. In view of many in the British Parliament, the American colonies were already in a state of rebellion, and harsh repressive measures were the result. The colonists were forbidden to trade with any nation other than Great Britain. Their fishing vessels were denied the right to work the waters off the New England coast.

In America, defiance of the crown was open and widespread. Massachusetts was the core of the Revolutionary movement. The patriotic Sons of Liberty were active throughout the colony; Committees of Safety were being organized in every town. Arms were being stored. The Minutemen, an informal (and illegal) militia, drilled for the inevitable. A chorus of Boston patriots including such men as Sam Otis, John Adams, John Hancock, and Samuel Adams spoke out defiantly.

Under orders to use force rather than allow the Colonies to prepare for war, the British military began to fortify Boston. Aware of these British moves, the Colonials organized to meet them. The point of no return was passed.

On April 18, 1775, in Boston, General Thomas Gage of the British Army, following a plan to seize arms stores set up by the Colonials, ordered his troops to march to Concord to destroy the military supplies he knew had been collected there.

Every movement of the Redcoats was now carefully observed by the Colonials, who had set up signals to alert the Minutemen by a series of lantern lights in a Boston church steeple. Three riders, Paul Revere, William Dawes, and Dr. Samuel Prescott, were to spread the word. At Lexington, about twenty miles from Boston, the British troops were intercepted, and after a brief skirmish the Redcoats moved on to Concord, where the main resistance was waiting. The battles of Lexington and Concord signaled the start of the Revolutionary War.

In May the war shifted to the mountain areas near the Canadian border, where Ethan Allen, a sometime soldier of the French and Indian War, and his band of Vermonters captured Fort Ticonderoga from the British.

"Don't one of you fire until you see the whites of their eyes," commanded Colonel William Prescott to his band of 1,600 Colonials as they watched British Redcoats ascend Breed's Hill (June 17, 1775).

Patrick Henry: "Give Me Liberty or Give Me Death"

Virginian Patrick Henry had tried his hand as a bartender, a storekeeper, and a tobacco farmer, not making a mark in any of those pursuits. But as an orator, even with that back-country accent, he could trigger a fire in the minds of men.

When he was twenty-four Henry started to practice law, and despite his ill-fitting clothes and frontier manner, he became one of the best lawyers in the land. By 1764 he had achieved a local reputation for his speeches, and a year later he became a member of the Virginia House of Burgesses. In that forum he tore into the Stamp Act ("If this be treason make the most of it"). And then in 1774, at the first Continental Congress, his oratory came right to the point: "The distinctions between Virginians, Pennsylvanians, New Yorkers, and New Englanders are no more. I am not a Virginian, but an American."

It was on March 23, 1775, in the Virginia House of Burgesses that Patrick Henry gave to the Revolutionary cause its most resounding slogan. Asserting that "no man thinks more highly than I do of patriotism," he denounced the arbitrary rules set down by the mother country and called for an armed force to resist, concluding with the immortal words: "Give me liberty or give me death."

Patrick Henry: Speech before the Virginia House of Burgesses (March 23, 1775)

Patrick Henry, the fiery orator from Virginia, is depicted in an 1857 engraving after a painting by Alonzo Chappel (1828–87).

Mr. President:

No man thinks more highly than I do of the patriotism, as well as abilities, of the very worthy gentlemen who have just addressed the House. But different men often see the same subject in different lights; and, therefore, I hope it will not be thought disrespectful to those gentlemen if, entertaining as I do opinions of a character very opposite to theirs, I shall speak forth my sentiments freely and without reserve. This is no time for ceremony. The question before the House is one of awful moment to this country. For my own part, I consider it as nothing less than a question of freedom or slavery; and in proportion to the magnitude of the subject ought to be the freedom of the debate. It is only in this way that we can hope to arrive at truth, and fulfill the great responsibility which we hold to God and our country. Should I keep back my opinions at such a time, through fear of giving offense, I should consider myself as guilty of treason toward my country, and of an act of disloyalty toward the Majesty of Heaven, which I revere above all earthly kings.

Mr. President, it is natural to man to indulge in the illusions of hope. We are apt to shut our eyes against a painful truth, and listen to the song of that siren till she transforms us into beasts. Is this the part of wise men, engaged in a great and arduous struggle for liberty? Are we disposed to be of the number of those who, having eyes, see not, and, having ears, hear not, the things which so nearly concern their temporal salvation? For my part, whatever anguish of spirit it may cost, I am willing to know the whole truth, to know the worst, and to provide for it.

I have but one lamp by which my feet are guided, and that is the lamp of experience. I know of no way of judging of the future but by the past. And judging by the past, I wish to know what there has been in the conduct of the British ministry for the last ten years to justify those hopes with which gentlemen have been pleased to solace themselves and the House. Is it that insidious smile with which our petition has been lately received? Trust it not, sir; it will prove a snare to your feet. Suffer not yourselves to be betrayed with a kiss. . . . And what have we to oppose to them [Britain's "navies and armies"]? Shall we try argument? Sir, we have been trying that for the last ten years. Have we anything new to offer upon the subject? Nothing. We have held the subject up in every light of which it is capable; but it has been all in vain. Shall we resort to entreaty and humble supplication? What terms shall we find which have not been already exhausted? Let us not, I beseech you, sir, deceive ourselves longer. Sir, we have done everything that could be done to avert the storm which is now coming on. We have petitioned; we have remonstrated; we have supplicated; we have prostrated ourselves before the throne, and have implored its interposition to arrest the tyrannical hands of the ministry and Parliament. Our petitions have been slighted; our remonstrances have produced additional violence and insult, our supplications have been disregarded; and we have been spurned, with contempt, from the foot of the throne! In vain, after these things, may we indulge the fond hope of peace and reconciliation. There is no longer any room for hope. If we wish to be free—if we mean to preserve inviolate those inestimable privileges for which we have been so long contending—if we mean not basely to abandon the noble struggle in which we have been so long engaged, and which we have pledged ourselves never to abandon until the glorious object of our contest shall be obtained—we must fight! I repeat it, sir, we must fight! An appeal to arms and to the God of Hosts is all that is left us!

They tell us, sir, that we are weak; unable to cope with so formidable an adversary. But when shall we be stronger? Will it be the next week, or the next year? Will it be when we are totally disarmed, and when a British guard shall be stationed in every house? Shall we gather strength by irresolution and inaction?

Shall we acquire the means of effectual resistance by lying supinely on our backs and hugging the delusive phantom of hope, until our enemies shall have bound us hand and foot? Sir, we are not weak if we make a proper use of those means which the God of nature hath placed in our power. Three millions of people, armed in the holy cause of liberty, and in such a country as that which we possess, are invincible by any force which our enemy can send against us. Besides, sir, we shall not fight our battles alone. There is a just God who presides over the destinies of nations, and who will raise up friends to fight our battles for us. The battle, sir, is not to the strong alone; it is to the vigilant, the active, the brave. Besides, sir, we have no election. If we were base enough to desire it, it is now too late to retire from the contest. There is no retreat but in submission and slavery! Our chains are forged! Their clanking may be heard on the plains of Boston! The war is inevitable—and let it come! I repeat it, sir, let it come.

It is in vain, sir, to extenuate the matter. Gentlemen may cry, Peace, Peace—but there is no peace. The war is actually begun! The next gale that sweeps from the north will bring to our ears the clash of resounding arms! Our brethren are already in the field! Why stand we here idle? What is it that gentlemen wish? What would they have? Is life so dear, or peace so sweet, as to be purchased at the price of chains and slavery? Forbid it, Almighty God! I know not what course others may take; but as for me, give me liberty or give me death!

The Midnight Ride of Paul Revere

Paul Revere worked as a silversmith, engraver, printer, and dentist, but, above all, it was a personal act of daring as a patriot that enabled him to leave his mark on history.

In mid-April of 1775, when Revere was about forty, the English general Thomas Gage, who was stationed in Boston, decided to seize the cache of military supplies that had been accumulated in nearby Concord. He was also determined to arrest rebel leaders Samuel Adams and John Hancock and send them off to Great Britain to stand trial.

With these objectives in mind, Gage assigned a contingent of seven hundred Redcoats, mainly light infantry and grenadiers out of guard duty, to prepare the small boats needed for the secret mission. Becoming aware of these preparations, the Boston patriots in turn set up plans to alert their comrades at Lexington and Concord and disrupt the British intentions.

Which route would the Redcoats take? By land across the Boston neck, or across the Charles River to Cambridge? The steeple atop the old North Church was the ideal vantage point from which to watch their movements.

The evening of April 18 proved damp and chilly for the New England spring. Revere and his companion, William Dawes, a rope maker, waited with their horses for a signal from the church tower. The sexton would hang a single lantern if the Redcoats marched by land, and two lanterns if they moved by sea. At about ten that night, the answer flashed through the darkness: two lights— the British were coming by sea. Revere and Dawes sprang onto their mounts for the long ride ahead. They reached Lexington, about twenty-one miles away, just after midnight. The alarm was sounded, enabling Adams and Hancock to make their escape.

When the British reached Lexington, the Minutemen were waiting. There was a short but sharp confrontation, with eight Americans killed in the exchange. Dr. Samuel Prescott, who had joined the alarm party at Lexington and was able to break through the Redcoat lines and make his way to Concord, alerted the militia there before the next skirmish. Revere was trapped by the British but was later released; Dawes eluded them and returned to Boston.

The efforts of Revere and his companions that April night provided the spark. The fervor would spread. The Colonies could no longer turn back.

PAUL REVERE'S RIDE (April 18–19, 1775)

Listen, my children, and you shall hear
Of the midnight ride of Paul Revere,
On the eighteenth of April, in Seventy-five;
Hardly a man is now alive
Who remembers that famous day and year.

He said to his friend, "If the British march
By land or sea from the town to-night,
Hang a lantern aloft in the belfry arch
Of the North Church tower as a signal light,—
One, if by land, and two, if by sea;
And I on the opposite shore will be,
Ready to ride and spread the alarm
Through every Middlesex village and farm,
For the country folk to be up and to arm."

Then he said, "Good night!" and with muffled oar
Silently rowed to the Charlestown shore,
Just as the moon rose over the bay,

Where swinging wide at her moorings lay
The Somerset, British man-of-war;
A phantom ship, with each mast and spar
Across the moon like a prison bar,
And a huge black hulk, that was magnified
By its own reflection in the tide.

Meanwhile, his friend, through alley and street,
Wanders and watches with eager ears,
Till in the silence around him he hears
The muster of men at the barrack door,
The sound of arms, and the tramp of feet,
And the measured tread of the grenadiers,
Marching down to their boats on the shore.

Then he climbed the tower of the Old North Church,
By the wooden stairs, with stealthy tread,
To the belfry-chamber overhead,
And startled the pigeons from their perch

In his **Midnight Ride of Paul Revere,** American artist Grant Wood (1891–1942) captured the urgency of Paul Revere's ride of April 19, 1775, to warn the Minutemen that the British were coming.

On the sombre rafters, that round him made
Masses and moving shapes of shade,—
By the trembling ladder, steep and tall,
To the highest window in the wall,
Where he paused to listen and look down
A moment on the roofs of the town,
And the moonlight flowing over all.

Beneath, in the churchyard, lay the dead,
In their night-encampment on the hill,
Wrapped in silence so deep and still
That he could hear, like a sentinel's tread,
The watchful night-wind, as it went
Creeping along from tent to tent,
And seeming to whisper, "All is well!"
A moment only he feels the spell
Of the place and the hour, and the secret dread
For suddenly all his thoughts are bent
On a shadowy something far away,
Where the river widens to meet the bay,—
A line of black that bends and floats
On the rising tide, like a bridge of boats.

Meanwhile, impatient to mount and ride,
Booted and spurred, with a heavy stride
On the opposite shore walked Paul Revere.
Now he patted his horse's side,
Now gazed at the landscape far and near,
Then, impetuous, stamped the earth,
And turned and tightened his saddle-girth;
But mostly he watched with eager search
The belfry-tower of the Old North Church,
As it rose above the graves on the hill,
Lonely and spectral and sombre and still.
And lo! as he looks, on the belfry's height
A glimmer, and then a gleam of light!
He springs to the saddle, the bridle he turns,
But lingers and gazes, till full on his sight
A second lamp in the belfry burns!

A hurry of hoofs in a village street,
A shape in the moonlight, a bulk in the dark,
And beneath, from the pebbles, in passing, a spark
Struck out by a steed flying fearless and fleet:
That was all! And yet, through the gloom and the light,
The fate of a nation was riding that night;
And the spark struck out by that steed, in his flight,
Kindled the land into flame with its heat.

He has left the village and mounted the steep,
And beneath him, tranquil and broad and deep,
Is the Mystic, meeting the ocean tides;

And under the alders that skirt its edge,
Now soft on the sand, now loud on the ledge,
Is heard the tramp of his steed as he rides.

It was twelve by the village clock,
When he crossed the bridge into Medford town.
He heard the crowing of the cock,
And the barking of the farmer's dog,
And felt the damp of the river fog,
That rises after the sun goes down.

It was one by the village clock,
When he galloped into Lexington.
He saw the gilded weathercock
Swim in the moonlight as he passed,
And the meeting-house windows, blank and bare,
Gaze at him with a spectral glare,
As if they already stood aghast
At the bloody work they would look upon.

It was two by the village clock,
When he came to the bridge in Concord town.
He heard the bleating of the flock,
And the twitter of birds among the trees,
And felt the breath of the morning breeze
Blowing over the meadows brown.
And one was safe and asleep in his bed
Who at the bridge would be first to fall,
Who that day would be lying dead,
Pierced by a British musket-ball.

You know the rest. In the books you have read,
How the British Regulars fired and fled,—
How the farmers gave them ball for ball,
From behind each fence and farm-yard wall,
Chasing the Redcoats down the lane,
Then crossing the fields to emerge again
Under the trees at the turn of the road,
And only pausing to fire and load.

So through the night rode Paul Revere;
And so through the night went his cry of alarm
To every Middlesex village and farm,—
A cry of defiance and not of fear,
A voice in the darkness, a knock at the door,
And a word that shall echo forevermore!
For, borne on the night-wind of the Past,
Through all our history, to the last,
In the hour of darkness and peril and need,
The people will waken and listen to hear
The hurrying hoof-beats of that steed,
And the midnight message of Paul Revere.

HENRY WADSWORTH LONGFELLOW

The Battle of Lexington, engraved in 1798 by New Yorker Cornelius Tiebout, depicts this first battle between the British and American troops. At dawn on April 19, 1775, a line of Redcoats approached the green at Lexington, Massachusetts, to face a motley corps of Minutemen.

The Shot Heard Around the World

"Disperse, ye rebels, disperse!"

Dawn on the village green at Lexington. The date was April 19, 1775. A sharp spring chill came with the early morning hour. The line of Redcoats, the best that Britain could muster, were weary after a twenty-one-mile all-night forced march from Boston. Now they faced a motley corps of seventy Minutemen. These men were assembled in a line facing the British troops and gave no sign of obeying the riot command of Major John Pitcairn. Stamping the ground with their dusty boots to warm their cold feet, they firmly gripped their weapons and refused to budge.

Major Pitcairn, annoyed, but eager to reach the final objective at Concord and complete the assignment to destroy the gunpowder and other supplies these rebels had gathered, repeated: "Disperse, go home!"

The ranks of the Minutemen seemed to be on the verge of breaking up. It had been a long wait since the alarm bell had sounded five hours earlier. The grim line began to sag.

Then, without a command, from a nearby stone wall a single shot rang out. There was first a moment of disbelief. And then the Redcoats, in the classic manner of the European battlefield, responded to that one shot with a series of volleys. The American Revolution had begun.

19

To mark the completion of the battle monument at Concord, a half century after the event, the noted pastor and poet Ralph Waldo Emerson wrote his "Concord Hymn," which was sung on April 19, 1836, as part of the dedication ceremony. In these few brief lines Emerson summed up the memories of that moment when "the embattled farmers stood, and fired the shot heard round the world." The "Concord Hymn" is engraved on the patriotic memory of America.

During that brief but violent exchange, eight Minutemen lost their lives and ten were wounded. One British trooper suffered a slight leg wound. The Redcoats, seeing a victory in this first encounter, cheered and swung down the road to Concord, five miles away.

On a slight rise beyond the North Bridge, the Minutemen of Concord, commanded by Colonel James Barrett, who was a veteran of the French and Indian War, had been waiting since two in the morning. The Redcoats, emboldened by the clash at Lexington, marched into view. Their attempt to rush the bridge was met by a prepared line of defenders who greeted the Redcoats with a withering volley. Confused and tired, the troops fell back, leaving fourteen dead. King George's best had been forced to retreat by a band of stubborn Massachusetts farmers who had defended their ground and then fought back.

The British retreat could have turned into an all-out rout were it not for the reinforcements who reached the Redcoats on their way back to Boston.

By the hour the Minutemen were building their forces. And those bright red coats of the enemy made excellent targets for the tenacious farmers, who harassed the British troops all the way back to Boston. From behind every tree stump, brick wall, and corner the rifle fire continued. The British losses totaled 73 dead and 174 wounded. The Americans had survived their baptism of fire and proved they could handle England's best regiments.

CONCORD HYMN

By the rude bridge that arched the flood,
Their flag to April's breeze unfurled,
Here once the embattled farmers stood,
And fired the shot heard round the world.

The foe long since in silence slept;
Alike the conqueror silent sleeps;
And Time the ruined bridge has swept
Down the dark stream which seaward creeps.

On this green bank, by this soft stream,
We set to-day a votive stone;
That memory may their deed redeem,
When, like our sires, our sons are gone.

Spirit, that made those heroes dare
To die, and leave their children free,
Bid Time and Nature gently spare
The shaft we raise to them and thee.

RALPH WALDO EMERSON

Alert and ready for action, musket in hand, and plow at his feet, the heroic sculpture **Minute Man of Concord** is one of Daniel Chester French's many patriotic works. Commissioned for the centennial of the battles of Lexington and Concord, this statue stands on the green at Concord, Massachusetts, a durable symbol of the nation's readiness to defend its liberty.

7. Call It Macaroni

It was born as an insult but grew into an expression of patriotism. This lively, defiant tune, with its multinational background—English, Dutch, Hungarian—and derisive verses, became a very American song.

Well before the Revolution, "Yankee Doodle" was being played and sung in London as an expression of anti-American sentiment. The British Redcoats were always dressed in splendor, while the Colonials, a ragamuffin band with the barest supply system, wore what was available.

Apparently, Dr. Richard Schuckburg, a British military surgeon, first put together the tune and the words properly, and the song quickly caught on. Published in Britain in 1775, it seems to have accompanied the British forces and was regularly played by their bands when they disembarked, "fifes playing and colours flying," for American duty.

Far from being insulted by the insolent satire, the Americans came to love the song and adopted it as their own. At the end of the Revolutionary War, at Yorktown, the tune had a place in the celebration among Washington's troops.

The term "Yankee" was originally used to denote a resident of New England; then, during the Civil War, it was a label for all Northerners. By World Wars I and II, it applied to all U.S. soldiers.

YANKEE DOODLE

1 Father and I went down to camp Along with Captain Gooding,
And there we see the men and boys, As thick as hasty pudding.
Yankee doodle keep it up, Yankee doodle dandy
Mind the music and the step, And with the girls be handy.

2 And there we see a swamping gun,
  Large as a log of maple,
Upon a duced little cart,
  A load for father's cattle.
Yankee doodle &c.

3 And every time they shoot it off,
  It takes a horn of powder;
It makes a noise like father's gun,
  Only a nation louder.
Yankee doodle &c.

4 I went as nigh to one myself
  As 'Siah's underpinning;
And father went as nigh again,
  I thought the duce was in him.
Yankee doodle &c.

5 Cousin Simon grew so bold,
  I thought he would have cocked it;
It scared me so I streaked it off,
  And hung by father's pocket.
Yankee doodle &c.

6 But Captain Davis has a gun,
  He kind of clapped his hand on't
And struck a crooked stabbing iron
  Upon the little end on't.
Yankee doodle &c.

7 And there I see a pumpkin shell,
  As big as mother's basin,
And every time they touched it off,
  They scamper'd like the nation.
Yankee doodle &c.

8 I see a little barrel too,
  The heads were made of leather;
They knocked upon it with little clubs,
  And called the folks together.
Yankee doodle &c.

9 And there was Captain Washington
  And gentlefolks about him;
They say he's grown so tarnal proud,
  He will not ride without 'em.
Yankee doodle &c.

8. Washington: Our First Leader

It was a fortunate circumstance of history that just as our nation was about to come into being there was available for leadership a Virginia gentleman named George Washington. No one else could have matched this man for integrity or ability to command respect. No one else could have risen so above political and personal rancor and set his own stamp on the nation. Washington's strength and his sense of purpose left a mark on our history that has lasted more than two centuries. In the stress of those closing years of the eighteenth century, in peace and in war, he proved himself a sound, dedicated leader for the new nation.

George Washington, according to eyewitness reports, was a solemn and shy man. Women seemed to have liked him, and he was reported to have been a dashing figure on the dance floor. But the men around him were properly awed by his air of dignity and a certain look in his blue eyes. At six feet three inches, he was, for the time, a very big man. In the uniforms he enjoyed wearing, his broad shoulders accented his muscular two hundred pounds. He had brown hair and large hands and feet, and on horseback he was truly an imposing figure.

Washington's formal schooling had been spasmodic, but he could handle arithmetic and he had a feeling for words. In manner he was direct and not always adroit, but beneath that mask of dignity one could sense a certain humility.

As a frontier fighter and a military commander, Washington had inspired confidence and displayed remarkable courage. As the first President, he adopted a national rather than provincial point of view, and succeeded in charting new paths for the great federal experiment. Washington was a forthright and an often stubborn man, who was always aware that he was setting precedents. He displayed ability to enlist the best talents for advisers, and brought those talents into harmony.

Washington was courageous, honest, and decisive. Despite his personal remoteness, he achieved and has retained his place as our greatest patriotic personality. Americans were fortunate that he was there when he was needed.

Rebellion was a reality on that June day in 1775 when George Washington, citizen-soldier, lieutenant colonel in the Virginia militia, delegate to the second Continental Congress, was named commander in chief of the newly born Continental Army.

Lexington, Concord, and Bunker Hill were already history. Boston was under siege by sixteen thousand ragged Colonials. John Adams had proposed that this army be recognized as the Continental Army. The British were bringing in reinforcements.

On June 14 the Congress voted to raise an additional six companies from Pennsylvania, Maryland, and Virginia to help the troops at Boston. The rough militia needed a commander, and on June 15 Maryland delegate Thomas Johnson nominated George Washington of Virginia as commander in chief. Elected unanimously, Washington accepted and agreed to serve without pay but with reimbursement for his expenses.

Who was this Virginia aristocrat in whose large, competent hands now rested the fate of a nation as yet unborn?

George Washington had spent much of his youth living at the home of his brothers. He was already working as a surveyor at age sixteen, and at twenty-one he was assigned to carry out a dangerous and delicate mission into the wilderness to warn the French they were encroaching on land belonging to the British crown. Then in 1775 he served as an aide to British General Thomas

Opposite page:
The first full-length portrait of Washington, showing the commander in chief at the Battle of Princeton. It is by Charles Willson Peale.

Braddock in an ill-fated expedition against the French and Indians. Young Washington's clothes were pierced by four enemy bullets, and he had two horses shot from under him. This firsthand experience in battle served him well.

George Washington dearly loved the Tidewater acres on the Potomac that he called home. At age eighteen he was already a landowner and a successful planter. He had, from his earliest days, a sense of purpose, a quality of leadership that marked him apart. When his moment came in the springtime of 1775, George Washington was ready for his role. Congress could not have chosen a better commander.

George Washington: Acceptance of His Appointment as General and Commander in Chief (June 16, 1775)

Mr. President:

Tho' I am truly sensible of the high Honour done me in this Appointment, yet I feel great distress from a consciousness that my abilities and Military experience may not be equal to the extensive and important Trust: However, as the Congress desires I will enter upon the momentous duty, and exert every power I Possess In their Service for the Support of the glorious Cause: I beg they will accept my most cordial thanks for this distinguished testimony of their Approbation.

But lest some unlucky event should happen unfavourable to my reputation, I beg it may be remembered by every Gentn. in the room, that I this day declare with the utmost sincerity, I do not think of my self equal to the Command I am honoured with.

As to pay, Sir, I beg leave to Assure the Congress that as no pecuniary consideration could have tempted me to have accepted this Arduous employment (at the expence of my domestt. ease and happiness) I do not wish to make any proffit from it: I will keep an exact Account of my expences; those I doubt not they will discharge and that is all I desire.

*   *   *

24

On January 6, 1759, when he was almost twenty-seven, the Virginia planter-soldier, George Washington, married Martha Dandridge Custis, a rich widow with two children. They were a remarkable pair, he over six feet, she short, slight, and brown-eyed, a serious woman who regarded herself as "an old-fashioned Virginian housekeeper, steady as a clock, busy as a bee, and cheerful as a cricket." George Washington loved his Virginia homestead with its six tobacco plantations. He was a good farmer and a capable businessman who enjoyed managing his acres.

Martha Washington was forty-four when husband George, then forty-three, signed up for military service. This did not stop her from accompanying the general on his Revolutionary campaigns.

George Washington: Letter to Martha Washington (Philadelphia, June 18, 1775)

My Dearest:

I am now set down to write to you on a subject, which fills me with inexpressible concern, and this concern is greatly aggravated and increased, when I reflect upon the uneasiness I know it will give you. It has been determined in Congress, that the whole army raised for the defence of the American cause shall be put under my care, and that it is necessary for me to proceed immediately to Boston to take upon me the command of it.

You may believe me, my dear Patsy, when I assure you, in the most solemn manner that, so far from seeking this appointment, I have used every endeavor in my power to avoid it, not only from my unwillingness to part with you and the family, but from a consciousness of its being a trust too great for my capacity, and that I should enjoy more real happiness in one month with you at home, than I have the most distant prospect of finding abroad, if my stay were to be seven years. But as it has been a kind of destiny, that has thrown me upon this service, I shall hope that my undertaking it is designed to answer some good purpose. You might, and I suppose did perceive, from the tenor of my letters, that I was apprehensive I could not avoid this appointment, as I did not pretend to intimate when I should return. That was the case. I was utterly out of my power to refuse this appointment, without exposing my character to such censures, as would have reflected dishonor upon myself, and given pain to my friends. This, I am sure, could not, and ought not, to be pleasing to you, and must have lessend me considerably in my own esteem. I shall rely, therefore, confidently on that Providence, which has heretofore preserved and been bountiful to me, not doubting but that I shall return safe to you in the fall. I shall feel no pain from the toil or the danger of the campaign, my unhappiness will flow from the uneasiness I know you will feel from being left alone. I therefore beg, that you will summon your whole fortitude, and pass your time as agreeably as possible. Nothing will give me so much sincere satisfaction as to hear this, and to hear it from your own pen. My earnest and ardent desire is, that you would pursue any plan that is most likely to produce content, and a tolerable degree of tranquillity; as it must add greatly to my uneasy feelings to hear, that you are dissatisfied or complaining at what I really could not avoid.

As life is always uncertain, and common prudence dictates to every man the necessity of settling his temporal concerns, while it is in his power, and while the mind is calm and undisturbed, I have, since I came to this place (for I had not time to do it before I left home) got Colonel Pendleton to draft a will for me, by the directions I gave him, which will I now enclose. The provision made for you in case of my death will, I hope, be agreeable.

I shall add nothing more, as I have several letters to write, but to desire that you will remember me to your friends, and to assure you that I am, with the most unfeigned regard, my dear Patsy, your affectionate, &c.

Martha Washington,
by Gilbert Stuart

George Washington,
by Gilbert Stuart

9. We Hold These Truths to Be Self-evident . . .

The debate over, the fighting had begun. It was time for the Colonies to break with the mother country. After all the speeches, resolutions, and correspondence, a statement of intent was needed to clarify for the whole world why these American colonies were fighting for independence. Much of the impetus for this declaration of independence came from Virginia, where a "united colonies, free and independent" was already being envisioned.

At the Second Continental Congress on June 7, 1776, a resolution for independence had reached the floor. It was followed by another on June 10. The delegates were now under some pressure to provide public expression to these sentiments. On June 11, a committee of five was named to prepare a declaration. The task was given to Thomas Jefferson, John Adams, Benjamin Franklin, Roger Sherman, and Robert Livingston.

The actual writing was assigned to Jefferson, the tall, red-haired scholar-architect from Monticello, who rented a nearby room and worked hard at the portable desk he had devised, battling the heat and insects of the Philadelphia summer.

Calling on his wide knowledge of classical thinkers to express his feelings about natural rights and self-evident truths, Jefferson fashioned a stirring rough draft of the declaration that was ready by June 28. His preamble of 200 words was a masterpiece of lucidity. The full Jefferson draft underwent eighty-six changes, and was finally cut by 480 words to a tight 1,337 words.

The result was an enduring masterpiece of political philosophy, an argument for revolution so precise and so forceful that it has flashed its lightning into every corner of the globe.

It was also as its author called it, a "declaration of the American mind," a logical outgrowth of the American colonial experience joined with enlightenment and reason. It synthesized ideas and purposes, based on bedrock "life, liberty and the pursuit of happiness," and those natural "unalienable" rights. It made sense out of the American Revolution.

On July 4, 1776, in the evening hours, the "Declaration of Independence" was adopted. A nation was born.

That evening the document was taken to a nearby print shop, where copies were prepared for distribution throughout the new nation. On July 8 the manifesto was read to the citizenry of Philadelphia from the balcony of the meeting hall; on July 9 Washington read it to his troops in New York, where a statue of King George was pulled down, to be made into forty thousand bullets.

Two weeks later, the signatures of all the delegates were added to an engrossed copy that now rests in the National Archives in Washington, D.C.

The Declaration of Independence
(July 4, 1776)

THE UNANIMOUS DECLARATION OF THE THIRTEEN UNITED STATES OF AMERICA

When in the Course of human events, it becomes necessary for one people to dissolve the political bands which have connected them with another, and to assume among the Powers of the earth, the separate and equal station to which the Laws of Nature and of Nature's God entitle them, a decent respect to the opinions of mankind requires that they should declare the causes which impel them to the separation.

John Hancock,
by John Singleton Copley

In his ***Signing of the
Declaration*** John Trumbull
(1756–1843) re-creates the
scene on July 4, 1776, at the
formal presentation of the
Declaration of Independence. As
members of the Continental
Congress look on, Thomas
Jefferson, author of the
Declaration, passes the
document to John Hancock
(*seated*), president of the
Congress, for his signature.
Jefferson stands with the group
of men responsible for
conceiving the Declaration.
From left to right: John Adams,
Roger Sherman, Robert R.
Livingston, and Benjamin
Franklin.

Signers of the Declaration of Independence

John Adams, Mass.
Samuel Adams, Mass.
Josiah Bartlett, N.H.
Carter Braxton, Va.
Chas. Carroll, Md.
Samuel Chase, Md.
Abraham Clark, N.J.
George Clymer, Pa.
William Emery, R.I.
William Floyd, N.Y.
Benjamin Franklin, Pa.
Elbridge Gerry, Mass.
Button Gwinnett, Ga.
Lyman Hall, Ga.
John Hancock, Mass.
Benjamin Harrison, Va.
John Hart, N.J.
Joseph Hewes, N.C.
Thos. Heyward, Jr., S.C.
William Hooper, N.C.
Stephen Hopkins, R.I.
Francis Hopkinson, N.J.
Samuel Huntington, Conn.
Thomas Jefferson, Va.
Richard Henry Lee, Va.
Francis Lightfoot Lee, Va.
Francis Lewis, N.Y.
Philip Livingston, N.Y.
Thomas Lynch, Jr., S.C.
Thomas McKean, Del.
Arthur S. Middleton, S.C.
Lewis Morris, N.Y.
Robert Morris, Pa.
John Morton, Pa.
Thos. Nelson, Jr., Va.
William Paca, Md.
Robert Treat Paine, Mass.
John Penn, N.C.
George Read, Del.
Caesar Rodney, Del.
George Ross, Pa.
Benjamin Rush, Pa.
Edward Rutledge, S.C.
Roger Sherman, Conn.
James Smith, Pa.
Richard Stockton, N.J.
Thomas Stone, Md.
George Taylor, Pa.
Matthew Thornton, N.H.
George Walton, Ga.
William Whipple, N.H.
William Williams, Conn.
James Wilson, Pa.
John Witherspoon, N.J.
Oliver Wolcott, Conn.
George Wythe, Va.

We hold these truths to be self-evident, that all men are created equal, that they are endowed by their Creator with certain unalienable Rights, that among these are Life, Liberty and the pursuit of Happiness. That to secure these rights, Governments are instituted among Men, deriving their just powers from the consent of the governed. That whenever any Form of Government becomes destructive of these ends, it is the Right of the People to alter or to abolish it, and to institute new Government, laying its foundation on such principles and organizing its powers in such form, as to them shall seem most likely to effect their Safety and Happiness. Prudence, indeed, will dictate that Governments long established should not be changed for light and transient causes; and accordingly all experience hath shown, that mankind are more disposed to suffer, while evils are sufferable, than to right themselves by abolishing the forms to which they are accustomed. But when a long train of abuses and usurpations, pursuing invariably the same Object evinces a design to reduce them under absolute Despotism, it is their right, it is their duty, to throw off such Government, and to provide new Guards for their future security.—Such has been the patient sufferance of these Colonies; and such is now the necessity which constrains them to alter their former Systems of Government. The history of the present King of Great Britain is a history of repeated injuries and usurpations, all having in direct object the establishment of an absolute tyranny over these States. To prove this, let Facts be submitted to a candid world.

He has refused to Assent to Laws, the most wholesome and necessary for the public good.

He has forbidden his Governors to pass Laws of immediate and pressing importance, unless suspended in their operation till his Assent should be obtained; and when so suspended, he has utterly neglected to attend to them.

He has refused to pass other Laws for the accommodation of large districts of people, unless those people would relinquish the right of Representation in the Legislature, a right inestimable to them and formidable to tyrants only.

He has called together legislative bodies at places unusual, uncomfortable, and distant from the depository of their Public Records, for the sole purpose of fatiguing them into compliance with his measures.

He has dissolved Representative Houses repeatedly, for opposing with manly firmness his invasions on the rights of the people.

He has refused for a long time, after such dissolutions, to cause others to be elected; whereby the Legislative Powers, incapable of Annihilation, have returned to the People at large for their exercise; the State remaining in the mean time exposed to all the dangers of invasion from without, and convulsions within.

He has endeavoured to prevent the population of these States; for that purpose obstructing the Laws of Naturalization of Foreigners; refusing to pass others to encourage their migration hither, and raising the conditions of new Appropriations of Lands.

He has obstructed the Administration of Justice, by refusing his Assent to Laws for establishing Judiciary Powers.

He has made Judges dependent on his Will alone, for the tenure of their offices, and the amount and payment of their salaries.

He has erected a multitude of New Offices, and sent hither swarms of Officers to harass our People, and eat out their substance.

He has kept among us, in times of peace, Standing Armies without the Consent of our legislature.

He has affected to render the Military independent of and superior to the Civil Power.

He has combined with others to subject us to a jurisdiction foreign to our constitution, and unacknowledged by our laws; giving his Assent to their acts of pretended legislation:

For quartering large bodies of armed troops among us:

For protecting them, by a mock Trial, from Punishment for any Murders which they should commit on the Inhabitants of these States:

For cutting off our Trade with all parts of the world:

For imposing taxes on us without our Consent:

For depriving us in many cases, of the benefits of Trial by Jury:

For transporting us beyond Seas to be tried for pretended offences:

For abolishing the free System of English Laws in a neighbouring Province, establishing therein an Arbitrary government, and enlarging its Boundaries so as to render it at once an example and fit instrument for introducing the same absolute rule into these Colonies:

For taking away our Charters, abolishing our most valuable Laws, and altering fundamentally the Forms of our Governments:

For suspending our own Legislature, and declaring themselves invested with Power to legislate for us in all cases whatsoever.

He has abdicated Government here, by declaring us out of his Protection and waging War against us.

He has plundered our seas, ravaged our Coasts, burnt our towns, and destroyed the lives of our people.

He is at this time transporting large armies of foreign mercenaries to compleat the works of death, desolation and tyranny, already begun with circumstances of Cruelty & perfidy scarcely paralleled in the most barbarous ages, and totally unworthy the Head of a civilized nation.

He has constrained our fellow Citizens taken Captive on the high Seas to bear Arms against their Country, to become the executioners of their friends and Brethren, or to fall themselves by their Hands.

He has excited domestic insurrections amongst us, and has endeavoured to bring on the inhabitants of our frontiers, the merciless Indian Savages, whose known rule of warfare, is an undistinguished destruction of all ages, sexes and conditions.

In every stage of these Oppressions We have Petitioned for Redress in the most humble terms: Our repeated Petitions have been answered only by repeated injury. A Prince, whose character is thus marked by every act which may define a Tyrant, is unfit to be the ruler of a free People.

Nor have We been wanting in attention to our British brethren. We have warned them from time to time of attempts by their legislature to extend an unwarrantable jurisdiction over us. We have reminded them of the circumstances of our emigration and settlement here. We have appealed to their native justice and magnanimity, and we have conjured them by the ties of our common kindred to disavow these usurpations, which, would inevitably interrupt our connections and correspondence. They too have been deaf to the voice of justice and of consanguinity. We must, therefore, acquiesce in the necessity, which denounces our Separation, and hold them, as we hold the rest of mankind, Enemies in War, in Peace Friends.

We, therefore, the Representatives of the United States of America, in General Congress, Assembled, appealing to the Supreme Judge of the world for the rectitude of our intentions, do, in the Name, and by Authority of the good People of these Colonies, solemnly publish and declare, That these United Colonies are, and of Right ought to be Free and Independent States; that they are Absolved from all Allegiance to the British Crown, and that all political connection between them and the State of Great Britain, is and ought to be totally dissolved; and that as Free and Independent States, they have full Power to levy War, conclude Peace, contract Alliances, establish Commerce, and to do all other Acts and Things which Independent States may of right do. And for the support of this Declaration, with a firm reliance on the Protection of Divine Providence, we mutually pledge to each other our Lives, our Fortunes and our sacred Honor.

Abigail Adams,
by Gilbert Stuart

John Adams: To His Wife, on the Birth of the New Nation
(Philadelphia, July 3, 1776)

Yesterday, the greatest question was decided, which ever was debated in America, and a greater, perhaps, never was nor will be decided among men. A resolution was passed without one dissenting colony, "that these United Colonies are, and of right ought to be, free and independent States, and as such they have, and of right ought to have, full power to make war, conclude peace,

John Adams,
by J. S. Copley

Letter writing was a widely practiced art in the Colonial years. Between John Adams, the persistent Revolutionary from New England, and his perceptive wife, there was a flow of letters that covered every possible subject. Abigail was talented, innovative, and as determined as her husband. She had a great feeling for words. She was also a feminist, and in a famous letter to her husband she wrote in a spirit of prophecy: "In the new code of law . . . remember the ladies and be more generous and favorable to them than your ancestors. Do not put such unlimited power into the hands of the husbands. Remember all men would be tyrants if they could. If particular attention is not paid to the ladies, we are determined to foment a rebellion and will not hold ourselves bound by any laws in which we have no voice or representation."

establish commerce, and to do all other acts and things which other States may rightfully do." You will see in a few days a Declaration setting forth the causes which have impelled us to this mighty revolution, and the reasons which will justify it in the sight of God and man. A plan of confederation will be taken up in a few days.

You will think me transported with enthusiasm, but I am not. I am well aware of the toil, and blood, and treasure, that it will cost us to maintain this declaration, and support and defend these States. Yet, through all the gloom, I can see the rays of ravishing light and glory. I can see that the end is more than worth all the means, and that posterity will triumph in that day's transaction, even although we should rue it, which I trust in God we shall not.

Independence Hall

Compared with most of the architectural historic monuments in Washington, London, Paris, or Rome, this stately Colonial structure in old Philadelphia lacks the imposing quality one might expect. But as visiting patriots enter its doors, history takes them by the hand. Here is where the Founding Fathers met to gather strength from each other, to spell out their grievances, to declare their independence, to seek unity to fashion a new nation.

The glow of history, long past but always new, hovers over these rooms, the chairs, desks, and inkwells; the hands of Washington, Jefferson, Franklin, Adams, and many others touched these places.

Originally the Pennsylvania State House, Independence Hall was started in 1732 and completed in 1753. In 1775, when the Minutemen of New England faced the British Redcoats, the State House was home to the Second Continental Congress, and it was here, on June 16, 1775, that George Washington of Virginia was given command of the new Continental Army. A year later, on July 4, 1776, the Declaration of Independence was signed at Independence Hall. In 1787, after the ordeal of the Revolution, a Constitution was framed there for the new nation.

Just to the west, in an adjoining hall, the fledgling Congress met for ten formative years, and to the east, in another hall, the U.S. Supreme Court conducted its early sessions.

There is no more revered building than Independence Hall. For the American patriot it is sacred ground.

Independence Hall,
Philadelphia

The Liberty Bell

"Proclaim Liberty Throughout All the Land unto all the Inhabitants Thereof." These words from Leviticus serve to remind Americans of the Liberty Bell's place in our history and to lend reverence to its place as a national symbol. We are the people of the bell.

The Liberty Bell was originally ordered to mark the fiftieth anniversary of the founding of the Commonwealth of Pennsylvania. It was cast by a London bell maker, Thomas Lister, and reached Philadelphia in August 1752. The bell had a circumference of twelve feet, measuring seven feet six inches from lip to crown, with a three-foot-two-inch clapper.

When the bell was being tested in September 1752, it cracked. A recasting was made by a Philadelphia foundry, Pass & Stow, where $1\frac{1}{2}$ ounces of copper was added for each of the bell's 2,080 pounds. That altered the tone and a second recast was ordered, after which it produced the right tone.

In June 1753, the huge bell was hung in the wooden steeple of the State House, later Independence Hall, where it was rung to announce defiance of British taxes, the Boston Tea Party, and then, in July 1776, the reading of the Declaration of Independence.

When British troops occupied Philadelphia during the grim days of the Revolution, the Liberty Bell was carted off to a hiding place in Allentown, Pennsylvania. In 1778 it was returned to Philadelphia. In 1835, when the great bell tolled the death of Chief Justice John Marshall, it cracked once again.

Today the Liberty Bell rests in its own enclosure in Independence National Park, close to Independence Hall, and Americans who come to this shrine can sense and thrill to the proud history it has proclaimed.

10. The Difficult Road to Independence

In August of 1776, despite those inspiring words coming out of Philadelphia, the Revolutionary Army had raised a bare eighteen thousand soldiers. With hardly a year of command experience, Washington saw that his forces were undermanned, underclothed, and underfed. His situation was nearly hopeless.

Washington's first objective was to prevent the king's forces from taking New York. Under the leadership of General William Howe, the British had brought in twenty-five thousand trained Redcoats and Hessians to face the Americans. The British fleet controlled the waterways surrounding New York, and the battle site was a Long Island plain, perfectly suited to the European open-field battle style. The date was August 27, 1776.

In addressing his men before the gunfire began, Washington made his call to battle in the classic mold of patriotic evocation, appealing to God and using the language of free men with a dedicated spirit, a vision of the future, and a grasp of the hour. His challenge: "To conquer or to die."

A thousand Americans died that day on Long Island. The British artillery punished the Revolutionary troops, the Hessian steel cut them down. Washington spent most of the day in his saddle, trying to save his battle lines, but it was close to a disaster. That night Washington managed to save the rest of his army—and the Revolution—by ferrying nine thousand men across the East River.

George Washington: To the American Troops Before the Battle of Long Island

The time is now near at hand which must probably determine whether Americans are to be freemen or slaves; whether they are to have any property they can call their own; whether their houses and farms are to be pillaged and destroyed, and themselves consigned to a state of wretchedness from which no human efforts will deliver them. The fate of unborn millions will now depend, under God, on the courage and conduct of this army. Our cruel and unrelenting enemy leaves us only the choice of a brave resistance, or the most abject submission. We have, therefore, to resolve to conquer or to die.

Our own, our country's honour, calls upon us for a vigorous and manly exertion; and if we now shamefully fail, we shall become infamous to the whole world. Let us, then, rely on the goodness of our cause, and the aid of the Supreme Being, in whose hands victory is, to animate and encourage us to great and noble actions. The eyes of all our countrymen are now upon us; and we shall have their blessings and praises, if happily we are the instruments of saving them from the tyranny meditated against them. Let us, therefore, animate and encourage each other, and show the whole world that a freeman contending for liberty on his own ground is superior to any slavish mercenary on earth.

Liberty, property, life and honour, are all at stake. Upon your courage and conduct rest the hopes of our bleeding and insulted country. Our wives, children and parents, expect safety from us only; and they have every reason to believe that Heaven will crown with success so just a cause. The enemy will endeavour to intimidate by show and appearance; but remember they have been repulsed on various occasions by a few brave Americans. Their cause is bad,—their men are conscious of it; and, if opposed with firmness and coolness on their first onset, with our advantage of works, and knowledge of the ground, the victory is most assuredly ours. Every good soldier will be silent and attentive, wait for orders, and reserve his fire until he is sure of doing execution.

The Gallant Hours

In the entire range of American patriotic iconography there are few more beloved paintings than that of General George Washington's daring crossing of the ice-filled Delaware River on Christmas night in 1776, and the drummer and fifer in *The Spirit of '76.*

Both of these paintings, produced long after the events they depict, epitomize the spirit of the American Revolution. They have become firmly rooted in the patriotic conscience of the nation, dramatizing our feelings without a written or a spoken word. Reproduced in many ways for many uses, they have appeared in literally millions of books and tens of thousands of schoolrooms and libraries around the nation. They speak directly to American patriotism, telling of that quality of spirit and of mind that can overcome all manner of stress and suffering and emerge triumphant. These paintings have achieved their own niche in the heart of Americans.

The Spirit of '76, Archibald M. Willard's patriotic evocation, was shown initially at the Centennial Exposition in Philadelphia in 1876. Willard, a prominent Cleveland artist, did fourteen additional versions of the painting in later years. In 1912 he was commissioned by the city to do a copy. For models he used his own father, Samuel Willard, a minister, as the drummer and a Civil War veteran, Hugh Mosher, to play the fife. That painting, eight feet by twelve feet, now hangs in the rotunda of the Cleveland City Hall. Willard was seventy-six when he completed that commission.

Emanuel Leutze's *Washington Crossing the Delaware* immortalizes the crucial episode in the Revolutionary War on Christmas night, December 25, 1776, when the American commander managed, with the help of former fishermen from Marblehead, Massachusetts, to ferry 2,400 troops across the icy Delaware at night and surprise the Hessians at Trenton. Leutze, remembered for his historical paintings, was born in Germany and settled in the United States just before the Civil War. This painting, twelve and a half by twenty-one feet, hangs in the Metropolitan Museum in New York.

Washington Crossing the Delaware, by Emanuel Leutze

11. Home-grown Heroes and Friends from Overseas

The Army of the United States was a myth, little more than a handful of ragtag volunteers facing the armed might of a world empire. To fight for a cause that not all of them entirely understood, farmers had left their plows, merchants their goods, fishermen their nets, teachers their classes. And, inspired by our Revolution, there were even those who came from abroad to help.

There were many heroes in that time. We do not know the names of most of them. These six whom we do remember have come to stand for the highest level of courage and devotion.

On the campus at Yale University in New Haven, Connecticut, stands a statue of **Captain Nathan Hale,** who was hanged as a spy by the British on September 22, 1776. The statue is the work of Bela Lyon Pratt.

Nathan Hale

Hale, a native of Connecticut, had graduated from Yale in 1773 and was teaching in a girls' school while looking forward to work in the ministry. Then in 1775 came the news from Lexington. Hale enlisted almost immediately in the Connecticut Rangers, declaring to the town meeting of his home in New London, Connecticut, "Liberty? Independence? Are they to remain only words? Gentlemen, let us make them *fighting* words!"

In the late summer of 1776, General Washington, encamped at Harlem Heights, desperately needed information about the British and their intentions on Long Island. The delicate assignment went to Hale, now a captain in the Rangers. Disguised as a Dutch schoolmaster, Hale managed to infiltrate the British lines, taking notes in Latin and drawing the appropriate sketches. All went well until Hale took a wrong boat trying to get back to the American encampment. He was captured, and readily admitted his identity.

At 11:00 A.M. the following day, September 22, 1776, Hale was executed by hanging, without trial and without even a Bible. There was sobbing among the witnesses, but the American never lost his composure. According to one report, Nathan Hale spoke as the noose was placed around his neck: "I only regret that I have but one life to lose for my country." Those words were to immortalize him in American history. Nathan Hale was twenty-one when he died.

Molly Pitcher at Monmouth, a lithograph done by Gilbert Gall in 1897 as an advertisement for the Union Metallic Cartridge Company.

Molly Pitcher

On June 28, 1778, a hot Sunday, a battle developed in the vicinity of Monmouth, New Jersey, not far from the home of one Mary Ludwig Hayes. Her husband, John, was a gunner in the engagement, and General Washington himself was supposed to have been there, mounted on his charger. The thirty-four-year-old housewife was helping the soldiers by drawing pitchers of cold water from the nearby spring. They started calling her "Molly Pitcher." When John Hayes fell, a victim of the heat, the cannon he had been manning was about to be carried off when Mary grabbed the rammer and proceeded to reload and fire the piece. In the heat of the action a British cannonball went right between Mary's legs and tore away part of her petticoat. That didn't stop her.

After the battle Washington asked her name, and Mary told him. General Washington said that thereafter Mary Ludwig Hayes was to be called "Sergeant Molly."

Marquis de Lafayette

Marie Joseph Paul Yves Roch Gilbert du Motier, Marquis de Lafayette (1757–1834) was a member of that small band of European military adventurers who came to participate in the American struggle for liberty.

Most of them asked for guaranteed rank and a good slice of pay. Lafayette was different. The wealthy scion of a noble French family, he came to Philadelphia in July 1777, asking only two favors: "One . . . to serve at my own expense, the other to commence by serving as a volunteer." Although not yet twenty, he was given the rank of major general.

During the crucial winter of 1777–78, with his own command of light infantry, Lafayette was at Valley Forge, where he bought comforts and clothing for his men. But his greatest contribution to the cause came in 1779, when he helped persuade the king of France to send military aid to the Revolution. That was the key to the victory at Yorktown and assured the Marquis de Lafayette an honored place in American history.

Lafayette,

Baron von Steuben

Baron Friederich Wilhelm von Steuben (1730–94) was forty-seven years old when he joined Washington's ragged troops at Valley Forge in February 1778.

Von Steuben, a German aristocrat, had served in the Seven Years' War, been an aide-de-camp to Frederick the Great, and filled a variety of military assignments throughout central Europe.

Persuaded by members of the French military to join the Americans, the tireless von Steuben tackled his task by writing a manual of arms for the Continentals and drilling a model company as an example. His special expertise helped to fashion a fighting force that could hold its own against the Redcoats.

Von Steuben

Thaddeus Kosciusko

"To fight for American independence." That was the direct answer young Thaddeus Kosciusko (1746–1817), fresh from Europe in the summer of 1776, gave to George Washington when the commander in chief asked the young Pole what he sought in America.

Kosciusko, from a noble line in Lithuania, was just twenty. At military schools in Warsaw and Paris he had studied engineering and fortifications. Then came a disappointing love affair in Paris, and, armed with a letter from Benjamin Franklin to George Washington, the young officer had come to America to fight and forget. He set up forts for the defense of the Delaware River and, with the rank of colonel in the Engineers of the Continental Army, he designed the initial defenses at West Point. Later he became a national hero of Poland for his efforts in one of her wars of liberation.

Kosciusko

Count Pulaski

Like many of his European colleagues in the American Army, Casimir Pulaski (1748–79) came of noble heritage. An experienced cavalry officer in his twenties, he came to America in 1777 with a letter of introduction from Benjamin Franklin to George Washington. Count Pulaski had fought in Poland against Russia; he had escaped to Prussia and then to France, where he met Franklin, who was assembling military expertise for the Continental Army.

Pulaski joined the Revolutionary forces and saw action at Brandywine and Germantown. Later, as a brigadier general, he formed his own cavalry unit, called Pulaski's Legion. He was mortally wounded in the Battle of Savannah on October 9, 1779.

Pulaski

12. Betsy Ross: A Flag for a New Nation

A full-fledged nation without an official flag? The notion may be preposterous, but it was not until 1912—136 years after the Declaration—that the Stars and Stripes received official approval establishing it as the flag of the United States of America.

At the start, there was a whole array of ensigns, regimental, state, local. There was the Rattlesnake Jack, a wriggling reptile against red and white bars, warning "Don't Tread on Me." It was used mainly by the navy, as were most of those flags. There was a flag with blue, red, and white bars, which John Paul Jones hoisted over the conquered *Serapis*. The Grand Union flag, used early by the Colonies, and bearing in the upper left corner the symbol of the British Union, was altered by the Continental Congress on June 14, 1777. The British crosses were replaced by "a new constellation" of stars representing the thirteen states. This flag was first used in 1783. Later, in 1818, Congress decreed the thirteen stripes. But only in 1912 was the final pattern made official.

History and legend have a way of blending in the crucible of time, and so it is with the story of our flag. The version we have is that told by Betsy Ross on her deathbed in 1836 to her eleven-year-old grandson, who, in turn, did not speak of it until 1870, when he passed it on to a meeting of the Pennsylvania Historical Society.

This painting, **The Birth of Our Nation's Flag,** by Charles H. Weisgerber, hangs in the Betsy Ross House in Philadelphia.

Elizabeth Griscom Ross was a Philadelphia seamstress married to John Ross, an upholsterer. Ross was killed in a munitions explosion in 1776. Betsy kept the upholstery shop going and lived on Arch Street, not too far from the State House on Chestnut, where history was being made almost every day. According to her story, a committee of the Continental Congress came to her in June 1777 and asked her to put together a new flag according to their instructions. The group included General Washington himself. Betsy had some experience in such matters, since she had made flags for the Navy. Her version of the flag for the new republic was not used until six years later.

If things did not happen precisely this way—if, in fact, Elizabeth Griscom Ross did not make that first flag—she did still sew a fine seam for a beloved legend.

13. Valley Forge: The Darkest Hour

Valley Forge—the very name brings a shiver. No American can hear it without conjuring up a vision of ragged soldiers huddled around a campfire, their feet leaving bloody marks in the snow, a desperate Washington in the saddle, head bowed in prayer, a council of officers deep in discussion of ways to hold an army together. There on that plateau on the banks of the Schuylkill, twenty miles northwest of Philadelphia, the American Revolution knew its darkest hour.

After the battles of Brandywine and Germantown, the general, over the objections of some who wanted this pitiful army to operate in the open, had set up this main encampment for his tired troops. In mid-December of 1777, there were about eleven thousand left in the Continental ranks. Desertion was a serious problem. The men needed shoes, food, shelter, blankets. There was, as some put it, "no pay, no clothes, no provisions, no rum."

The decision was to "hut" the army in its own cabins. During those grim weeks, 2,600 troops died of exposure and disease. Faith in Washington did much to hold the troops together even while they had to forage for food. The general countered his critics, noting that it was a lot easier to level objections from "a comfortable room by a good fireside, then to occupy a cold, bleak hill, and sleep under frost and snow without clothes or blankets."

Meantime, under the vigilant eyes of the Prussian drillmaster, Baron von Steuben, the ragged Continentals were being whipped into a capable fighting force. By June of 1777, when Washington was preparing for action against the Tommy Lobsters and their Hessian hirelings, the Americans were ready.

14. "These Are the Times That Try Men's Souls"

Thomas Paine (1737–1809) wrote of freedom and liberty with thunder and lightning in his words. They were not the conventional words of pleading and humility; they were forthright and uncomfortably bold. He had come to America from England in 1775, armed with a letter from Benjamin Fanklin, and was promptly caught up in the tide toward revolution.

His historic pamphlet, *Common Sense,* published anonymously, appeared on January 9, 1776. It sold half a million copies and stirred the patriotic fervor of every reader. *Common Sense* called for immediate independence from Great Britain. It labeled monarchy a corrupt form of government and insisted that Great Britain was restraining the growth of the American colonies.

Paine joined the Revolutionary Army but continued to write a series of pamphlets under the title *The Crisis.* The opening passage of the first of these carried the immortal words: "These are the times that try men's souls." At the request of George Washington, the publication was read to the Colonial troops. By the sheer force of its language and its eloquent patriotism, Paine's words pointed the way for many who were hesitant about the Colonial cause.

In 1787 Thomas Paine returned to England and began to write in defense of the French Revolution and the rights of man. Almost imprisoned in England, he fled to France and became a French citizen. Imprisoned there for certain unpopular views, he was finally released with the help of James Monroe and returned to America, where he died in 1809. Thomas Paine wrote, "Where freedom is not, there is my country." He lived by that credo.

Thomas Paine,
by John Wesley Jarvis

From *Common Sense* (1776)

I have heard it asserted by some that, as America has flourished under her former connection with Great Britain, the same connection is necessary towards her future happiness, and will always have the same effect. Nothing can be more fallacious than this kind of argument. We may as well assert that, because a child has thrived upon milk, it is never to have meat, or that the first twenty years of our lives is to become a precedent for the next twenty. But even this is admitting more than is true. For I answer roundly that America would have flourished as much, and probably much more, had no European power taken any notice of her. . . .

But Britain is the parent country, say some. Then the more shame upon her conduct. Even brutes do not devour their young, nor savages make war upon their families; wherefore the assertion, if true, turns to her reproach. . . .

Everything that is right or reasonable pleads for separation. The blood of the slain, the weeping voice of nature, cries, 'TIS TIME TO PART. Even the distance at which the Almighty hath placed England and America is a strong and natural proof that the authority of the one over the other was never the design of Heaven. . . .

But if you say, you can still pass the violations over, then I ask, Hath your house been burnt? Hath your property been destroyed before your face? Are your wife and children destitute of a bed to lie on, or bread to live on? Have you lost a parent or a child by their hands, and yourself the ruined and wretched survivor? If you have not, then are you not a judge of those who have. But if you have, and can still shake hands with the murderers, then are you unworthy the name of husband, father, friend, or lover; and whatever may be your rank or title in life, you have the heart of a coward, and the spirit of a sycophant. . . .

Small islands, not capable of protecting themselves, are the proper objects for government to take under their care. But there is something absurd in supposing a continent to be perpetually governed by an island. In no instance hath nature made the satellite larger than its primary planet; and as England and America, with respect to each other, reverse the common order of nature, it is evident that they belong to different systems. England to Europe: America to itself. . . .

You that tell us of harmony and reconciliation, can you restore to us the time that is past? Can you give to prostitution its former innocence? Neither can you reconcile Britain and America. . . . There are injuries which nature cannot forgive; she would cease to be nature if she did. As well can the lover forgive the ravisher of his mistress as the continent forgive the murders of Britain. The Almighty hath implanted in us these unextinguishable feelings for good and wise purposes. . . . They distinguish us from the herd of common animals. . . .

O! you that love mankind! You that dare oppose not only the tyranny but the tyrant, stand forth! Every spot of the old world is overrun with oppression. Freedom hath been hunted around the globe. Asia and Africa have long expelled her. Europe regards her like a stranger, and England hath given her warning to depart. O! receive the fugitive, and prepare in time an asylum for mankind.

From *The Crisis* (1776)

These are the times that try men's souls. The summer soldier and the sunshine patriot will, in this crisis, shrink from the service of their country; but he that stands it now, deserves the love and thanks of man and woman. Tyranny, like hell, is not easily conquered; yet we have this consolation with us, that the harder the conflict, the more glorious the triumph. What we obtain too cheap, we esteem too lightly: it is dearness only that gives every thing its value. Heaven knows how to put a proper price upon its goods; and it would be strange indeed if so celestial an article as FREEDOM should not be highly rated. Britain, with an army to enforce her tyranny, has declared that she has a right (not only to TAX) but "to BIND us in CASES WHATSOEVER," and if being bound in that manner, is not slavery, then there is not such a thing as slavery upon earth. Even the expression is impious; for so unlimited a power can belong only to God. . . .

I have as little superstition in me as any man living, but my secret opinion has ever been, and still is, that God Almighty will not give up a people to military destruction, or leave them unsupportedly to perish, who have so earnestly and so repeatedly sought to avoid the calamities of war, by every decent method which wisdom could invent. Neither have I so much of the infidel in me, as to suppose that He has relinquished the government of the world, and given us up to the care of devils; and as I do not, I cannot see on what grounds the king of Britain can look up to heaven for help against us: a common murderer, a highwayman, or a housebreaker, has as good a pretence as he.

'Tis surprising to see how rapidly a panic will sometimes run through a country. All nations and ages have been subject to them. Britain has trembled like an ague at the report of a French fleet of flat bottomed boats; and in the fourteenth century the whole English army, after ravaging the kingdom of France, was driven back like men petrified with fear; and this brave exploit was performed by a few broken forces collected and headed by a woman, Joan of Arc. Would that heaven might inspire some Jersey maid to spirit up her countrymen, and save her fair fellow sufferers from ravage and ravishment! Yet panics, in some cases, have their uses; they produce as much good as hurt. Their duration is always short; the mind soon grows through them, and acquires a firmer habit than before. But their peculiar advantage is, that they are the touchstones of sincerity and hypocrisy, and bring things and men to light, which might otherwise have lain forever undiscovered. In fact, they have the same effect on secret traitors, which an imaginary apparition would have upon a private murderer. They sift out the hidden thoughts of man, and hold them up in public to the world. Many a disguised Tory has lately shown his head, that shall penitentially solemnize with curses the day on which Howe arrived upon the Delaware. . . .

I shall conclude this paper with some miscellaneous remarks on the state of our affairs; and shall begin with asking the following question, Why is it that the enemy have left the New England provinces, and made these middle ones the seat of war? The answer is easy: New England is not infested with Tories, and we are. I have been tender in raising the cry against these men, and used numberless arguments to show them their danger, but it will not do to sacrifice a world either to their folly or their baseness. The period is now arrived, in which either they or we must change our sentiments, or one or both must fall. And what is a Tory? Good God! what is he? I shall not be afraid to go with a hundred Whigs against a thousand Tories, were they to attempt to get into arms. Every Tory is a coward; for servile, slavish, self-interested fear is the foundation of Toryism; and a man under such influence, though he may be cruel, never can be brave.

But, before the line of irrecoverable separation be drawn between us, let us reason the matter together: Your conduct is an invitation to the enemy, yet not one in a thousand of you has heart enough to join him. Howe is as much deceived by you as the American cause is injured by you. He expects you will all take up arms, and flock to his standard, with muskets on your shoulders. Your opinions are of no use to him, unless you support him personally, for 'tis soldiers, and not Tories, that he wants.

15. A New Nation Victorious

After six years of fighting, the Revolutionary cause was at low ebb, and there was little reason to hope that victory was possible. Washington's men were badly fed and badly clothed, and some had even mutinied. Washington, however, had faith—and a plan. He felt that the key to victory was sea power, and seeking a naval force to deal a stunning blow, he at last got his help from France, which was eager to tangle with the British again, having been defeated by them in 1763, in the French and Indian War.

Just where the confrontation would take place was left in the hands of the French admiral Comte de Grasse, who selected the village of Yorktown in Virginia, located near the mouth of the York River and Chesapeake Bay. It was here that the British commander, Lord Cornwallis, after a winning campaign in North Carolina, had dug in with fortifications for his 7,500 men.

The British, who had believed the blow would fall on New York, were decoyed successfully and then trapped in Yorktown. Washington's strategy involved a well-orchestrated military-naval campaign that made full use of the powerful French fleet and its four thousand men, along with combined American and French land forces of six thousand, who were moved in from the north.

After a preliminary sea skirmish, the ring around Yorktown was tightened. Cornwallis tried to escape the net, but a storm prevented the move. After a siege of ten days, he sent word of his capitulation and asked for terms. On October 19, 1781, the surrender ceremony took place. Cornwallis himself did

The Surrender of Lord Cornwallis at Yorktown is a large painting (twelve by eighteen feet) by John Trumbull depicting the events of October 19, 1781. Trumbull (1756–1843), the son of a governor of Connecticut, had served as an aide to General Washington in the Continental Army. After the Revolution John Trumbull was a diplomat for the new nation and later painted four pictures in the U.S. Capitol Rotunda.

not appear, saying he was ill. An aide, Brigadier Charles O'Hara, delivered the commander's sword. As the British troops stacked their arms, the Redcoat band played "The World Turned Upside Down." Marquis de Lafayette wrote: "The play is over; the fifth act has come to an end." The Colonies had won their Revolution.

General Washington Resigns

It was at noon on November 23, 1783, that the officers of the Continental Army assembled at Fraunces Tavern on Pearl Street in New York for a final meeting with their commander in chief. Washington lifted his glass and turned to face the men in the room:

"With a heart full of love and gratitude I now take leave of you. I most devoutly wish that your later days may be as prosperous and happy as your former ones have been glorious and honorable." The general paused, then added:

"I cannot come to each of you but shall be obliged if each of you will come and take me by the hand."

General Knox was first. They clasped hands and embraced in silence. Every officer in the room followed. No words were exchanged.

Washington left the room and walked to a waiting barge. The Continental Army was history.

General George Washington resigning his commission as commander in chief at a meeting of the Continental Congress, Annapolis, Maryland, December 23, 1783. The portrayal of this significant episode in the painting by John Trumbull is in the U.S. Capitol.

General Washington: Resignation (December 23, 1783)

Mr. President:

The great events on which my resignation depended having at length taken place, I have now the honor of offering my sincere congratulations to Congress, and of presenting myself before them to surrender into their hands the trust committed to me, and to claim the indulgence of retiring from the service of my country.

Happy in the confirmation of our independence and sovereignty, and pleased with the opportunity afforded the United States of becoming a respectable nation, I resign with satisfaction the appointment I accepted with diffidence,—a diffidence in my abilities to accomplish so arduous a task, which, however, was superseded by a confidence in the rectitude of our cause, the support of the supreme power of the Union, and the patronage of Heaven.

The successful termination of the war has verified the most sanguine expectations; and my gratitude for the interposition of Providence, and the assistance I have received from my countrymen, increases with every review of the momentous contest. While I repeat my obligations to the Army in general, I should do injustice to my own feelings not to acknowledge, in this place, the peculiar services and distinguished merits of the gentlemen who have been attached to my person during the war. It was impossible the choice of confidential officers to compose my family should have been more fortunate. Permit me, Sir, to recommend in particular those who have continued in the service to the present moment, as worthy of the favorable notice and patronage of Congress.

I consider it an indispensable duty to close this last solemn act of my official life by commending the interests of our beloved country to the protection of Almighty God; and those who have the superintendence of them, to His holy keeping.

Having now finished the work assigned me, I retire from the great theatre of action; and, bidding an affectionate farewell to this august body, under whose orders I have so long acted, I here offer my commission, and take my leave of all the employments of public life.

16. Franklin and Hamilton: Men Who Charted the Course of a Nation

Benjamin Franklin

The son of a Boston soap maker, Ben Franklin (1706–90) left school when he was ten years old and at twelve apprenticed to his brother, a printer. At seventeen he left Boston for Philadelphia, and after some years in the printing trade there and in London, Franklin became, at twenty-two, the owner and editor of a publication called the *Pennsylvania Gazette.* This was the first outlet for the down-to-earth philosophy and witty aphorisms that after 1732 appeared in his *Poor Richard's Almanack.*

Benjamin Franklin,
painted in London in 1767 by
David Martin.

A self-taught man, Franklin learned French, Italian, German, Spanish, and Latin, founded an academy that later became the University of Pennsylvania, experimented with electricity, and invented a stove, bifocals, a harmonica, and a lightning rod. He represented the Congress in France during the Revolution and helped draft the Constitution, and his views helped guide the fledgling nation. Franklin died in 1790 at the age of eighty-four.

The "Wisest American," as he was sometimes known, wrote an epitaph for himself. It read: "The body of Benjamin Franklin, Printer (like the cover of an old book, its contents torn out and stripped of its lettering and gilding), lies here, food for worms; but the work shall not be lost, for it will (as he believed) appear once more in a new and more elegant edition, revised and corrected by the Author."

Benjamin Franklin to the Constitutional Convention (September 17, 1787)

Mr. President:

I confess that I do not entirely approve of this Constitution at present, but sir, I am not sure I shall never approve it: For having lived long, I have experienced many instances of being obliged by better information, or fuller consideration, to change opinions even on important subjects, which I once thought right, but found to be otherwise. It is therefore that the older I grow, the more apt I am to doubt my own judgment, and to pay more respect to the judgment of others. Most men indeed, as well as most sects in religion, think themselves in possession of all truth, and that wherever others differ from them it is so far error.

But though many private persons think almost as highly of their own infallibility as of that of their sect, few express it so naturally as a certain French lady who, in a little dispute with her sister, said, "I don't know how it happens, sister, but I meet with nobody but myself that's always in the right. Il n'y a que moi qui a toujours raison."

In these sentiments, sir, I agree to this Constitution with all its faults, if they are such; because I think a general government necessary for us, and there is no form of government but what may be a blessing to the people if well administered, and I believe further that this is likely to be well administered for a course of years, and can only end in despotism, as other forms have done before it, when people shall become so corrupted as to need despotic government, being incapable of any other. I doubt too whether any other Convention we can obtain may be able to make a better Constitution. For when you assemble a number of men to have the advantage of their joint wisdom, you inevitably assemble with those men all their prejudices, their passions, their errors of opinion, their local interests, and their selfish views. From such an assembly can a perfect production be expected? It therefore astonishes me, sir, to find this system approaching so near to perfection as it does.

If every one of us in returning to our constituents were to report the objections he has had to it, and use his influence to gain partisans in support of them, we might prevent its being generally received, and thereby lose all the salutary effects and great advantages resulting naturally in our favor among foreign nations as well as among ourselves from our real or apparent unanimity. Much of the strength and efficiency of any government in procuring and securing happiness to the people depends on opinion, on the general opinion of the goodness of the government, as well as of the wisdom and integrity of its governors. I hope therefore that for our own sakes as a part of the people, and for the sake of posterity, we shall act heartily and unanimously in recommending this Constitution, wherever our influence may extend, and turn our future thoughts and endeavors to the means of having it well administered.

Alexander Hamilton

Alexander Hamilton (1755–1804) possessed a logical, legal, and fiscal mind, and while others argued, he acted. He had not only a total vision of the structure of government but the genius for planning its operation.

In 1772, when he was only seventeen years old, young Hamilton came to New York from his native West Indies. During most of the Revolution he served as George Washington's secretary, but at the siege of Yorktown he was in uniform and saw significant action. After the war he practiced law in New York City and became an articulate advocate of a strong central government. Hamilton wrote many of the *Federalist Papers* in favor of the United States Constitution and was the chief spokesman for the Federalist party. While serving in Washington's first cabinet as secretary of the treasury, his was a firm voice in shaping responsible fiscal policy.

His talent for planning was so precise and his convictions were so unshakable that his political enemies, who included Thomas Jefferson's vice-president, Aaron Burr, called him "dangerous." Hamilton died of a bullet wound after engaging in a duel with Burr.

Alexander Hamilton, whose fiscal views influenced the founding fathers, is depicted in this painting by John Trumbull. Hamilton died in a duel with rival politician Aaron Burr in 1804.

17. The Constitution: Cornerstone of the Republic

The summer of 1787 was very hot, especially in Philadelphia. In that historic city a monumental political document was taking shape, drawing on the philosophies, prejudices, pride, opinions, and hopes of a remarkable group of men.

The document was the Constitution of the United States, and it has not only survived two hundred years of history but has actually grown over those years. When George Washington, revered leader of the recent Revolution, called the meeting to order on May 25, 1787, the new nation had been struggling for six years with an ineffective organization of loosely confederated states. The new country needed an expression of authority and order. It needed a workable mechanism of self-government.

The document that emerged from that Constitutional Convention, and out of that summer of argument and the heat of political differences, was ratified in June 1788. Twelve states were represented by fifty-five delegates; Rhode Island was absent. The venerable Benjamin Franklin, eighty-one, was the oldest of the delegates; Jonathan Drayton from New Jersey, only twenty-one, was the youngest. Alexander Hamilton of New York was thirty.

Of the fifty-five delegates, twenty-nine were college-educated, knowledgeable about the political literature of Greece and Rome. The convention was, in effect, a brain trust, gathering the best minds of the Colonies at that time. The proceedings were held in great secrecy, for fear of political repercussion.

The framers represented a mood of thought far removed from the fiery discussions of the Continental Congress, but, always aware that the new freedom had been won at great cost, they fashioned a document designed to protect that freedom.

The ***Scene at the Signing of the Constitution of the United States***, which hangs at the east stairway in the House Wing of the U.S. Capitol, was painted by the artist Howard Chandler Christy in the Sail Loft of the U.S. Navy Yard in Washington, D.C., and was completed in April 1940. The principal figures—Washington, Madison, Franklin, Hamilton, and others—can all be identified.

John Langdon
New Hampshire

Rufus King
Massachusetts

David Brearley,
New Jersey
(Portrait unobtainable)

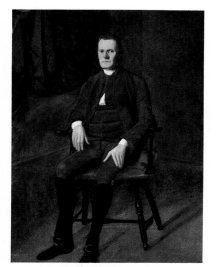

Roger Sherman
Connecticut

THE CONSTITUTION OF THE UNITED STATES OF AMERICA*

We the People of the United States in Order to form a more perfect Union, establish Justice, insure domestic Tranquility, provide for the common defence, promote the general Welfare, and secure the Blessings of Liberty to ourselves and our Posterity, do ordain and establish this Constitution for the United States of America.

Article. I.

Section. 1. All legislative Powers herein granted shall be vested in a Congress of the United States, which shall consist of a Senate and House of Representatives.

Section. 2. The House of Representatives shall be composed of Members chosen every second Year by the People of the several States and the Electors in each State shall have the Qualifications requisite for Electors of the most numerous Branch of the State Legislature.

No Person shall be a Representative who shall not have attained to the Age of twenty five Years, and been seven Years a Citizen of the United States, and who shall not, when elected, be an Inhabitant of that State in which he shall be chosen.

Representatives and direct Taxes shall be apportioned among the several States which may be included within this Union, according to their respective Numbers, which shall be determined by adding to the whole Number of free Persons, including those bound to Service for a Term of Years, and excluding Indians not taxed, three fifths of all other Persons. The actual Enumeration shall be made within three Years after the first Meeting of the Congress of the United States, and within every subsequent Term of ten Years, in such Manner as they shall by Law direct. The Number of Representatives shall not exceed one for every thirty Thousand, but each State shall have at Least one Representative; and until such enumeration shall be made, the State of New Hampshire shall be entitled to chuse three; Massachusetts eight; Rhode Island and Providence Plantations one; Connecticut five; New York six; New Jersey four; Pennsylvania eight; Delaware one; Maryland six; Virginia ten; North Carolina five; South Carolina five; and Georgia three.

When vacancies happen in the Representation from any State, the Executive Authority thereof shall issue Writs of Election to fill such Vacancies.

The House of Representatives shall chuse their Speaker and other Officers; and shall have the sole Power of Impeachment.

Section. 3. The Senate of the United States shall be composed of two Senators from each State, chosen by the Legislature thereof, for six Years; and each Senator shall have one Vote.

Immediately after they shall be assembled in Consequence of the first Election, they shall be divided as equally as may be into three Classes. The Seats of the Senators of the first Class shall be vacated at the Expiration of the second Year, of the second Class at the Expiration of the fourth Year, and of the third Class at the Expiration of the sixth Year, so that one third may be chosen every second Year; and if Vacancies happen by Resignation, or otherwise, during the Recess of the Legislature of any State, the Executive thereof may make temporary Appointments until the next Meeting of the Legislature, which shall then fill such Vacancies.

No Person shall be a Senator who shall not have attained to the Age of thirty Years, and been nine Years a Citizen of the United States, and who shall not, when elected, be an Inhabitant of that State for which he shall be chosen.

The Vice President of the United States shall be President of the Senate, but shall have no Vote, unless they be equally divided.

The Senate shall chuse their other Officers, and also a President pro tempore, in the Absence of the Vice President, or when he shall exercise the Office of President of the United States.

The Senate shall have the sole Power to try all Impeachments. When sitting for that Purpose, they shall be on Oath or Affirmation. When the President of the United States is tried, the Chief Justice shall preside: And no Person shall be convicted without the Concurrence of two thirds of the Members present.

Judgment in Cases of Impeachment shall not extend further than to removal from Office, and disqualification to hold and enjoy any Office of honor, Trust or Profit under the United States: but the Party convicted shall nevertheless be liable and subject to Indictment, Trial, Judgment and Punishment, according to Law.

Section. 4. The Times, Places and Manner of holding Elections for Senators and Representatives, shall be prescribed in each State by the Legislature thereof; but the Congress may at any time by Law make or alter such Regulation, except as to the Places of chusing Senators.

The Congress shall assemble at least once in every Year, and such Meetings shall be on the first Monday in December, unless they shall by Law appoint a different Day.

Section. 5. Each House shall be the Judge of the Elections, Returns and Qualifications of its own Members, and a Majority of each shall constitute a Quorum to do Business; but a smaller Number may adjourn from day to day, and may be authorized to compel the Attendance of absent Members, in such Manner, and under such Penalties as each House may provide.

Each House may determine the Rules of its Proceedings, punish its Members for disorderly Behaviour, and, with the Concurrence of two thirds, expel a Member.

Each House shall keep a Journal of its Proceedings, and from time to time publish the same, excepting such Parts as may in their Judgment require Secrecy; and the Yeas and Nays of the Members of either House on any question shall, at the Desire of one fifth of those Present, be entered on the Journal.

Neither House, during the Session of Congress, shall, without the Consent of the other, adjourn for more than three days, nor to any other Place than that in which the two Houses shall be sitting.

Section. 6. The Senators and Representatives shall receive a Compensation for their Services, to be ascertained by Law, and paid out of the Treasury of the United States. They shall in all Cases, except Treason, Felony and

*Transcribed with original spelling, capitalization, and punctuation from the copy of the Constitution in the National Archives.

Breach of the Peace, be privileged from Arrest during their Attendance at the Session of their respective Houses, and in going to and returning from the same; and for any Speech or Debate in either House, they shall not be questioned in any other Place.

No Senator or Representative shall, during the Time for which he was elected, be appointed to any civil Office under the Authority of the United States, which shall have been created, or the Emoluments whereof shall have been encreased during such time; and no Person holding any Office under the United States, shall be a Member of either House during his Continuance in Office.

Section. 7. All Bills for raising Revenue sh. ll originate in the House of Representatives; but the Senate may propose or concur with Amendments as on other Bills.

Every Bill which shall have passed the House of Representative and the Senate shall, before it become a Law, be presented to the President of the United States; If he approve he shall sign it, but if not he shall return it, with his Objections to that House in which it shall have originated, who shall enter the Objections at large on their Journal, and proceed to reconsider it. If after such Reconsideration two thirds of that House shall agree to pass the Bill, it shall be sent, together with the Objections, to the other House, by which it shall likewise be reconsidered, and if approved by two thirds of that House, it shall become a Law. But in all such Cases the Votes of both Houses shall be determined by Yeas and Nays, and the Names of the Persons voting for and against the Bill shall be entered on the Journal of each House respectively. If any Bill shall not be returned by the President within ten Days (Sundays excepted) after it shall have been presented to him, the Same shall be a Law, in like Manner as if he had signed it, unless the Congress by their Adjournment prevent its Return, in which Case it shall not be a Law.

Every Order, Resolution, or Vote to which the Concurrence of the Senate and House of Representatives may be necessary (except on a question of Adjournment) shall be presented to the President of the United States; and before the Same shall take Effect, shall be approved by him, or being disapproved by him shall be repassed by two thirds of the Senate and House of Representatives, according to the Rules and Limitations prescribed in the Case of a Bill.

Section. 8. The Congress shall have Power To lay and collect Taxes, Duties, Imposts and Excises, to pay the Debts and provide for the common Defence and general Welfare of the United States; but all Duties, Imposts and Excises shall be uniform throughout the United States;

To borrow Money on the credit of the United States;

To regulate Commerce with foreign Nations, and among the several States, and with the Indian Tribes;

To establish an uniform Rule of Naturalization, and uniform Laws on the subject of Bankruptcies throughout the United States;

To coin Money, regulate the Value thereof, and of foreign Coin, and fix the Standard of Weights and Measures;

To provide for the Punishment of counterfeiting the Securities and current Coin of the United States;

To establish Post Offices and post Roads;

To promote the Progress of Science and useful Arts, by securing for limited Times to Authors and Inventors the exclusive Right to their respective Writings and Discoveries;

To constitute Tribunals inferior to the supreme Court;

To define and punish Piracies and Felonies committed on the high Seas, and Offences against the law of Nations;

To declare War, grant Letters of Marque and Reprisal, and makes Rules concerning Captures on Land and Water;

To raise and support Armies, but no Appropriation of Money to that Use shall be for a longer Term than two Years;

To provide and maintain a Navy;

To make Rules for the Government and Regulation of the land and naval Forces;

To provide for organizing, arming, and disciplining, the Militia, and for governing such Part of them as may be employed in the Service of the United States, reserving to the States respectively, the Appointment of the Officers, and the Authority of training the Militia according to the discipline prescribed by Congress;

To exercise exclusive Legislation in all Cases whatsoever, over such District (not exceeding ten Miles square) as may, by Cession of particular States, and the Acceptance of Congress, become the Seat of the Government of the United States, and to exercise like Authority over all Places purchased by the Consent of the Legislature of the State in which the Same shall be, for the Erection of Forts, Magazines, Arsenals, dock-Yards, and other needful Buildings;—And

To make all Laws which shall be necessary and proper for carrying into Execution the foregoing Powers, and all other Powers vested by this Constitution in the Government of the United States, or in any Department or Officer thereof.

Section. 9. The Migration or Importation of such Persons as any of the States now existing shall think proper to admit, shall not be prohibited by the Congress prior to the Year one thousand eight hundred and eight, but a Tax or duty may be imposed on such Importation, not exceeding ten dollars for each Person.

The Privilege of the Writ of Habeas Corpus shall not be suspended, unless when in Cases of Rebellion or Invasion the public Safety may require it.

No Bill of Attainder or ex post facto Law shall be passed.

No Capitation, or other direct, Tax shall be laid, unless in Proportion to the Census or Enumeration herein before directed to be taken.

No Tax or Duty shall be laid on Articles exported from any State.

No Preference shall be given by any Regulation of Commerce or Revenue to the Ports of one State over those of another.

No Money shall be drawn from the Treasury, but in Consequence of Appropriations made by Law, and a regular Statement and Account of the Receipts and Expenditures of all public Money shall be published from time to time.

No Title of Nobility shall be granted by the United States: And no Person holding any Office of Profit or Trust under them, shall, without the Consent of the Congress, accept of any present, Emolument, Office, or Title, of any kind whatever, from any King, Prince, or foreign State.

Section. 10. No State shall enter into any Treaty, Alliance, or Confederation; grant Letters of Marque and Reprisal; coin Money; emit Bills of Credit; make any Thing but gold and silver Coin a Tender in Payment of

Thomas Mifflin
Pennsylvania

Jared Ingersoll
Pennsylvania

James Wilson
Pennsylvania

55

John Dickinson
Delaware

Richard Bassett
Delaware

James McHenry
Maryland

James Madison, Jr.
Virginia

Debts; pass any Bill of Attainder, ex post facto Law, or Law impairing the Obligation of Contracts, or grant any Title of Nobility.

No State shall, without the Consent of the Congress, lay any Imposts or Duties on Imports or Exports, except what may be absolutely necessary for executing its inspection Laws: and the net Produce of all Duties and Imposts, laid by any State on Imports or Exports, shall be for the Use of the Treasury of the United States; and all such Laws shall be subject to the Revision and Controul of the Congress.

No State shall, without the Consent of Congress, lay any Duty of Tonnage, keep Troops, or Ships of War in time of Peace, enter into any Agreement or Compact with another State, or with a foreign Power, or engage in War, unless actually invaded, or in such imminent Danger as will not admit of delay.

Article. II.

Section. 1. The executive Power shall be vested in a President of the United States of America. He shall hold his Office during the Term of four Years, and, together with the Vice President, chosen for the same Term, be elected, as follows:

Each State shall appoint, in such Manner as the Legislature thereof may direct, a Number of Electors, equal to the whole Number of Senators and Representatives to which the State may be entitled in the Congress: but no Senator or Representative, or Person holding an Office of Trust or Profit under the United States, shall be appointed an Elector.

The Electors shall meet in their respective States, and vote by Ballot for two Persons, of whom one at least shall not be an Inhabitant of the same State with themselves. And they shall make a List of all the Persons voted for, and of the Number of Votes for each; which List they shall sign and certify, and transmit sealed to the Seat of the Government of the United States, directed to the President of the Senate. The President of the Senate shall, in the Presence of the Senate and House of Representatives, open all the Certificates, and the Votes shall then be counted. The Person having the greatest Number of Votes shall be the President, if such Number be a Majority of the whole Number of Electors appointed; and if there be more than one who have such Majority, and have an equal Number of Votes, then the House of Representatives shall immediately chuse by Ballot one of them for President; and if no Person have a Majority, then from the five highest on the List the said House shall in like Manner chuse the President. But in chusing the President, the Votes shall be taken by States, the Representation from each State having one Vote; A quorum for this Purpose shall consist of a Member or Members from two thirds of the States, and a Majority of all the States shall be necessary to a Choice. In every Case, after the Choice of the President, the Person having the greatest Number of Votes of the Electors shall be the Vice President. But if there should remain two or more who have equal Votes, the Senate shall chuse from them by Ballot the Vice President.

The Congress may determine the Time of chusing the Electors, and the Day on which they shall give their Votes; which Day shall be the same throughout the United States.

No Person except a natural born Citizen, or a Citizen of the United States, at the time of the Adoption of this Constitution, shall be eligible to the Office of President; neither shall any Person be eligible to that Office who shall not have attained to the Age of thirty five Years, and been fourteen Years a Resident within the United States.

In Case of the Removal of the President from Office, or of his Death, Resignation, or Inability to discharge the Powers and Duties of the said Office, the Same shall devolve on the Vice President, and the Congress may by Law provide for the Case of Removal, Death, Resignation or Inability, both of the President and Vice President, declaring what Officer shall then act as President, and such Officer shall act accordingly, until the Disability be removed, or a President shall be elected.

The President shall, at stated Times, receive for his Services, a Compensation, which shall neither be encreased nor diminished during the Period for which he shall have been elected, and he shall not receive within that Period any other Emolument from the United States, or any of them.

Before he enter on the Execution of his Office, he shall take the following Oath or Affirmation:—"I do solemnly swear (or affirm) that I will faithfully execute the Office of President of the United States, and will to the best of my Ability, preserve, protect and defend the Constitution of the United States."

Section. 2. The President shall be Commander in Chief of the Army and Navy of the United States, and of the Militia of the several States, when called into the actual Service of the United States; he may require the Opinion, in writing, of the principal Officer in each of the executive Departments, upon any Subject relating to the Duties of their respective Offices, and he shall have Power to grant Reprieves and Pardons for Offences against the United States, except in Cases of Impeachment.

He shall have Power, by and with the Advice and Consent of the Senate, to make Treaties, provided two thirds of the Senators present concur; and he shall nominate, and by and with the Advice and Consent of the Senate, shall appoint Ambassadors, other public Ministers and Consuls, Judges of the supreme Court, and all other Officers of the United States, whose Appointments are not herein otherwise provided for, and which shall be established by Law: but the Congress may by Law vest the Appointment of such inferior Officers, as they think proper, in the President alone, in the Courts of Law, or in the Heads of Departments.

The President shall have Power to fill up all Vacancies that may happen during the Recess of the Senate, by granting Commissions which shall expire at the End of their next Session.

Section. 3. He shall from time to time give to the Congress Information of the State of the Union, and recommend to their Consideration such Measures as he shall judge necessary and expedient; he may, on extraordinary Occasions, convene both Houses, or either of them, and in Case of Disagreement between them, with Respect to the Time of Adjournment, he may adjourn them to such Time as he shall think proper; he shall receive Ambassadors and other public Ministers; he shall take Care that the Laws be faithfully executed, and shall Commission all the Officers of the United States.

Section. 4. The President, Vice President and all civil Officers of the United States, shall be removed from Office on Impeachment for, and Conviction of, Treason, Bribery, or other high Crimes and Misdemeanors.

Article. III.

Section. 1. The judicial Power of the United States, shall be vested in one supreme Court, and in such inferior Courts as the Congress may from time to time ordain and establish. The Judges, both of the supreme and inferior Coaurts, shall hold their Offices during good Behaviour, and shall, at stated Times, receive for their Services, a Compensation, which shall not be diminished during their Continuance in Office.

Section. 2. The judicial Power shall extend to all Cases, in Law and Equity, arising under this Constitution, the Laws of the United States, and Treaties made, or which shall be made, under their Authority;—to all Cases affecting Ambassadors, other public Ministers and Consuls;—to all Cases of admiralty and maritime Jurisdiction;—to Controversies to which the United States shall be a Party;—to Controversies between two or more States;—between a State and Citizens of another State;—between Citizens of different States,—between Citizens of the same State claiming Lands under Grants of different States, and between a State, or the Citizens thereof, and foreign States, Citizens or Subjects.

In all Cases affecting Ambassadors, other public Ministers and Consuls, and those in which a State shall be Party, the supreme Court shall have original Jurisdiction. In all the other Cases before mentioned, the supreme Court shall have appellate Jurisdiction, both as to Law and Fact, with such Exceptions, and under such Regulations as the Congress shall make.

The Trial of all Crimes, except in Cases of Impeachment, shall be by Jury; and such Trial shall be held in the State where the said Crimes shall have been committed; but when not committed within any State, the Trial shall be at such Place or Places as the Congress may by Law have directed.

Section. 3. Treason against the United States, shall consist only in levying War against them, or in adhering to their Enemies, giving them Aid and Comfort. No Person shall be convicted of Treason unless on the Testimony of two Witnesses to the same overt Act, or on Confession in open Court.

The Congress shall have Power to declare the Punishment of Treason, but no Attainder of Treason shall work Corruption of Blood, or Forfeiture except during the Life of the Person attainted.

William Blount
North Carolina

Article. IV.

Section. 1. Full Faith and Credits shall be given in each State to the public Acts, Records, and judicial Proceedings of every other State. And the Congress may by general Laws prescribe the Manner in which such Acts, Records and Proceedings shall be proved, and the Effect thereof.

Section. 2. The Citizens of each State shall be entitled to all Privileges and Immunities of Citizens in the several States.

A Person charged in any State with Treason, Felony, or other Crime, who shall flee from Justice, and be found in another State, shall on Demand of the executive Authority of the State from which he fled, be delivered up, to be removed to the State having Jurisdiction of the Crime.

No Person held to Service or Labour in one State, under the Laws thereof, escaping into another, shall, on Consequence of any Law or Regulation therein, be discharged from such Service or Labour, but shall be delivered up on Claim of the Party to whom such Service or Labour may be due.

Section. 3. New States may be admitted by the Congress into this Union; but no new State shall be formed or erected within the Jurisdiction of any other State, nor any State be formed by the Junction of two or more States, or Parts of States, without the Consent of the Legislatures of the States concerned as well as of the Congress.

The Congress shall have Power to dispose of and make all needful Rules and Regulations respecting the Territory or other Property belonging to the United States; and nothing in this Constitution shall be so construed as to Prejudice any Claims of the United States, or of any particular State.

Section. 4. The United States shall guarantee to every State in this Union a Republican Form of Government, and shall protect each of them against Invasion; and on Application of the Legislature, or of the Executive (when the Legislature cannot be convened) against domestic violence.

Richard Dobbs Spaight, Sr.
North Carolina

Article. V.

The Congress, whenever two thirds of both Houses shall deem it necessary, shall propose Amendments to this Constitution, or, on the Application of the Legislatures of two thirds of the several States, shall call a Convention for proposing Amendments, which, in either Case, shall be valid to all Intents and Purposes, as Part of this Constitution, when ratified by the Legislatures of three fourths of the several States, or by Conventions in three fourths thereof, as the one or the other Mode of Ratification may be proposed by the Congress; Provided that no Amendment which may be made prior to the Year One thousand eight hundred and eight shall in any Manner affect the first and fourth Clauses in the Ninth Section of the first Article; and that no State, without its Consent, shall be deprived of its equal Suffrage in the Senate.

Article. VI.

All Debts contracted and Engagements entered into, before the Adoption of this Constitution, shall be as valid against the United States under this Constitution, as under the Confederation.

Pierce Butler
South Carolina

This Constitution, and the Laws of the United States which shall be made in Pursuance thereof; and all Treaties made, or which shall be made, under the Authority of the United States, shall be the supreme Law of the Land; and the Judges in every State shall be bound thereby, any Thing in the Constitution or Laws of any State to the Contrary notwithstanding.

The Senators and Representatives before mentioned, and the Members of the several State Legislatures, and all executive and judicial Officers, both of the United States and of the several States, shall be bound by Oath or Affirmation, to support this Constitution; but no religious Test shall ever be required as a Qualification to any Office or public Trust under the United States.

Article. VII.

The Ratification of the Conventions of nine States, shall be sufficient for the Establishment of this Constitution between the States so ratifying the Same.

done in Convention by the Unanimous Consent of the States present the Seventeenth Day of September in the Year of our Lord one thousand seven hundred and Eighty seven and of the Independence of the United States of America the Twelfth. **In witness** whereof We have hereunto subscribed our Names,

Articles in Addition to, and Amendment of, the Constitution of the United States of America, Proposed by Congress, and Ratified by the Legislatures of the Several States, Pursuant to the Fifth Article of the Original Constitution.

William Few
Georgia

Amendment I

Congress shall make no law respecting an establishment of religion, or prohibiting the free exercise thereof; or abridging the freedom of speech, or of the press; or the right of the people peaceably petition the Government for a redress of grievances.

Amendment II

A well regulated Militia, being necessary to the security of a free State, the right of the people to keep and bear Arms shall not be infringed.

Amendment III

No Soldier shall, in time of peace, be quartered in any house, without the consent of the Owner, nor in time of war, but in a manner to be prescribed by law.

Amendment IV

The right of the people to be secure in their persons, houses, papers, and effects against unreasonable searches and seizures, shall not be violated, and no Warrants shall issue, but upon probable cause, supported by Oath or affirmation, and particularly describing the place to be searched, and the persons or things to be seized.

Amendment V

No person shall be held to answer for a capital or otherwise infamous crime, unless on a presentment or indictment of a Grand Jury, except in cases arising in the land or naval forces, or in the Militia, when in actual service in time of War or public danger; nor shall any person be subject for the same offence to be twice put in jeopardy of life or limb; nor shall be compelled in any criminal case to be a witness against himself, nor be deprived of life, liberty, or property, without due process of law; nor shall private property be taken for public use, without just compensation.

Amendment VI

In all criminal prosecutions, the accused shall enjoy the right to a speedy and public trial, by an impartial jury of the State and district wherein the crime shall have been committed, which district shall have been previously ascertained by law, and to be informed of the nature and cause of the accusation; to be confronted with the witnesses against him; to have compulsory process for obtaining witnesses in his favor, and to have the Assistance of Counsel for his defence.

Amendment XVII

In suits at common law, where the value in controversy shall exceed twenty dollars, the right of trial by jury shall be preserved, and no fact tried by a jury, shall be otherwise reexamined in any Court of the United States, than according to the rules of the common law.

Amendment VIII

Excessive bail shall not be required, nor excessive fines imposed, nor cruel and unusual punishments inflicted.

Amendment IX

The enumeration in the Constitution, of certain rights, shall not be construed to deny or disparage others retained by the people.

Amendment X

The powers not delegated to the United States by the Constitution; nor prohibited by it to the States, are reserved to the States respectively, or to the people.

Amendment XI

The Judicial power of the United States shall not be construed to extend to any suit in law or equity, commenced or prosecuted against one of the United States by Citizens of another State, or by Citizens or Subjects of any Foreign State.

Amendment XII

The Electors shall meet in their respective States and vote by ballot for President and Vice-President, one of whom, at least, shall not be an inhabitant of the same State with themselves; they shall name in their ballots the person voted for as President, and in distinct ballots the person voted for as Vice-President, and they shall make distinct lists of all persons voted for as President, and of all persons voted for as Vice-President, and of the number of votes for each, which lists they shall sign and certify, and transmit sealed to the seat of the government of the United States, directed to the President of the Senate; The President of the Senate shall, in the presence of the Senate and House of Representatives, open all the certificates and the votes shall then be counted;—The person having the greatest number of votes for President, shall be the President, if such number be a majority of the whole number of Electors appointed; and if no person have such majority, then from the persons having the highest numbers not exceeding three on the list of those voted for as President, the House of Representatives shall choose immediately, by ballot, the President. But in choosing the President, the votes shall be taken by states, the representation from each state having one vote; a quorum for this purpose shall consist of a member or members from two-thirds of the states, and a majority of all the states shall be necessary to a choice. And if the House of Representatives shall not choose a President whenever the right of choice shall devolve upon them, before the fourth day of March next following, then the Vice-President shall act as President, as in the case of the death or other constitutional disability of the President.—The person having the greatest number of votes as Vice-President, shall be the Vice-President, if such number be a majority of the whole number of Electors appointed, and if no person have a majority, then from the two highest numbers on the list, the Senate shall choose the Vice-President; a quorum for the purpose shall consist of two-thirds of the whole number of Senators, and a majority of the whole number shall be necessary to a choice. But no person constitutionally ineligible to the office of President shall be eligible to that of Vice-President of the United States.

Amendment XIII

SECTION 1. Neither slavery nor involuntary servitude, except as a punishment for crime whereof the party shall have been duly convicted, shall exist within the United States, or any place subject to their jurisdiction.

SECTION 2. Congress shall have power to enforce this article by appropriate legislation.

Amendment XIV

SECTION 1. All persons born or naturalized in the United States, and subject to the jurisdiction thereof, are citizens of the United States and of the State wherein they reside. No State shall make or enforce any law which shall abridge the privileges or immunities of citizens of the United States; nor shall any State deprive any person of life, liberty, or property, without due process of law; nor deny to any person within its jurisdiction the equal protection of the laws.

SECTION 2. Representatives shall be apportioned among the several States according to their respective numbers, counting the whole number of persons in each State, excluding Indians not taxed. But when the right to vote at any election for the choice of electors for President and Vice-President of the United States, Representatives in Congress, the Executive and Judicial officers of a State, or the members of the Legislature thereof, is denied to any of the male inhabitants of such State, being twenty-one years of age, and citizens of the United States, or in any way abridged, except for participation in rebellion, or other crime, the basis of representation therein shall be reduced in the proportion which the number of such male citizens shall bear to the whole number of male citizens twenty-one years of age in such State.

SECTION 3. No person shall be a Senator or Representative in Congress, or elector of President and Vice-President, or hold any office, civil or military, under the United States, or under any State, who, having previously taken an oath, as a member of Congress, or as an officer of the United States, or as a member of any State legislature, or as an executive or judicial officer of any State, to support the Constitution of the United States, shall have engaged in insurrection or rebellion against the same, or given aid or comfort to the enemies thereof. But Congress may by a vote of two-thirds of each House, remove such disability.

SECTION 4. The validity of the public debt of the United States, authorized by law, including debts incurred for payment of pensions and bounties for services in suppressing insurrection or rebellion, shall not be questioned. But neither the United States nor any State shall assume or pay any debt or obligation incurred in aid of insurrection or rebellion against the United States, or any claim for the loss or emancipation of any slave; but all such debts, obligations, and claims shall be held illegal and void.

SECTION 5. The Congress shall have the power to enforce, by appropriate legislation, the provisions of this article.

Amendment XV

SECTION 1. The right of citizens of the United States to vote shall not be denied or abridged by the United States or by an State on account of race, color, or previous condition of servitude—

SECTION 2. The Congress shall have power to enforce this article by appropriate legislation.

Amendment XVI

The Congress shall have power to lay and collect taxes of incomes, from whatever source derived, without apportionment among the several States, and without regard to any census or enumeration.

Amendment XVII

The Senate of the United States shall be composed of two Senators from each State, elected by the people thereof, for six years; and each Senator shall have one vote. The electors in each State shall have the qualifications requisite for electors of the most numerous branch of the State legislatures.

When vacancies happen in the representation of any State in the Senate, the executive authority of such State shall issue writs of election to fill such vacancies: *Provided,* That the legislature of any State may empower the executive thereof to make temporary appointments until the people fill the vacancies by election as the legislature may direct.

This amendment shall not be so construed as to affect the election or term of any Senator chosen before it becomes valid as part of the Constitution.

Amendment XVIII

SECTION 1. After one year from the ratification of this article the manufacture, sale, or transportation of intoxicating liquors within, the importation thereof into, or the exportation thereof from the United States and all territory subject to the jurisdiction thereof for beverage purposes is hereby prohibited.

SECTION 2. The Congress and the several States shall have concurrent power to enforce this article by appropriate legislation.

SECTION 3. This article shall be inoperative unless it shall have been ratified as an amendment to the Constitution by the legislatures of the several States, as provided in the Constitution, within seven years from the date of the submission hereof to the States by the Congress.

Amendment XIX

The right of citizens of the United States to vote shall not be denied or abridged by the United States or by any State on account of sex.

Congress shall have power to enforce this article by appropriate legislation.

Amendment XX

SECTION 1. The terms of the President and Vice-President shall end at noon on the 20th day of January, and the terms of Senators and Representatives at noon on the 3rd day of January, of the years in which such terms would have ended if this article had not been ratified; and the terms of their successors shall then begin.

SECTION 2. The Congress shall assemble at least once in every year, and such meeting shall begin at noon on the 3rd day of January, unless they shall by law appoint a different day.

SECTION 3. If, at the time fixed for the beginning of the term of the President, the President elect shall have died, the Vice-President elect shall become President. If a President shall not have been chosen before the time fixed for the beginning of his term, or if the President elect shall have failed to qualify, then the Vice-President elect shall act as President until a President shall have qualified; and the Congress may by law provide for the case wherein neither a President elect nor a Vice-President elect shall have qualified, declaring who shall then act as President, or the manner in which one who is to act shall be selected, and such person shall act accordingly until a President or Vice-President shall have qualified.

SECTION 4. The Congress may by law provide for the case of the death of any of the persons from whom the House of Representatives may choose a President whenever the right of choice shall have devolved upon them, and for the case of the death of any of the persons from whom the Senate may choose a Vice-President whenever the right of choice shall have devolved upon them.

SECTION 5. Sections 1 and 2 shall take effect on the 15th day of October following the ratification of this article.

SECTION 6. This article shall be inoperative unless it shall have been ratified as an amendment to the Constitution by the legislatures of three-fourths of the several States within seven years from the date of its submission.

Amendment XXI

SECTION 1. The eighteenth article of amendment to the Constitution of the United States is hereby repealed.

SECTION 2. The transportation or importation into any State, Territory, or possession of the United States for delivery or use therein of intoxicating liquors, in violation of the law thereof, is hereby prohibited.

SECTION 3. This article shall be inoperative unless it shall have been ratified as an amendment to the Constitution by conventions in the several States, as provided in the Constitution, within seven years from the date of the submission hereof to the States by the Congress.

Amendment XXII

No person shall be elected to the office of the President more than twice, and no person who has held the office of President, or acted as President, for more than two years of a term to which some other person was elected President shall be elected to the office of the President more than once.

But this Article shall not apply to any person holding the office of President when this Article was proposed by the Congress, and shall not prevent any person who may be holding the office of President, or acting as President, during the term within which this Article becomes operative from holding the office of President or acting as President during the remainder of such term.

Amendment XXIII

SECTION 1. The District constituting the seat of Government of the United States shall appoint in such manner as the Congress may direct:

A number of electors of President and Vice President equal to the whole number of Senators and Representatives in Congress to which the District would be entitled if it were a State, but in no event more than the least populous State; they shall be in addition to those appointed by the States, but they shall be considered, for the purposes of the election of President and Vice President, to be electors appointed by the State; and they shall meet in the District and perform such duties as provided by the twelfth article of amendment.

SECTION 2. The Congress shall have power to enforce this article by appropriate legislation.

Amendment XXIV

SECTION 1. The right of citizens of the United States to vote in any primary or other election for President or Vice President, or for Senator or Representative in Congress, shall not be denied or abridged by the United States or any State by reason of failure to pay any poll tax or other tax.

SECTION 2. The Congress shall have power to enforce this article by appropriate legislation.

Amendment XXV

SECTION 1. In case of the removal of the President from office or of his death or resignation, the Vice President shall become President.

SECTION 2. Whenever there is a vacancy in the office of the Vice President, the President shall nominate a Vice President who shall take office upon confirmation by a majority vote of both Houses of Congress.

SECTION 3. Whenever the President transmits to the President pro tempore of the Senate and the Speaker of the House of Representatives his written declaration that he is unable to discharge the powers and duties of his office, and until he transmits to them a written declaration to the contrary, such powers and duties shall be discharged by the Vice President as Acting President.

SECTION 4. Whenever the Vice President and a majority of either the principal officers of the executive department or of such other body as Congress may by law provide, transmit to the President pro tempore of the Senate and the Speaker of the House of Representatives their written declaration that the President is unable to discharge the powers and duties of his office, the Vice President shall immediately assume the powers and duties of the office of Acting President.

Thereafter, when the President transmits to the President pro tempore of the Senate and the Speaker of the House of Representatives his written declaration that no inability exists, he shall resume the powers and duties of his office unless the Vice President and a majority of either the principal officers of the executive department or of such other body as Congress may by law provide, transmit within four days to the President pro tempore of the Senate and the Speaker of the House of Representatives their written declaration that the President is unable to discharge the powers and duties of his office. Thereupon Congress shall decide the issue, assembling within forty-eight hours for that purpose if not in session. If the Congress within twenty-one days after receipt of the latter written declaration, or, if Congress is not in session, within twenty-one days after Congress is required to assemble, determines by two-thirds vote of both Houses that the President is unable to discharge the powers and duties of his office, the Vice President shall continue to discharge the same as Acting President; otherwise, the President shall resume the powers and duties of his office.

Amendment XXVI

SECTION 1. The right of citizens of the United States, who are eighteen years of age or older, to vote shall not be denied or abridged by the United States or by any State on account of age.

SECTION 2. The Congress shall have power to enforce this article by appropriate legislation.

18. The First President

On April 6, 1789, under the New Constitution, the House of Representatives, meeting in New York, cast the electoral vote that named George Washington President. A week later at Mount Vernon the General received notice that he was to be sworn in on April 30. Comfortably retired, the planter from Virginia was not too sure he wanted this job. Mount Vernon, an eight-thousand-acre estate stretching along the Potomac for about ten miles, was a haven of peace, and the General would have been happy to remain there caring for his wheat, flax, and root crops. But, once again, duty called.

No man had ever filled the new post he was offered. The new Constitution established the vague outlines of the presidency, but it would be up to the first President to define the real nature of the office and to set its tone and style for the years ahead.

Sometime during those final days before he took the oath, Washington wrote: "... unwilling am I, in the evening of a life nearly consumed in public cares, to quit a peaceful abode for an ocean of difficulties, without that competency of political skill, abilities, and inclination, which are necessary to manage the helm. I am sensible that I am embarking the voice of the people, and a good name of my own, on this voyage; but what returns will be made for them, Heaven alone can foretell. Integrity and Firmness are all I can promise."

George Washington takes the presidential oath, 1789. This is a contemporary painting by an unknown artist.

George Washington: First Inaugural Address (April 30, 1789)

Fellow Citizens of the Senate and the House of Representatives:

Among the vicissitudes incident to life, no event could have filled me with greater anxieties than that of which the notification was transmitted by your order, and received on the fourteenth day of the present month. On the one hand, I was summoned by my Country, whose voice I can never hear but with veneration and love, from a retreat which I had chosen with the fondest predilection, and, in my flattering hopes, with an immutable decision, as the asylum of my declining years: a retreat which was rendered every day more necessary as well as more dear to me, by the addition of habit to inclination, and of frequent interruptions in my health to the gradual waste committed on it by time. On the other hand, the magnitude and difficulty of the trust to which the voice of my Country called me, being sufficient to awaken in the wisest and most experienced of her citizens, a distrustful scrutiny into his qualifications, could not but overwhelm with dispondence, one, who, inheriting inferior endowments from nature and unpractised in the duties of civil administration, ought to be peculiarly conscious of his own deficiencies. In this conflict of emotions, all I dare aver, is, that it has been my faithful study to collect by duty from a just appreciation of every circumstance, by which it might be affected. All I dare hope, is, that, if in executing this task I have been too much swayed by a grateful remembrance of former instances, or by an affectionate sensibility to this transcendent proof, of the confidence of my fellow-citizens; and have thence too little consulted my incapacity as well as disinclination for the weighty and untried cares before me; my *error* will be palliated by the motives which misled me, and its consequences be judged by my Country, with some share of the partiality in which they originated.

Such being the impressions under which I have, in obedience to the public summons, repaired to the present station; it would be peculiarly improper to omit in this first official Act, my fervent supplications to that Almighty Being who rules over the Universe, who presides in the Councils of Nations, and whose providential aids can supply every human defect, that his benediction may consecrate to the liberties and happiness of the People of the United States, a Government instituted by themselves for these essential purposes: and may enable every instrument employed in its administration to execute with success, the functions allotted to his charge. In tendering this homage to the Great Author of every public and private good, I assure myself that it expresses your sentiments not less than my own; nor those of my fellow-citizens at large, less than either. No People can be bound to acknowledge and adore the invisible hand, which conducts the Affairs of men more than the People of the United States. Every step, by which they have advanced to the character of an independent nation, seems to have been distinguished by some token of providential agency. And in the important revolution just accomplished in the system of their United Government, the tranquil deliberations and voluntary consent of so many distinct communities, from which the event has resulted, cannot be compared with the means by which most Governments have been established, without some return of pious gratitude along with an humble anticipation of the future blessings which the past seem to presage. These reflections, arising out of the present crisis, have forced themselves too strongly on my mind to be suppressed. You will join with me I trust in thinking, that there are none under the influence of which, the proceedings of a new and free Government can more auspiciously commence.

By the article establishing the Executive Department, it is made the duty of the President "to recommend to your consideration, such measures as he shall judge necessary and expedient." The circumstances under which I now meet you, will acquit me from entering into that subject, farther than to refer to the Great Constitutional Charter under which you are assembled; and which, in

Robert R. Livingston, first chancellor of the state of New York, administered the presidential oath to George Washington. A member of the Continental Congress, Livingston was a strong supporter of the new U.S. Constitution. He was later involved in the negotiations that brought about the Louisiana Purchase.

defining your powers, designates the objects to which your attention is to be given. It will be more consistent with those circumstances, and far more congenial with the feelings which actuate me, to substitute, in place of a recommendation of particular measures, the tribute that is due to the talents, the rectitude, and the patriotism which adorn the characters selected to devise and adopt them. In these honorable qualifications, I behold the surest pledges, that as on one side, no local prejudices, or attachments; no separate views, nor party animosities, will misdirect the comprehensive and equal eye which ought to watch over this great assemblage of communities and interests: so, on another, that the foundations of our National policy will be laid in the pure and immutable principles of private morality; and the pre-eminence of a free Government, be exemplified by all the attributes which can win the affections of its Citizens, and command the respect of the world.

I dwell on this prospect with every satisfaction which an ardent love for my Country can inspire: since there is no truth more thoroughly established, than that there exists in the economy and course of nature, an indissoluble union between virtue and happiness, between duty and advantage, between the genuine maxims of an honest and magnanimous policy, and the solid rewards of public prosperity and felicity: Since we ought to be no less persuaded that the propitious smiles of Heaven, can never be expected on a nation that disregards the eternal rules of order and right, which Heaven itself has or-dained: And since the preservation of the sacred fire of liberty, and the destiny of the Republican model of Government, are justly considered as *deeply*, perhaps as *finally* staked, on the experiment entrusted to the hands of the American people.

Besides the ordinary objects submitted to your care, it will remain with your judgment to decide, how far an exercise of the occasional power delegated by the Fifth article of the Constitution is rendered expedient at the present juncture by the nature of objections which have been urged against the System, or by the degree of inquietude which has given birth to them. Instead of undertaking particular recommendations on this subject, in which I could be guided by no lights derived from official opportunities, I shall again give way to my entire confidence in your discernment and pursuit of the public good: For I assure myself that whilst you carefully avoid every alteration which might endanger the benefits of an United and effective Government, or which ought to await the future lessons of experience; a reverence for the characteristic rights of free-men, and a regard for the public harmony, will sufficiently influence your deliberations on the question how far the former can be more impregnably fortified, or the latter be safely and advantageously promoted.

To the preceding observations I have one to add, which will be most properly addressed to the House of Representatives. It concerns myself, and will therefore be as brief as possible. When I was first honoured with a call into the Service of my Country, then on the eve of an arduous struggle for its liberties, the light in which I contemplated my duty required that I should renounce every pecuniary compensation. From this resolution I have in no instance departed. And being still under the impressions which produced it, I must decline as inapplicable to myself, any share in the personal emoluments, which may be indispensably included in a permanent provision for the Executive Department; and must accordingly pray that the pecuniary estates for the Station in which I am placed, may, during my continuance in it, be limited to such actual expenditures as the public good may be thought to require.

Having thus imparted to you my sentiments, as they have been awakened by the occasion which brings us together, I shall take my present leave; but not without resorting once more to the benign parent of the human race, in humble supplication that since He has been pleased to favour the American people, with opportunities for deciding with unparalleled unanimity on a form of Government, for the security of their Union, and the advancement of their happiness; so His divine blessing may be equally *conspicuous* in the enlarged views, the temperate consultations, and the wise measures on which the success of this Government must depend.

19. First in the Hearts of His Countrymen

George Washington brought a firm, even hand to the helm of the new Republic. Gifted with a keen political overview, he sensed he was creating precedents and establishing tradition. He was a leader of rare determination, as he had showed so often in his conduct of the hit-and-run warfare that marked the years of the Revolution. In his approach to the presidency he was careful to follow a democratic rather than aristocratic way, although he had every right to assume the latter.

Washington was well organized and creative and had a sense of fair play and the knowledge that, as he did in his youth, he could blaze fresh trails. No experiment in federal government on so large a scale had ever worked. He was a cool administrator, direct in his approach to problems and deliberate in decision.

With all his achievements, Washington could inspire respect, and this helped him rise above the stresses that surrounded his position, in which he had to face enormous fiscal problems and crucial foreign policy decisions.

When he had reached the end of his second term, he thought of himself as a "wearied traveller who seeks a resting place." At last he could go home to Mount Vernon.

Washington was a man of serious mien. There is no record of his telling a joke, or even repeating a funny anecdote. That was not his way. Despite his place in the public eye and his fondness for traveling in his coach, he showed a certain humility. He also enjoyed dancing, but he invariably conducted himself with dignity.

A bit uncomfortable amid the sparkling talents of such men as Hamilton and Jefferson, Washington recognized his role as the even-tempered helmsman and was sustained by his faith in himself and his religion. When his task as President was completed in March 1797, he wanted only to go home to his beloved Virginia farm, to his field, his barns, his crops, and his friends.

George Washington died in December 1799, and Henry Lee of Virginia, a former cavalry officer who was known as Light Horse Harry and was now serving in the House of Representatives, honored him with these words: "To the memory of the Man, first in war, first in peace, and first in the hearts of his countrymen."

President Washington: Farewell Address
(September 17, 1796)

Friends, and Fellow-Citizens:

The period for a new election of a Citizen, to administer the Executive government of the United States, being not far distant, and the time actually arrived, when your thoughts must be employed in designating the person, who is to be clothed with that important trust, it appears to me proper, especially as it may conduce to a more distinct expression of the public voice, that I should now apprise you of the resolution I have formed, to decline being considered among the number of those, out of whom a choice is to be made.

I beg you, at the same time, to do me the justice to be assured, that this resolution has not been taken, without a strict regard to all the considerations appertaining to the relation, which binds a dutiful citizen to his country, and that, in withdrawing the tender of service which silence in my situation might imply, I am influenced by no diminution of zeal for your future interest, no deficiency of grateful respect for your past kindness; but am supported by a full conviction that the step is compatible with both.

Mount Vernon, George Washington's home in Virginia, was in every sense a working farm.

Washington had inherited this land along the Potomac in 1754, adding over time 5,500 acres to his original 2,500. As a farmer he kept in close touch with the latest developments in agricultural science.

The main house, built in 1743 by George's half brother Lawrence, was named for Admiral Edward Vernon, Lawrence's commander in the British navy. George made numerous additions to the two-and-a-half-story structure, with its wide lawn and gardens. The main mansion was restored on Washington's detailed orders. In 1860 the Mount Vernon Ladies Association became its permanent custodian.

The house is seen from the less familiar aspect, looking toward the Potomac.

The acceptance of, and continuance hitherto in, the office to which your Suffrages have twice called me, have been a uniform sacrifice of inclination to the opinion of duty, and to a deference for what appeared to be your desire. I constantly hoped, that it would have been much earlier in my power, consistently with motives, which I was not at liberty to disregard, to return to that retirement, from which I had been reluctantly drawn. The strength of my inclination to do this, previous to the last election, had even led to the preparation of an address to declare it to you; but mature reflection on the then perplexed and critical posture of our affairs with foreign nations, and the unanimous advice of persons entitled to my confidence, impelled me to abandon the idea.

I rejoice, that the state of your concerns, external as well as internal, no longer renders the pursuit of inclination incompatible with the sentiment of duty, or propriety; and am persuaded whatever partiality may be retained for my services, that in the present circumstances of our country, you will not disapprove my determination to retire.

The impressions, with which I first undertook the arduous trust, were explained on the proper occasion. In the discharge of this trust, I will only say, that I have, with good intentions, contributed towards the organization and administration of the government, with best exertions of which a very fallible judgment was capable. Not unconscious, in the outset, of the inferiority of my qualifications, experience in my own eyes, perhaps still more in the eyes of others, has strengthened the motives to diffidence of myself; and every day the increasing weight of years admonishes me more and more, that the shade of retirement is as necessary to me as it will be welcome. Satisfied that if any circumstances have given peculiar value to my services, they were temporary, I have the consolation to believe, that while choice and prudence invite me to quit the political scene, patriotism does not forbid it. . . .

A solicitude for your welfare, which cannot end but with my life, and the apprehension of danger, natural to that solicitude, urge me on an occasion like

the present, to offer to your solemn contemplation, and to recommend to your frequent review, some sentiments; which are the result of much reflection, of no inconsiderable observation, and which appear to me all important to the permanency of your felicity as a People. These will be offered to you with the more freedom, as you can only see in them the disinterested warnings of a parting friend, who can possibly have no personal motive to bias his counsel. . . .

It is of infinite moment that you should properly estimate the immense value of your national Union to your collective and individual happiness; that you should cherish a cordial, habitual and immoveable attachment to it; accustoming yourselves to think and speak of it as of the Palladium of your political safety and prosperity; watching for its preservation with jealous anxiety; discountenancing whatever may suggest even a suspicion that it can in any event be abandoned, and indignantly frowning upon the first dawning of every attempt to alienate any portion of our country from the rest, or to enfeeble the sacred ties which now link together the various parts.

For this you have every inducement of sympathy and interest. Citizens by birth or choice, of a common country, that country has a right to concentrate your affections. The name of AMERICAN, which belongs to you in your national capacity, must always exalt the just pride of patriotism, more than any appellation derived from local discriminations. . . .

While then every part of our country thus feels an immediate and particular interest in Union, all the parts combined cannot fail to find in the united mass of means and efforts greater strength, greater resources, proportionably greater security from external danger, a less frequent interruption of their peace by foreign nations; and, what is of inestimable value! they must derive from Union an exemption from those broils and wars between themselves which so frequently afflict neighboring countries, not tied together by the same government; which their own rivalships alone would be sufficient to produce, but which opposite foreign alliances, attachments and intrigues would stimulate and imbitter. Hence likewise they will avoid the necessity of those overgrown Military establishments, which under any form of government are inauspicious to liberty, and which are to be regarded as particularly hostile to Republican Liberty: In this sense it is, that your Union ought to be considered as a main prop of your liberty and that the love of the one ought to endear to you the preservation of the other. . . .

In contemplating the causes which may disturb our Union, it occurs as a matter of serious concern that any ground should have been furnished for characterizing parties by *geographical* discriminations: *Northern* and *Southern;* *Atlantic* and *Western;* whence designing men may endeavor to excite a belief that there is a real difference of local interests and views. One of the expedients of Party to acquire influence, within particular districts, is to misrepresent the opinions and aims of other Districts. You cannot shield yourselves too much against the jealousies and heart burnings which spring from these misrepresentations. They tend to render alien to each other those who ought to be bound together by fraternal affection. . . .

To the efficacy and permanency of your Union, a Government for the whole is indispensable. No alliances however strict between the parts can be an adequate substitute. They must inevitably experience the infractions and interruptions which all alliances in all times have experienced. Sensible of this momentous truth, you have improved upon your first essay, by the adoption of a Constitution of Government, better calculated than your former for an intimate Union, and for the efficacious management of your common concerns. This Government, the offspring of our own choice uninfluenced and unawed, adopted upon full investigation and mature deliberation, completely free in its principles, in the distribution of its powers, uniting security with energy, and containing within itself a provision for its own amendment, has a just claim to your confidence and your support. Respect for its authority, compliance with its laws, acquiescence in its measures, are duties enjoined by the fundamental maxims of true Liberty. The basis of our political systems is the right of the people to make and to alter their Constitutions of Government. But the Constitution which at any time exists, 'till changed by an explicit and authentic act of the whole people, is sacredly obligatory upon all. The very idea of the power and the right of the people to establish Government presupposes the duty of every individual to obey the established Government. . . .

Towards the preservation of your government and the permanency of your present happy state, it is requisite, not only that you steadily discountenance irregular oppositions to its acknowledged authority, but also that you resist with care the spirit of innovation upon its principles however specious the pretexts. One method of assault may be to effect, in the forms of the Constitution, alterations which will impair the energy of the system and thus to undermine what cannot be directly overthrown. In all the changes to which you may be invited, remember that time and habit are at least as necessary to fix the true character of governments, as of other human institutions; that experience is the surest standard, by which to test the real tendency of the existing Constitution of a country. . . .

I have already intimated to you the danger of Parties in the State, with particular reference to the founding of them on geographical discriminations. Let me now take a more comprehensive view, and warn you in the most solemn manner against the baneful effects of the spirit of Party, generally. . . .

Without looking forward to an extremity . . . the common and continual mischiefs of the spirit of Party are sufficient to make it in the interest and the duty of a wise people to discourage and restrain it.

It serves always to distract the Public Councils and enfeeble the Public administration. It agitates the community with ill-founded jealousies and false alarms, kindles the animosity of one part against another, foments occasionally riot and insurrection. It opens the door to foreign influence and corruption, which finds a facilitated access to the government itself and [*sic*] the will of one country, are subjected to the policy and will of another.

There is an opinion that parties in free countries are useful checks upon the administration of the government and serve to keep alive the spirit of liberty. This within certain limits is probably true, and in governments of monarchical cast patriotism may look with indulgence, if not with favor, upon the spirit of party. But in those of the popular character, in governments purely elective, it is a spirit not to be encouraged. . . .

It is important, likewise, that the habits of thinking in a free country should inspire caution in those entrusted with its administration to confine themselves within their respective Constitutional spheres; avoiding in the exercise of the powers of one department to encroach upon another. The spirit of encroachment tends to consolidate the powers of all the departments in one, and thus to create whatever the form of government a real despotism. A just estimate of that love of power, and proneness to abuse it, which predominates in the human heart is sufficient to satisfy us of the truth of this position. . . .

Of all the dispositions and habits which lead to political prosperity, religion and morality are indispensable supports. In vain would that man claim the tribute of patriotism who should labor to subvert these great pillars of human happiness, these firmest props of the duties of men and citizens. . . .

'Tis substantially true, that virtue or morality is a necessary spring of popular government. . . .

As a very important source of strength and security, cherish public credit. One method of preserving it is to use it as sparingly as possible: avoiding occasions of expense by cultivating peace, but remembering also that timely disbursements to prepare for danger frequently prevent much greater disbursements to repel it; avoiding likewise the accumulation of debt, not only by shunning occasions of expense, but by vigorous exertions in time of peace to discharge the debts which unavoidable wars may have occasioned, not ungenerously throwing upon posterity the burden which we ourselves ought to bear. The executive of these maxims belongs to your Representatives, but it is necessary that public opinion should cooperate. To facilitate to them the performance of their duty, it is essential that you should practically bear in mind that towards the payment of debts there must be revenue; that to have revenue there must be taxes; that no taxes can be devised which are not more or less inconvenient and unpleasant; that the intrinsic embarrassment inseparable from the selection of the proper objects (which is always a choice of difficulties) ought to be a decisive motive for a candid construction of the Conduct of the Government in making it, and for a spirit of acquiescence in the measures for obtaining revenue which the public exigencies may at any time dictate.

Observe good faith and justice towards all nations. Cultivate peace and harmony with all. Religion and morality enjoin this conduct; and can it be that good policy does not equally enjoin it? It will be worthy of a free, enlightened, and, at no distance period, a great Nation, to give to mankind the magnanimous and too novel example of a people always guided by an exalted justice and benevolence. . . .

The nation which indulges towards another an habitual hatred or an habitual fondness is in some degree a slave. It is a slave to its animosity or to its affection, either of which is sufficient to lead it astray from its duty and its interest. Antipathy in one nation against another disposes each more readily to offer insult and injury, to lay hold of slight causes of umbrage, and to be haughty and intractable, when accidental or trifling occasions of dispute occur. Hence frequent collisions, obstinate envenomed and bloody contests. The nation prompted by ill will and resentment sometimes impels to war the Government, contrary to the best calculations of policy. The Government sometimes participates in the national propensity and adopts through passion what reason would reject; at other times, it makes the animosity of the nation subservient to projects of hostility instigated by pride, ambition and other sinister and pernicious motives. The peace often, sometimes perhaps the liberty, of nations has been the victim. . . .

Against the insidious wiles of foreign influence (I conjure you to believe me fellow citizens) the jealousy of a free people ought to be *constantly* awake;

Rising 555 feet at the west end of the Mall, the Washington Monument dominates the District of Columbia skyline.

Architect Robert Mills's elaborate design for an obelisk was accepted, and on July 4, 1848, the cornerstone was laid. But work was continuously delayed until, in 1876, Congress took over the building of the monument and appropriated the necessary money. The shaft was completed in 1884 and an aluminum top was placed in position. Because of the lengthy delays in construction, the stones of the lower level of the monument differ in color from those higher up. The structure was opened in 1888. The top can be reached by stairs or by elevator.

since history and experience prove that foreign influence is one of the most baneful foes of Republican government. . . .

The great rule of conduct for us in regard to foreign nations is in extending our commercial relations to have with them as little *political* connection as possible. So far as we have already formed engagements let them be fulfilled, with perfect good faith. Here let us stop.

Europe has a set of primary interests, which to us have none, or a very remote relation. Hence she must be engaged in frequent controversies, the causes of which are essentially foreign to our concerns. Hence therefore it must be unwise in us to implicate ourselves, by artificial ties, in the ordinary vicissitudes of her politics, or the ordinary combinations and collisions of her friendships, or enmities:

Our detached and distance situation invites and enables us to pursue a different course. If we remain one people, under an efficient government, the period is not far off when we may defy material injury from external annoyance; when we may take such an attitude as will cause the neutrality we may at any time resolve upon to be scrupulously respected; when belligerent nations, under the impossibility of making acquisitions upon us, will not lightly hazard the giving us provocation; when we may choose peace or war, as our interest guided by our justice shall counsel.

Why forego the advantages of so peculiar a situation? Why quit our own to stand upon foreign ground? Why, by interweaving our destiny with that of any part of Europe, entangle our peace and prosperity in the toils of European ambition, rivalship, interest, humor or caprice?

'Tis our true policy to steer clear of permanent alliances, with any portion of the foreign world. So far, I mean, as we are now at liberty to do it, for let me not be understood as capable of patronising infidelity to existing engagements. . . .

Harmony, liberal intercourse with all nations, are recommended by policy, humanity and interest. But even our commercial policy should hold an equal and impartial hand: neither seeking nor granting exclusive favors or preferences. . . . There can be no greater error than to expect, or calculate upon real favors from nation to nation. 'Tis an illusion which experience must cure, which a just pride ought to discard.

In offering to you, my Countrymen, these counsels of an old and affectionate friend, I dare not hope they will make the strong and lasting impression, I could wish; that they will control the usual current of the passions, or prevent our nation from running the course which has hitherto marked the destiny of nations: But if I may even flatter myself, that they may be productive of some partial benefit, some occasional good; that they may now and then recur to moderate the fury of party spirit, to warn against the mischiefs of foreign intrigue, to guard against the impostures of pretended patriotism; this hope will be a full recompense for the solicitude for your welfare, by which they have been dictated. . . .

Though in reviewing the incidents of my administration, I am unconscious of intentional error, I am nevertheless too sensible of my defects not to think it probable that I may have committed many errors. Whatever they may be I fervently beseech the Almighty to avert or mitigate the evils to which they may tend. I shall also carry with me the hope that my country will never cease to view them with indulgence; and that after forty-five years of my life dedicated to its service, with an upright zeal, the faults of incompetent abilities will be consigned to oblivion, as myself must soon be to the mansions of rest.

Relying on its kindness in this as in other things, and actuated by that fervent love towards it which is so natural to a man, who views in it the native soil of himself and his progenitors for several generations; I anticipate with pleasing expectation that retreat, in which I promise myself to realize, without alloy, the sweet enjoyment of partaking, in the midst of my fellow Citizens, the benign influence of good laws under a free government, the ever favorite object of my heart, and the happy reward, as I trust, of our mutual cares, labors and dangers.

20. "Eternal Hostility Toward Every Form of Tyranny": Thomas Jefferson

If there was one among the founders whose personal philosophy and passionate faith in mankind left a durable imprint on the new nation, that man was Thomas Jefferson.

Endowed with broad vision and a rare sense of the future, Jefferson, whose hand and heart seemed to be everywhere in those formative years, remains among the greatest of great Americans.

Shy, awkward, and slightly disheveled, with red hair and hazel eyes, Jefferson, six feet two inches tall, strode onto the stage of history at precisely the right moment, emerging at that place and at that time when his beliefs, and his great talent for expressing them, produced the greatest good.

Although he was an aristocrat completely dedicated to the democratic philosophy, Jefferson believed absolutely in the common man and in that man's ability to govern himself. He distrusted concentration of power, pomp of office, and centralized authority, and he admired "republican simplicity."

He was a statesman, philosopher, and lawyer; he was also an architect, a writer, a musician, and an inventor. That bland exterior hid a far-ranging mind that explored every corner of human knowledge and was mirrored in exquisite taste and a special "felicity of expression." It was this unique feeling for words that served him especially well when in the summer of 1776, at the age of thirty-three, working in the rented room of a Philadelphia bricklayer's home, he wrote the immortal "Declaration of Independence," an assertion of basic human dignity that was to affect history in every corner of the globe.

Thomas Jefferson: First Inaugural Address (March 4, 1801)

Friends and Fellow-Citizens:

Called upon to undertake the duties of the first executive office of our country, I avail myself of the presence of that portion of my fellow-citizens which is here assembled to express my grateful thanks for the favor with which they have been pleased to look toward me, to declare a sincere consciousness that the task is above my talents, and that I approach it with those anxious and awful presentiments which the greatness of the charge and the weakness of my powers so justly inspire. A rising nation, spread over a wide and fruitful land, traversing all the seas with the rich productions of their industry, engaged in commerce with nations who feel power and forget right, advancing rapidly to destinies beyond the reach of mortal eye—when I contemplate these transcendent objects, and see the honor, the happiness, and the hopes of this beloved country committed to the issue and the auspices of this day, I shrink from the contemplation, and humble myself before the magnitude of the undertaking. Utterly, indeed, should I despair did not the presence of many whom I here see remind me that in the other high authorities provided by our Constitution I shall find resources of wisdom, of virtue, and of zeal on which to rely under all difficulties. To you, then, gentlemen, who are charged with the sovereign functions of legislation, and to those associated with you, I look with encouragement for that guidance and support which may enable us to steer with safety the vessel in which we are all embarked amidst the conflicting elements of a troubled world.

During the contest of opinion through which we have passed the animation of discussions and of exertions has sometimes worn an aspect which might impose on strangers unused to think freely and to speak and to write what they

Monticello, or "Little Mountain," designed and built by Thomas Jefferson himself, was the grandest house in all of Virginia, the glittering product of four decades of a very busy life. Situated on ten thousand acres of rich Virginia land, Monticello became the focal point of Jefferson's vast and varied interests, the repository for his genius and his good taste.

Of a distinctly practical mind, Jefferson installed a dumbwaiter that could bring up food from the basement, an air shaft for ventilation, a device that could write two letters at the same time, a new kind of clock, and a swivel chair. To keep track of progress in construction of the new University of Virginia, rising in the valley below under his personal guidance, Jefferson installed a telescope.

Monticello has become an American symbol.

think; but this being now decided by the voice of the nation, announced according to the rules of the Constitution, all will, of course, arrange themselves under the will of the law, and united in common efforts for the common good. All, too, will bear in mind this sacred principle, that though the will of the majority is in all cases to prevail, that will to be rightful must be reasonable; that the minority possess their equal rights, which equal law must protect, and to violate would be oppression. Let us, then, fellow-citizens, unite with one heart and one mind. Let us restore to social intercourse that harmony and affection without which liberty and even life itself are but dreary things. And let us reflect that, having banished from our land that religious intolerance under which mankind so long bled and suffered, we have yet gained little if we countenance a political intolerance as despotic, as wicked, and capable of as bitter and bloody persecutions. During the throes and convulsions of the ancient world, during the agonizing spasms of infuriated man, seeking through blood and slaughter his long-lost liberty, it was not wonderful that the agitation of the billows should reach even this distant and peaceful shore; that this should be more felt and feared by some and less by others, and should divide opinions as to measures of safety. But every difference of opinion is not a difference of principle. We have called by different names brethren of the same principle. We are all Republicans, we are all Federalists. If there be any among us who would wish to dissolve this Union or to change its republican form, let them stand undisturbed as monuments of the safety with which error of opinion may be tolerated where reason is left free to combat it. I know, indeed, that some honest men fear that a republican government can not be strong, that this Government is not strong enough; but would the honest patriot, in the full tide of successful experiment, abandon a government which has so far kept us free and firm on the theoretic and visionary fear that this Government, the world's best hope, may by possibility want energy to preserve itself? I trust not. I believe this, on the contrary, the strongest Government on earth. I believe it the only one where every man, at the call of the law, would fly to the standard of the law, and would meet invasions of the public order as his own personal concern. Sometimes it is said that man can not be trusted with the government

Statue of **Thomas Jefferson,** holding in his left hand a rolled copy of the Declaration of Independence. The nineteen-foot sculpture is at the center of the Jefferson Memorial located on the Tidal Basin in Washington's East Potomac Park. It is the work of Rudulph Evans.

of himself. Can he, then, be trusted with the government of others? Or have we found angels in the forms of kings to govern him? Let history answer this question.

Let us, then, with courage and confidence pursue our own Federal and Republican principles, our attachment to union and representative government. Kindly separated by nature and a wide ocean from the exterminating havoc of one quarter of the globe; too high-minded to endure the degradations of the others; possessing a chosen country, with room enough for our descendants to the thousandth and thousandth generation; entertaining a due sense of our equal right to the use of our own faculties, to the acquisitions of our own industry, to honor and confidence from our fellow-citizens, resulting not from birth, but from our actions and their sense of them; enlightened by a benign religion, professed, indeed, and practiced in various forms, yet all of them inculcating honesty, truth, temperance, gratitude, and the love of man; acknowledging and adoring an overruling Providence, which by all its dispensations proves that it delights in the happiness of man here and his greater happiness hereafter—with all these blessings, what more is necessary to make us a happy and a prosperous people? Still one thing more, fellow-citizens—a wise and frugal Government, which shall restrain men from injuring one another, shall leave them otherwise free to regulate their own pursuits of

71

I have sworn upon the altar of God, eternal hostility against every form of tyranny over the mind of man.

Letter to Dr. Benjamin Rush, September 23, 1800

The Jefferson Memorial follows the architectural style of the Rotunda at Jefferson's own University of Virginia. Circular in design, the memorial building incorporates four panels of Jefferson quotations, with a fifth quote at the base of the dome.

industry and improvement, and shall not take from the mouth of labor the bread it has earned. This is the sum of good government, and this is necessary to close the circle of our felicities.

About to enter, fellow-citizens, on the exercise of duties which comprehend everything dear and valuable to you, it is proper you should understand what I deem the essential principles of our Government, and consequently those which ought to shape its Administration. I will compress them within the narrowest compass they will bear, stating the general principle, but not all its limitations. Equal and exact justice to all men, of whatever state or persuasion, religious or political; peace, commerce, and honest friendship with all nations, entangling alliances with none; the support of the State governments in all their rights, as the most competent administrations for our domestic concerns and the surest bulwarks against antirepublican tendencies; the preservation of the General Government in its whole constitutional vigor, as the sheet anchor of our peace at home and safety abroad; a jealous care of the right of election by the people—a mild and safe corrective of abuses which are lopped by the sword of revolution where peaceable remedies are unprovided; absolute acquiescence in the decision of the majority, the vital principle of republics, from which is no appeal but to force, the vital principle and immediate parent of despotism; a well-disciplined militia, our best reliance in peace and for the first moments of war, till regulars may relieve them; the supremacy of the civil over the military authority; economy in the public expense, that labor may be lightly burthened; the honest payment of our debts and sacred preservation of the public faith; encouragement of agriculture, and of commerce as its handmaid; the diffusion of information and arraignment of all abuses at the bar of the public reason; freedom of religion; freedom of the press, and freedom of person under the protection of the habeas corpus, and trial by juries impartially selected. These principles form the bright constellations which has gone before us and guided our steps through an age of revolution and reformation. The wisdom of our sages and blood of our heroes have been devoted to their attainment. They should be the creed of our political faith, the text of civic instruction, the touchstone by which to try the services of those we trust; and should we

wander from them in moments of error or of alarm, let us hasten to retrace our steps and to regain the road which alone leads to peace, liberty, and safety.

I repair, then, fellow-citizens, to the post you have assigned me. With experience enough in subordinate offices to have seen the difficulties of this the greatest of all, I have learnt to expect that it will rarely fall to the lot of imperfect man to retire from this station with the reputation and the favor which bring him into it. Without pretensions to that high confidence you reposed in our first and greatest revolutionary character, whose preeminent services had entitled him to the first place in his country's love and destined for him the fairest page in the volume of faithful history, I ask so much confidence only as may give firmness and effect to the legal administration of your affairs. I shall often go wrong through defect of judgment. When right, I shall often be thought wrong by those whose positions will not command a view of the whole ground. I ask your indulgence for my own errors, which will never be intentional, and your support against the errors of others, who may condemn what they would not if seen in all its parts. The approbation implied by your suffrage is a great consolation to me for the past, and my future solicitude will be to retain the good opinion of those who have bestowed it in advance, to conciliate that of others by doing them all the good in my power, and to be instrumental to the happiness and freedom of all.

Relying, then, on the patronage of your good will, I advance with obedience to the work, ready to retire from it whenever you become sensible how much better choice it is in your power to make. And may that infinite Power which rules the destinies of the universe lead our councils to what is best, and give them a favorable issue for your peace and prosperity.

This bright new nation, the United States of America, just born and scarcely united, would, Thomas Jefferson hoped, develop into a strong agrarian democracy. The land and those who worked to make it produce would be the foundation on which this republic would rest. No king, nor anyone who would be king, could seize the power.

Such was the base of Jeffersonian idealism. Each man would fully enjoy those rights that were his by nature. Strong central government control could be a danger. There would be freedom of the press and freedom of religion. Popular education would in time lift the ability of the general population to live in harmony and common purpose.

Before he entered the White House as the third President, Thomas Jefferson had served as governor of Virginia, U.S. minister to France, and secretary of state. On February 17, 1801, he was elected to the presidency by the House of Representatives on the thirty-sixth ballot, emerging victorious after tying with Aaron Burr on seventy-three votes in the electoral college.

Jefferson was the first President to be inaugurated in Washington. He walked through the muddy streets to the ceremonies at the Capitol Building, then under construction.

President Jefferson saw the federal government as a tool in the handling of foreign affairs, while local and state governments concerned themselves with domestic matters. He trimmed expenditures and cut down the national debt. But his major achievement in office was the historic purchase of the Louisiana Territory from Napoleon of France in the year 1803. That transaction, for $15 million, brought 828,000 square miles to the territorial expansion of the United States and doubled the size of the country. The territory eventually became thirteen new states.

Jefferson died on July 4, 1826, the fiftieth anniversary of the Declaration of Independence. His epitaph, written by himself, reflected the way he regarded his own life:

HERE WAS BURIED THOMAS JEFFERSON
AUTHOR OF THE DECLARATION OF AMERICAN INDEPENDENCE
OF THE STATUTE OF VIRGINIA FOR RELIGIOUS FREEDOM
AND FATHER OF THE UNIVERSITY OF VIRGINIA

We confide in our strength, without boasting of it; we respect that of others, without fearing it.

Letter to William Carmichael and William Short, 1793

The care of human life and happiness, and not their destruction, is the first and only legitimate object of good government.

To the Republican citizens of Washington County, Maryland, March 31, 1809

The basis of our government being the opinion of the people, the very first object should be to keep that right; and were it left to me to decide whether we should have a government without newspapers, or newspapers without a government, I should not hesitate a moment to prefer the latter.

Letter to Colonel Edward Carrington, January 16, 1787

21. Sea of Glory

From the earliest years of the Republic, the American Navy developed its own service traditions and its own roster of heroes. Those heroes of the U.S. Navy have always occupied a special place of honor in the hearts of Americans.

In the nation's formative years the fledgling sea force of the Continental Congress—frigates under construction, small state fleets flying state flags, converted merchantmen, privateers—were hardly a match for the formidable Royal Navy, nearly three hundred men-of-war, more than amply supplied with both gunpower and manpower.

So the newborn Continental Navy resorted to a kind of naval guerrilla war. While Britain guarded the sea lanes to supply its troops in America, the speedy American frigates and the converted merchantmen ranged the Atlantic, bagging no fewer than six hundred prize ships, including sixteen British men-of-war. When heavy French sea power, under Admiral Count François de Grasse, was thrown into the fight before Yorktown, the British forces finally gave way.

Out of these tentative Revolutionary beginnings there developed in those years of trial and test a first-rate American sea power that could meet a challenge in any quarter of the globe. It was to be directed by a group of valiant naval commanders, ready for battle action on any bridge, on any sea front.

In 1830, "Old Ironsides" was deemed "unseaworthy" and was scheduled to be scrapped. When he learned of this, the great Oliver Wendell Holmes wrote the poem "Old Ironsides," which helped popularize the cause of saving the old ship from the wrecking crew. She was rebuilt, used as a training vessel, and, in 1877, again rebuilt and used in Atlantic crossings. Finally, in 1897, she was put into storage at the Boston Navy yard, where she was rebuilt for the third time. Now, the proud symbol of our patriotic heritage, she serves as a museum.

John Paul Jones

This painting of John Paul Jones aboard the *Bonhomme Richard* during the battle with the *Serapis* was done by Ben Stahl.

He was born John Paul in Scotland in 1747 and went to sea when he was only twelve. By the time he arrived in Philadelphia in 1775 as an experienced sea captain, he had changed his name to John Paul Jones.

After conducting sea raids on the coast of Britain, he took command in 1779 of a rebuilt French merchant ship, renamed the *Bonhomme Richard* to honor Benjamin Franklin. On September 23, 1779, Jones engaged the British frigate *Serapis* in the North Sea, daringly sailing in close, lashing his vessel to the British ship, and fighting the battle at point-blank range. During the fight two of his cannon burst, and the British captain asked Jones if he was ready to surrender. Replied Jones: "Sir, I have not yet begun to fight." The American crew finally boarded the *Serapis* after the British vessel had struck her colors, and from the deck of the *Serapis* they watched the *Bonhomme Richard* sink into the North Sea.

Stephen Decatur

This heroic portrait of Stephen Decatur was done by the American painter Alonzo Chappel (1828–87).

In the early years of the nineteenth century the Barbary States along the coast of North Africa had been committing piracy and exacting tribute for the passage of ships and cargo in the Mediterranean. In 1801 Tripoli, believing the young United States was not sufficiently compliant, declared war. The frigate USS *Philadelphia* was boarded, her captain and crew were imprisoned, and the pirates began to refit the vessel for their own use. On the night of February 16, 1804, Lieutenant Stephen Decatur (1779–1820) entered Tripoli harbor aboard the ketch *Intrepid.* Decatur boarded and burned the captured *Philadelphia* with her thirty-eight guns, a daring and well-planned exploit to warn the Tripolitans of the kind of enemy they had provoked.

That was only the first of Decatur's many deeds. In 1812, commanding the *United States*, he took the British frigate *Macedonian*, operating off Morocco, and in 1815 he forced all the Barbary pirates to sign a treaty of peace. At a banquet in 1816 celebrating his victory, he offered a classic patriotic toast: "Our Country! In her intercourse with foreign nations, may she always be in the right; but our country, right or wrong."

Oliver Hazard Perry

This engraving of Commodore Perry, by Henry Meyer is from an original portrait by John W. Jarvis.

Most of the very brief life of Oliver Hazard Perry (1785–1819) was spent in the service of his country. At the age of fourteen he became a midshipman in the new Navy. After service in the war against the Barbary pirates, he was named a lieutenant in 1807 and spent much of the following two years building gunboats. During the War of 1812 he was assigned to build a fleet for use on Lake Erie. It was there in September 1813, near Put-in-Bay, that his ships met a British squadron. When his flagship, the *Lawrence*, was rendered useless, he transferred command to the *Niagara* and from her deck won the victory that meant control of the strategic Lake Erie. Perry's famous message to General William Henry Harrison was "We have met the enemy and they are ours." He had earned a hero's laurels. Perry died in Venezuela of yellow fever at the age of thirty-four.

This painting of the USS *Constitution* by Salisbury Tuckerman hangs in the Knicker-bocker Club in New York City.

There are few patriotic thrills equal to those you sense when you step on the hallowed deck of Old Ironsides, the nickname given to the forty-four gun frigate originally christened the USS *Constitution*. This is the most honored vessel ever to serve in the U.S. Navy. Authorized in 1794, three years in the building, launched in 1797, and commissioned in 1798, she began her career in the undeclared war against the French, saw action in the conflict with the Barbary pirates, and fought the British in the War of 1812.

OLD IRONSIDES
(September 14, 1830)

Ay, tear her tattered ensign down!
Long has it waved on high,
And many an eye has danced to see
That banner in the sky;
Beneath it rung the battle shout,
And burst the cannon's roar;—
The meteor of the ocean air
Shall sweep the clouds no more!

Her deck, once red with heroes' blood,
Where knelt the vanquished foe,
When winds were hurrying o'er the flood,
And waves were white below,

No more shall feel the victor's tread,
Or know the conquered knee;—
The harpies of the shore shall pluck
The eagle of the sea!

Oh better that her shattered hulk
Should sink beneath the wave;
Her thunders shook the mighty deep,
And there should be her grave;
Nail to the mast her holy flag,
Set every threadbare sail,
And give her to the god of storms,
The lightning and the gale!

OLIVER WENDELL HOLMES

22. What So Proudly We Hail

We found our national anthem about thirty-eight years after we gained our independence. It was the work of a Washington lawyer-poet, Francis Scott Key, who indicated that his lines should be combined with the music of an English song, "To Anacreon in Heaven," with music by John Stafford Smith. Key had tried that music, first published about 1780, with a previous poem of his, "When the Warrior Returns." Anacreon was an ancient Greek poet who wrote mainly about wine and love.

During the War of 1812, Key, a lawyer in his early thirties, was retained to obtain the release of a physician, Dr. William Beanes, who had been taken by the British in Washington. Their troops had burned the White House in late August, when President Madison and his First Lady, Dolley, in their last-minute rush to leave, had had to rip the Stuart portrait of George Washington from the walls without its frame.

In Chesapeake Bay, the British fleet was maneuvering to take the city of Baltimore. On September 5, Key went out to the fleet under a flag of truce. The negotiations were not easy, but finally an arrangement was reached. However, by that time the British were ready to move, and Key, along with his party, was held through the night of September 13–14 as the British ships bombarded Fort McHenry, guarding Baltimore.

Key witnessed the attack in which the British used the new Congreve rockets. Smoke and fog hid the results, but by morning the U.S. flag, with its fifteen stars, clearly was still flying over the fort. Inspired by the sights and sounds of that night, Key wrote his lines on his way back to the shore. A day later his poem, "The Defense of Fort McHenry," was published as a handbill, and it was reprinted in the *Baltimore Patriot* on September 20, 1814. America had its own national anthem.

It is not an easy song for an untrained singer, and yet, when "The Star-spangled Banner" is sung by a large and enthusiastic crowd, it manages to lift the hearts of everyone.

"The Star-spangled Banner" was first issued as a song by a Baltimore music publisher, Joseph Carr, and identified simply as a "patriotic song." The U.S. Army and Navy regarded the song as the national anthem, but it was not until 1916 that "The Star-spangled Banner" received official recognition. On March 3, 1931, President Herbert Hoover confirmed this by signing a proclamation that read: "That the composition consisting of the words and music known as 'The Star-spangled Banner' is designated as the national anthem of the United States of America."

Then conquer we must, for our cause it is just, And this be our motto: "In God is our Trust!"

"Star-spangled Banner," 1814

Francis Scott Key, author of "The Star-spangled Banner"

23. The New Nation Spans a Mighty Continent

For three hundred years after Columbus and two hundred after the Pilgrims landed, the sheer bigness of North America was a mystery. Then, almost suddenly, after the first trails had been blazed, the first roads opened, and the first rails set, it took less than a hundred years for a great nation to be carved out of this vast landscape.

The fact is, though, the lure of the open country to the west exerted its pull almost from the beginning. Even before the Revolution, the British crown, seeking to lock up the lucrative fur trade, had forbidden settlement west of the Allegheny crest. But many settlers ignored the so-called Proclamation Line, which became just another irritant in the Revolutionary cause.

The Treaty of Paris, ending the Revolution in 1783, set the westward boundary of the new nation at the Mississippi, but the situation was confused, and the waves of immigration continued from the east. Finally, under the Northwest Ordinance, Congress organized the vast new territory, dealt with state claims to the western lands, and set the framework for new states to be admitted to the Union.

Not quite twenty-seven years after Independence came the biggest real estate transaction in history, the Louisiana Purchase from France—828,000 square miles west of the Mississippi, from the Sabine River to the forty-ninth parallel, a block of territory that enabled the new nation to more than double its size for just $15 million. Then, between 1818 and 1819, the U.S. acquired the Florida territory from Spain. In 1845 the vast territory of Texas was taken into the Union, after that Republic had won its independence from Mexico. The subsequent U.S. war with Mexico resulted in the acquisition of California and the Southwest, and this was supplemented by the purchase of the Gadsden strip in 1862.

From the earliest tentative thrusts into the western wilderness, there were attempts to set trails to the Pacific. By the 1840s, certain routes were accepted as the trails to follow: to the north the road marked by the explorers Meriwether Lewis and William Clark, the Oregon Trail, or the Mormon trail blazed by the followers of Brigham Young; to the south the Butterfield Overland and the Santa Fe, each with its wheel ruts and lonely graves to mark the arduous passage.

A bare four years after the close of the Civil War there was an event that capped the westward migrations and secured the nation's geographical unity. On May 10, 1869, at Promontory, Utah, a golden spike was hammered into a set of railroad tracks linking the lines of the Union Pacific, coming from the east, and the Central Pacific, coming from the west. The nation had been joined, sea to sea. The news of a transcontinental railroad sputtered on telegraph keys all over the country.

In 1861, traveling by stage and railroad, it would have taken twenty-six days to cross the continent. In 1869 you could do it all by rail for a $190 fare. The first air service took twenty-four hours. Today, it takes five hours. The saga is one of the most thrilling chapters in our history. It is truly the American Odyssey.

West, always west, across the rivers, mountains, and plains, on foot, on horseback, by wagon. That was the direction in which the new nation set its face.

The West was geographically inevitable, a magnet, a challenge, just beyond the next horizon. And the stories were haunting—abundant game, endless forest, mighty rivers, shimmering prairies. Even before they had achieved independence, the Americans were reaching out, were looking far beyond the strip of seaboard where they had first landed.

For more than a century after independence, each generation pushed farther, each discovering for itself the wonders of a fresh and untouched land. There was something for every dream and every talent. You could remake the land, even as the land might remake you.

In that trek westward a nation was molding its character, carving out its own image. By the year 1800, less than twenty-five years after the Declaration, there were already 45,000 residents in Ohio and 5,600 in neighboring Indiana. By 1840 there would be more than 6 million settlers living on the frontier.

But to sink those roots into the terra incognita of the West demanded of the settlers something beyond a restless spirit and a certain strength and stamina. It called for boundless faith in themselves and their new land. And as generation followed generation, the land itself proved to be a source of renewed strength. In the West there was a sense of independence that could make one stand straighter. Life was unfettered. There was a kind of mental and physical freedom, uniquely American, that spoke directly to one's patriotic impulses. Your neighbor was miles away, yet close enough if you needed help. You could band together for community decisions, for leadership, and for some voice in your destiny.

The West became a symbol. In such an environment patriotism took deep root. Beyond the love of the land you came to cherish the untouched stretches where you could breathe and find yourself or your God.

Explorers Meriwether Lewis and William Clark, commissioned by President Jefferson, reached the mouth of the Columbia River and claimed the vast territory between the Missouri River and the Pacific Ocean for the United States. Painting by Frederic Remington.

This heroic painting, **Daniel Boone Escorting Settlers through the Cumberland Gap,** was done in 1851 by George Caleb Bingham (1811–79).

Daniel Boone (1734–1820) was a real-life person whose exploits as a frontiersman lifted him into the pantheon of American folklore.

Boone first made his reputation as a "long hunter," one of the wilderness people who used the famous Kentucky rifle, with its formidable four-foot barrel, to bag vast numbers of the wild turkeys and deer that enriched the forests of Kentucky, Tennessee, and the Carolinas.

In 1775 Boone and a group of companions hacked out a 208-mile trail over the Cumberland Gap through the Appalachian Mountains from Kentucky to Tennessee in three weeks. The pathway became known as the Wilderness Road, and that achievement alone assures Daniel Boone's place in U.S. history, since it opened a door to the West.

From *The Significance of the Frontier in American History* by Frederick Jackson Turner (1893)

From the conditions of frontier life came intellectual traits of profound importance. The works of travelers along each frontier from Colonial days onward describe for each certain traits, and these traits have, while softening down, still persisted as survivals in the place of their origin, even when a higher social organization succeeded. The result is that to the frontier the American intellect owes its striking characteristics. That coarseness and strength combined with acuteness and inquisitiveness, that practical, inventive turn of mind, quick to find expedients, that masterful grasp of material things, lacking in the artistic but powerful to effect great ends, that restless, nervous energy, that dominant individualism, working for good and for evil, and withal that buoyancy and exuberance which comes with freedom, these are traits of the frontier, or traits called out elsewhere because of the existence of the frontier. Since the days when the fleet of Columbus sailed into the waters of the New World, America has been another name for opportunity, and the people of the United States have taken their tone from the incessant expansion which has not only been open but has even been forced upon them. He would be a rash prophet who should assert that the expansive character of American life has now entirely ceased. Movement has been its dominant fact, and, unless this training has no effect upon a people, the American intellect will continually demand a wider field for its exercise. But never again will such gifts of free land offer themselves. For a moment at the frontier the bonds of custom are broken, and unrestraint is triumphant. There is not *tabula rasa.* The stubborn American environment is there with its imperious summons to accept its conditions; the inherited ways of doing things are also there; and yet, in spite of environment, and in spite of custom, each frontier did indeed furnish a new field of opportunity, a gate of escape from the bondage of the past; and freshness, and confidence, and scorn of older society, impatience of its restraints and its ideas, and indifference to its lessons, have accompanied the frontier. What the Mediterranean Sea was to the Greeks, breaking the bond of custom, offering new experiences, calling out new institutions and activities, that, and more, the ever retreating frontier has been to the United States directly, and to the nations of Europe more remotely. And now, four centuries from the discovery of America, at the end of a hundred years of life under the Constitution, the frontier has gone, and with its going has closed the first period of American history.

Thomas Hart Benton's dramatic mural **Independence and the Opening of the West** was done between 1959 and 1962. It is located in the museum of the Harry S Truman Library in Independence, Missouri. Benton (1889–1975) was a regionalist painter who chose American historical and folklore themes for his murals.

24. Two Presidents Who Helped Shape the Nation

James Monroe

James Monroe (1758–1831), fifth President of the United States, served in the Revolutionary War and was twice wounded in action. One of the negotiating team that helped to arrange the Louisiana Purchase in 1803, Monroe later served as Jefferson's minister to Great Britain and was Madison's secretary of state.

During Monroe's presidency (1817–25) the country was flourishing. Industry was being developed and western settlement was expanding. Monroe was active in firming up the nation's borders by acquiring Florida from Spain and settling the boundary with Canada. With these issues resolved, he was able to dismantle the forts guarding the borders.

However, it was on foreign affairs that Monroe left his deepest mark. As Spain's former colonies in Central and South America gained their independence, Monroe lost no time in recognizing them. When he learned that there were plans for reconquest, Monroe drafted a warning to European powers that "any attempt to extend their system to any portion of this hemisphere" would be met by war. The pronouncement, delivered in 1823, became known as the Monroe Doctrine. It has served as a cornerstone of U.S. policy.

The Monroe Doctrine
(President Monroe's Seventh Annual Message to Congress, December 2, 1823)

The occasion has been judged proper for asserting, as a principle in which the rights and interests of the United States are involved, that the American continents, by the free and independent condition which they have assumed and maintain, are henceforth not to be considered as subjects for future colonization by any European powers. . . .

It was stated at the commencement of the last session that a great effort was then making in Spain and Portugal to improve the condition of the people of those countries, and that it appeared to be conducted with extraordinary moderation. It need scarcely be remarked that the result has been so far very different from what was then anticipated. Of events in that quarter of the globe, with which we have so much intercourse and from which we derive our origin, we have always been anxious and interested spectators. The citizens of the United States cherish sentiments of the most friendly in favor of the liberty and happiness of their fellow-men on that side of the Atlantic. In the wars of the European powers in matters relating to themselves we have never taken any part, nor does it comport with our policy to do so. It is only when our rights are invaded or seriously menaced that we resent injuries or make preparation for our defense. With the movements in this hemisphere we are of necessity more immediately connected, and by causes which must be obvious to all enlightened and impartial observers. The political system of the allied powers is essentially different in this respect from that of America. This difference proceeds from that which exists in their respective Governments; and to the defense of our own, which has been achieved by the loss of so much blood and treasure, and matured by the wisdom of their most enlightened citizens, and under which we have enjoyed unexampled felicity, this whole nation is devot-

James Monroe,
an early engraving

ed. We owe it, therefore, to candor and to the amicable relations existing between the United States and those powers to declare that we should consider any attempt on their part to extend their system to any portion of this hemisphere as dangerous to our peace and safety. With the existing colonies or dependencies of any European power we have not interfered and shall not interfere. But with the Governments who have declared their independence and maintained it, and whose independence we have, on great consideration and on just principles, acknowledged, we could not view any interposition for the purpose of oppressing them, or controlling in any other manner their destiny, by any European power in any other light than as the manifestation of an unfriendly disposition toward the United States. In the war between those new Governments and Spain we declared our neutrality at the time of their recognition, and to this we have adhered, and shall continue to adhere, provided no change shall occur which in the judgment of the competent authorities of this Government, shall make a corresponding change on the part of the United States indispensable to their security.

The late events in Spain and Portugal show that Europe is still unsettled. Of this important act no stronger proof can be adduced than that the allied powers should have thought it proper, on any principle satisfactory to themselves, to have interposed by force in the internal concerns of Spain. To what extent such interposition may be carried, on the same principle, is a question in which all independent powers whose governments differ from theirs are interested, even those most remote, and surely none more so than the United States. Our policy in regard to Europe, which was adopted at an early stage of the wars which have so long agitated that quarter of the globe, nevertheless remains the same, which is, not to interfere in the internal concerns of any of its powers; to consider the government *de facto* as the legitimate government for us; to cultivate friendly relations with it, and to preserve those relations by a frank, firm, and manly policy, meeting in all instances the just claims of every power, submitting to injuries from none. But in regard to those continents circumstances are eminently and conspicuously different. It is impossible that the

allied powers should extend their political system to any portion of either continent without endangering our peace and happiness; nor can anyone believe that our southern brethren, if left to themselves, would adopt it of their own accord. It is equally impossible, therefore, that we should behold such interposition in any form with indifference. If we look to the comparative strength and resources of Spain and those new Governments, and their distance from each other, it must be obvious that she can never subdue them. It is still the true policy of the United States to leave the parties to themselves, in the hope that other powers will pursue the same course. . . .

Andrew Jackson

Andrew Jackson (1767–1845), seventh President of the United States, was popularly regarded as the first "people's President," though his opponents often called him "King Andrew." He emerged as a national hero in March 1814, when he defeated the Creek Indians in a battle at Horseshoe Bend, Alabama. His victory over the British at New Orleans, Louisiana, in January 1815, pushed the Tennessee lawyer-soldier to the top of the pantheon of heroes.

Jackson's victories in the field helped to signal even greater expansion to the West from the fringe of pioneer settlements that clung to the banks of the Ohio.

As President, starting in 1829, Jackson was not quite the frontiersman he was so often painted. He did ride on horseback to his inauguration, and the punch bowls had to be moved out to the White House lawns in order to get rid of the guests, but "Old Hickory" proved a capable chief executive endowing the voters with a sense of participation. Only 27 percent voted in the presidential election of 1824, but 58 percent voted in 1828, and the percentage rose to 80 in 1840, reflecting feelings of national pride and individual responsibility.

25. "Remember the Alamo"

In San Antonio, Texas, not too far from the Mexican border, stands a small mission built by the Franciscan missionaries in 1722. It is called the Alamo. In 1836 the Alamo became the site of a brief siege in late February and early March. Here a band of 187 Texans, protesting the violation of their rights and seeking separation from Mexico, faced a force of three thousand Mexican troops under General Santa Anna. It was a showdown for about ten days; then the weight of Mexican numbers told, the garrison was overwhelmed, and in the hand-to-hand fighting that followed was slaughtered to a man. Among those who died was the commander, Colonel William B. Travis, and such legendary frontier figures as Jim Bowie and Davy Crockett. "Remember the Alamo" became etched into the hearts of all embattled Texans. The land became a republic and then a state in the Union in 1845. And the Alamo became a national patriotic shrine.

Davy Crockett

Davy Crockett was one of the legendary backwoodsman in our era of national growth. His heroic stand against the Mexican Army at the Alamo has become one of the inspiring chapters in the history of the American Southwest. This picture is an engraving from a portrait by S. S. Osgood. Crockett asserted that it was the only correct likeness of him.

Fall of the Alamo---Death of Crockett.

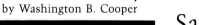

Sam Houston,
by Washington B. Cooper

Sam Houston

It was Virginia-born Samuel Houston (1793–1863)—American soldier, Tennessee lawyer, first President of the Republic of Texas—who was the link that brought the vast spaces of Texas into the American Union.

Houston had moved to Texas in 1833. He was a leader among the sparse groups of settlers who determined on separation from an oppressive Mexican government and the brutality of military chief Santa Anna. After the siege of the Alamo, the Texans under Houston regrouped their forces and met Santa Anna in the battle of San Jacinto. With the battle cry "Remember the Alamo," they defeated the Mexicans and captured Santa Anna himself.

Texas joined the Union in 1845. Houston was elected governor of Texas in 1859 but was deposed when he refused to take an oath supporting the Confederacy in 1861.

26. Daniel Webster:
"Liberty and Union, Now and Forever"

There was something in his ability to sway people that was almost mystical. In fact, those who listened to him insisted that in a showdown argument with the Devil himself, you should bet on Daniel Webster. In a day when oratory was a national passion, "Black Dan" was the greatest orator of his time. He was of swarthy complexion, rotund in stature, with a large head and eyes that reflected a special glow under fierce eyebrows. Dressed in his favorite speaking suit of dark blue with brass buttons, he could make his voice roll and clap with thunder. Listeners were mesmerized.

Daniel Webster was born in New Hampshire in 1782, the son of a farmer. As a young man he tried schoolteaching, then turned to politics. At thirty-one, he already was a congressman, and later he served as a senator, as secretary of state, and as head of the Whig party of his time. Webster was also a very successful lawyer. His lasting fame, however, rests on his speeches.

In debate, Webster was at once majestic and lethal. He could devastate an opponent with oratorical force bulwarked by well-organized thinking. While other statesmen and orators might burn with the love of the land, Daniel Webster's great passion was for the Union. At that moment in our early history, when some in power still argued for the right of the states to refuse to obey federal law, Daniel Webster rose to the challenge. He viewed slavery as an evil but disunion as a greater danger.

The pinnacle of Webster's oratory was reached on January 26, 1830, when he replied in a crowded Senate chamber to Senator Robert Hayne of South Carolina, who had turned a debate on public-lands policy into an argument of the states'-rights question. The room was jammed with visitors who had learned that a crucial argument was taking place. In what has been rated one of the greatest examples of American oratory, a patriotic declamation repeated for years after on a thousand school platforms, "Black Dan" Webster defined his concept of the Union, for all posterity.

Daniel Webster on the Union (January 26, 1830)

It is to that Union we owe our safety at home, and our consideration and dignity abroad. It is to that Union that we are chiefly indebted for whatever makes us most proud of our country. That Union we reached only by the discipline of our virtues in the severe school of adversity. It had its origin in the necessities of disordered finance, prostrate commerce, and ruined credit. Under its benign influences, these great interests immediately awoke as from the dead, and sprang forth with newness of life. Every year of its duration has teemed with fresh proofs of its utility and its blessings; and although our territory has stretched out wider and wider, and our population spread farther and farther, they have not outrun its protection or its benefits. It has been to us all a copious fountain of national, social, and personal happiness.

I have not allowed myself, Sir, to look beyond the Union, to see what might lie hidden in the dark recess behind. I have not coolly weighed the chances of preserving liberty when the bonds that unite us together shall be broken asunder. I have not accustomed myself to hang over the precipice of disunion, to see whether, with my short sight, I can fathom the depth of the abyss below; nor could I regard him as a safe counselor in the affairs of this government, whose thoughts shall be mainly bent on considering, not how the Union may be best preserved, but how tolerable might be the condition of the

Daniel Webster, who raised oratory to an art, relaxes at his farm in this portrait by an unknown artist.

The tune for the song we call "America," or "My Country, 'tis of Thee," probably goes back to Elizabethan times. In 1744 it became the anthem "God Save Our Lord, the King."

The music found its way into print in America about 1761, and was used for a variety of patriotic verses. In 1831 Samuel Francis Smith, a student at Andover Theological Seminary, was asked to write a school song, and composed the words for "My Country, 'tis of Thee." The song was first used in a July Fourth celebration that same year.

Smith, who later became a clergyman, editor, and poet, claimed that when he wrote words for his poem, he did not realize that the tune he had in mind was that of the British national anthem. He was under the impression that he was using an old German song.

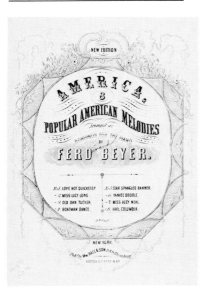

people when it should be broken up and destroyed. While the Union lasts we have high, exciting, gratifying prospects spread out before us, for us and our children. Beyond that I seek not to penetrate the veil. God grant that in my day at least that curtain may not rise! God grant that on my vision never may be opened what lies behind! When my eyes shall be turned to behold for the last time the sun in heaven, may I not see Him shining on the broken and dishonored fragments of a once glorious Union; on States dissevered, discordant, belligerent; on a land rent with civil feuds, or drenched, it may be, in fraternal blood! Let their last feeble and lingering glance rather behold the gorgeous ensign of the republic, now known and honored throughout the earth, still full high advanced, its arms and trophies streaming in their original lustre, not a stripe erased or polluted, not a single star obscured, bearing for its motto, no such miserable interrogatory as "What is all this worth?" nor those other words of delusion and folly, "Liberty first and Union afterwards"; but everywhere, spread all over in characters of living light, blazing on all its ample folds, as they float over the sea and over the land, and in every wind under the whole heavens, that other sentiment, dear to every true American heart,—Liberty *and* Union, now and forever, one inseparable!

27. Columbia, the Gem of the Ocean

From the earliest years there was a close link between the adventurers of the new nation and the beckoning sea. Though sometimes hostile and treacherous, the sea provided a source of food, an easy avenue of travel and commerce, and an opportunity for quick wealth.

Around those who went down to the sea in ships, legends grew up, and if their glory years were hazardous and often short, still they were filled with proud vitality. They were years when our sea captains and our sailors could be found in any part of the globe and a national tradition of high adventure was born.

The ten years between 1847 and 1857 marked the peak period of the clipper ships, so named for their sleek design and great speed. Theirs were the years of the westward thrust, when the pressure for swift passage to the California gold mines was high, when profits from the trade with China might enable a shipowner or a captain to retire before he was forty.

From shipbuilders all along the East Coast came a steady flotilla of clippers, designed with skill and built with pride. These clippers could speed down to Cape Horn and around to California, with a stop at San Francisco, in less than ninety days. Then on to Canton and back in seventy-four days. The clippers were sometimes 250 feet long and could reach 22 nautical miles per hour.

With reasonable luck and favoring weather, and with a steady hand at the helm, these clippers could go anywhere. Visions of beauty, they bore such names as *Flying Cloud, Cutty Sark, Stag Hound,* and *Seawitch.* They moved with speed and grace under a thundering spread of magnificent sail, fashioned to make the most of every line in or out of the water.

With the advent of steam, the clippers disappeared, almost overnight. However, they have remained a part of our heritage, and more than a hundred years after their demise the age of the clipper ships is still a bright spot in our national memory.

Columbia with shield was a proper figurehead for a fast-flying clipper.

Flying Cloud, an incomparable clipper that broke the ninety-day record from New York to San Francisco. Josiah Cressy was among her noted captains. This painting is by J. Warren Sheppard.

28. Honest Abe Lincoln

B y 1860, conflict over the slavery issue was coming closer. The Abolitionists were waging their own war, their exhortations at fever pitch. Virginia had already called out its militia. Secession was only weeks away.

Politically the Whigs were split. The Democrats settled on Stephen Douglas, and the Seceders nominated former Vice-President John C. Breckenridge of Kentucky for the presidency. The so-called Constitution party picked John Bell of Tennessee.

The new Republicans sensed victory. On their third ballot the nomination went to a lawyer from Illinois, a man known as "Honest Abe" Lincoln.

Abraham Lincoln had been born in Kentucky, son of Thomas and Nancy Hanks Lincoln, and while he was still a child his family had moved first to Indiana and then, in 1830, on to Illinois.

Young Lincoln had been a storekeeper, surveyor, postmaster, then had studied law. He served a term in Congress from 1847 to 1849, left political life for five years, and returned to it as a candidate for the Senate. Lincoln argued in his campaign that the Constitution was a binding and irrevocable contract between the states. His "House Divided" speech attacking compromise with slavery was initially delivered at Springfield, Illinois, and later at Peoria, Illinois. Lincoln was defeated for the Senate by Stephen A. Douglas, his opponent in a series of campaign debates.

Although Abraham Lincoln had no formal education, he had read widely. He had a special flair for storytelling and a grasp of the nuances and mood of language. To help in his campaign for the presidency, Lincoln wrote a brief autobiography. In its way it has served to reinforce his image. In its simplicity and directness, it brought Lincoln into sharp focus. It reflected the character of the man. Though millions of words have been written about Lincoln, many of them contributions to a massive mythology, nothing has matched this straight-to-the-mark statement he wrote himself. It helped to elect him President, giving the nation the kind of leader it needed.

Abraham Lincoln: Autobiography (December 20, 1859)

I was born February 12, 1809, in Hardin County, Kentucky. My parents were both born in Virginia, of undistinguished families—second families, perhaps I should say. My mother, who died in my tenth year, was of a family of the name of Hanks, some of whom now reside in Adams, and others in Macon County, Illinois. My paternal grandfather, Abraham Lincoln, emigrated from Rockingham County, Virginia, to Kentucky about 1781 or 1782, where a year or two later he was killed by the Indians, not in battle, but by stealth, when he was laboring to open a farm in the forest. His ancestors, who were Quakers, went to Virginia from Berks County, Pennsylvania. An effort to identify them with the New England family of the same name ended in nothing more definite than a similarity of Christian names of both families, such as Enoch, Levi, Mordecai, Solomon, Abraham, and the like.

My father, at the death of his father, was but six years of age, and he grew up literally without education. He moved from Kentucky to what is now Spencer County, Indiana, in my eighth year. We reached our new home about the time the state came into the Union. It was a wild region, with many bears and other wild animals still in the woods. There I grew up. There were some schools, so called, but no qualification was ever required of a teacher beyond "readin', writin', and cipherin'," to the rule of three. If a straggler supposed to

Here American artist Eastman Johnson (1824–1906) pictures *The Boy Lincoln* reading by a light from the fireplace. Lincoln's early struggles to acquire an education became a substantial part of the legend that surrounded the sixteenth President.

Young Abraham Lincoln, axe in hand, pauses in his chores as a rail-splitter. This engraving is after a rather romanticized painting by Jean L. G. Ferris.

understand Latin happened to sojourn in the neighborhood, he was looked upon as a wizard. There was absolutely nothing to excite ambition for education. Of course, when I came of age I did not know much. Still, somehow, I could read, write, and cipher to the rule of three, but that was all. I have not been to school since. The little advance I now have upon this store of education, I have picked up from time to time under the pressure of necessity.

I was raised to farm work, which I continued till I was twenty-two. At twenty-one I came to Illinois, Macon County. Then I got to New Salem, at that time in Sangamon, now in Menard County, where I remained a year as a sort of clerk in a store. Then came the Black Hawk War; and I was elected a captain of volunteers, a success which gave me more pleasure than any I have had since. I went the campaign, was elected, ran for the legislature the same year (1832), and was beaten—the only time I have ever been beaten by the people. The next and three succeeding biennial elections I was elected to the legislature. I was not a candidate afterward. During this legislative period I had studied law, and removed to Springfield to practice it. In 1846 I was once elected to the lower House of Congress. Was not a candidate for reelection. From 1849 to 1854, both inclusive, practiced law more assiduously than ever before. Always a Whig in politics; and generally on the Whig electoral tickets, making active canvasses. I was losing interest in politics when the repeal of the Missouri Compromise aroused me again. What I have done since that is pretty well known.

If any personal description of me is thought desirable, it may be said I am, in height, six feet four inches, nearly; lean in flesh, weighing on an average one hundred and eighty pounds; dark complexion with coarse black hair and gray eyes. No other marks or brands recollected.

29. A House Divided

"I believe this government cannot endure," declared the gaunt man from Springfield, "permanently half slave and half free."

It was June 16, 1858, and Abraham Lincoln was addressing the closing session of the Republican State Convention in the hall of the Illinois House of Representatives. The focus of the speech was the phrase: "A house divided against itself cannot stand." There, in a few memorable words, was the entire problem as Lincoln saw it.

The "House Divided" speech was the springboard for a flood of argument that swept the country in its aftermath. It was a prologue to the nine Lincoln-Douglas debates, from which Lincoln emerged a national figure. To a country upset by the tumult over slavery, Lincoln had found the words and philosophy to clarify the issue. He said, in effect, that there would be no rest from the slavery question until the nation had passed through a crisis. He made it clear that he did not expect the Union to collapse. However the end was reached, the nation would be one way or the other, slave or free.

Lincoln Argues That a House Divided Against Itself Cannot Stand (June 16, 1858)

Mr. President, and Gentlemen of the Convention:

If we could first know where we are, and whither we are tending, we could better judge what to do, and how to do it. We are now far into the fifth year since a policy was initiated with the avowed object and confident promise of putting an end to slavery agitation. Under the operation of that policy, that agitation has not only not ceased, but has constantly augmented. In my opinion, it will not cease until a crisis shall have been reached and passed. "A house divided against itself cannot stand." I believe this government cannot endure permanently half slave and half free. I do not expect the Union to be dissolved—I do not expect the house to fall—but I do expect it will cease to be divided. It will become all one thing or all the other. Either the opponents of slavery will arrest the further spread of it, and place it where the public mind shall rest in the belief that it is in the course of ultimate extinction; or its advocates will push it forward till it shall become alike lawful in all the states, old as well as new—North as well as South. . . .

While the Nebraska Bill was passing through Congress, a law case involving the question of a Negro's freedom, by reason of his owner having voluntarily taken him first into a free state and then into a territory covered by the Congressional prohibition, and held him as a slave for a long time in each, was passing through the United States Circuit Court for the District of Missouri; and both the Nebraska Bill and lawsuit were brought to a decision in the same month of May 1854. The Negro's name was "Dred Scott," which name now designates the decision finally made in the case. Before the then next presidential election, the law case came to, and was argued in, the Supreme Court of the United States; but the decision of it was deferred until after the election. Still, before the election, Senator Trumbull, on the floor of the Senate, requested the leading advocate of the Nebraska Bill to state his opinion whether the people of a territory can constitutionally exclude slavery from their limits, and the latter answered: "That is a question for the Supreme Court." . . .

The several points of the Dred Scott decision, in connection with Senator Douglas' "care-not" policy, constitute the piece of machinery, in its present

state of advancement. This was the third point gained. The working points of that machinery are:

First, that no Negro slave, imported as such from Africa, and no descendant of such slave, can ever be a citizen of any state, in the sense of that term as used in the Constitution of the United States. This point is made in order to deprive the Negro, in every possible event, of the benefit of that provision of the United States Constitution which declares that: "The citizens of each state shall be entitled to all privileges and immunities of citizens in the several states."

Second, that "subject to the Constitution of the United States," neither Congress nor a territorial legislature can exclude slavery from any United States territory. This point is made in order that individual men may fill up the territories with slaves, without danger of losing them as property, and thus to enhance the chances of permanency to the institution through all the future.

Third, that whether the holding a Negro in actual slavery in a free state makes him free, as against the holder, the United States courts will not decide, but will leave to be decided by the courts of any slave state the Negro may be forced into by the master. This point is made, not to be pressed immediately; but, if acquiesced in for a while, and apparently endorsed by the people at an election, then to sustain the logical conclusion that what Dred Scott's master might lawfully do with Dred Scott, in the free state of Illinois, every other master may lawfully do with any other one, or one thousand slaves, in Illinois or in any other free state. . . .

While the opinion of the court, by Chief Justice Taney, in the Dred Scott case, and the separate opinions of all the concurring judges, expressly declare that the Constitution of the United States neither permits Congress nor a territorial legislature to exclude slavery from any United States territory, they

93

all omit to declare whether or not the same Constitution permits a state, or the people of a state, to exclude it. Possibly this is a mere omission; but who can be quite sure, if McLean or Curtis [Supreme Court Justices] had sought to get into the opinion a declaration of unlimited power in the people of a state to exclude slavery from their limits, just as Chase and Mace [Supreme Court Justices] sought to get such declaration, in behalf of the people of a territory, into the Nebraska Bill—I ask, who can be quite sure that it would not have been voted down in the one case as it had been in the other? The nearest approach to the point of declaring the power of a state over slavery is made by Judge Nelson. . . . Put this and that together, and we have another nice little niche, which we may ere long see filled with another Supreme Court decision, declaring that the Constitution of the United States does not permit a state to exclude slavery from its limits. . . .

Such a decision is all that slavery now lacks of being alike lawful in all the states. Welcome or unwelcome, such decision is probably coming, and will soon be upon us, unless the power of the present political dynasty shall be met and overthrown. We shall lie down pleasantly dreaming that the people of Missouri are on the verge of making their state free, and we shall wake to the reality instead that the Supreme Court has made Illinois a slave state. To meet and overthrow the power of that dynasty is the work now before all those who would prevent that consummation. This is what we have to do. How can we best do it?

There are those who denounce us openly to their own friends, and yet whisper us softly, that Senator Douglas is the aptest instrument there is with which to effect that object. They wish us to infer all from the fact that he now has a little quarrel with the present head of the dynasty; and that he has regularly voted with us on a single point, upon which he and we have never differed. They remind us that he is a great man, and that the largest of us are very small ones. Let this be granted. But "a living dog is better than a dead lion." Judge Douglas, if not a dead lion, for this work, is at least a caged and toothless one. How can he oppose the advances of slavery? He does not care anything about it. His avowed mission is impressing the "public heart" to care nothing about it. A leading Douglas Democrat newspaper thinks Douglas' superior talent will be needed to resist the revival of the African slave trade. Does Douglas believe an effort to revive that trade is approaching? He has not said so. Does he really think so? But if it is, how can he resist it? For years he has labored to prove it a sacred right of white men to take Negro slaves into the new territories. Can he possibly show that it is less a sacred right to buy them where they can be bought cheapest? And unquestionably they can be bought cheaper in Africa than in Virginia. He had done all in his power to reduce the whole question of slavery to one of a mere right of property; and, as such, how can he oppose the foreign slave trade—how can he refuse that trade in that "property" shall be "perfectly free"—unless he does it as a protection to the home production? And as the home producers will not ask the protection, he will be wholly without a ground of opposition.

Senator Douglas holds, we know, that a man may rightfully be wiser today than he was yesterday—that he may rightfully change when he finds himself wrong. But can we, for that reason, run ahead and infer that he will make any particular change, of which he, himself, has given no intimation? Can we safely base our action upon any such vague interference? Now, as ever, I wish not to misrepresent Judge Douglas' position, question his motives, or do aught that can be personally offensive to him. Whenever, if ever, he and we can come together on principle so that our cause may have assistance from his great ability, I hope to have interposed no adventitious obstacle. But clearly, he is not now with us—he does not pretend to be—he does not promise ever to be.

Our cause, then, must be intrusted to, and conducted by, its own undoubted friends—those whose hands are free, whose hearts are in the work—who do care for the result. Two years ago the Republicans of the nation mustered over thirteen hundred thousand strong. We did this under the single impulse of resistance to a common danger, with every external circumstance against us. Of strange, discordant, and even hostile elements, we gathered from the four winds, and formed and fought the battle through, under the constant hot fire of a disciplined, proud, and pampered enemy. Did we brave all then to falter now?—now, when that same enemy is wavering, dissevered, and belligerent? The result is not doubtful. We shall not fail—if we stand firm, we shall not fail. Wise counsels may accelerate, or mistakes delay it, but, sooner or later, the victory is sure to come.

President-Elect Lincoln Bids Farewell to Springfield, Illinois (February 11, 1861)

My Friends:

No one, not in my situation, can appreciate my feeling of sadness at this parting. To this place, and the kindness of these people, I owe everything. Here I have lived a quarter of a century, and have passed from a young to an old man. Here my children have been born, and one is buried. I now leave, not knowing when or whether ever I may return, with a task before me greater than that which rested upon Washington. Without the assistance of that Divine Being who ever attended him, I cannot succeed. With that assistance, I cannot fail. Trusting in Him who can go with me, and remain with you, and be everywhere for good, let us confidently hope that all will yet be well. To His care commending you, as I hope in your prayers you will commend me, I bid you an affectionate farewell.

In the light of his final destiny, Lincoln's brief farewell to his friends in Springfield on February 11, 1861, is truly poignant. It captures in Lincoln's typical style the mood of that moment. Here was the lawyer from Illinois, at the crossroads of his personal life, on the eve of his fifty-second birthday, about to leave his home and to step onto the stage of history. The nation was on the brink of disintegration, the South was preparing for secession. Lincoln was aware of the task that had fallen on him. He believed that he would have the help of God and that the Union would be preserved.

Abraham Lincoln on horseback as he appeared before his Springfield, Illinois, residence at the close of the campaign with Stephen Douglas.

30. The Union Must Be Preserved

The years of debate, the clash of political philosophies, the abortive attempts at compromise were over. The Secessionists made their moves, chipping off state after state. The Republic was splitting up.

Some saw the coming war as an "irrepressible conflict" generated by differing social theories, by opposed economic forces. In Abraham Lincoln's view, it would be, simply, a war to preserve the Union.

The North had the cannon; the South had cotton. Population and wealth were against the South but the Confederacy, summoning up a call for liberty and self-government, had an emotional edge. The South also had interior lines of communication and a social system that would allow for maximum use of its manpower. Many felt that the South had only to stay alive to win. But they failed to reckon with Abraham Lincoln, to whose vision of a united nation, North and South rejoined, in unbreakable union, the people would eventually rally.

In the fateful election of November 1860, the six-foot-four-inch lawyer from Illinois won with a popular vote of 1,866,452 and an electoral vote of 180.

On Inauguration Day, March 4, 1861, the Federal City was nervous. Rumor had it that Secessionists from Maryland or Virginia were about to invade, even as the sixteenth President was being inaugurated. A fringe of derricks surrounded the incomplete Capitol dome. It was almost symbolic. Somehow in the midst of the ceremony the dignitaries that surrounded Lincoln seemed almost out of place. The new President made it clear he was not going to bow. The states were bound together—irrevocably.

On April 12, the first gun of the Civil War was fired at Fort Sumter in Charleston. It came from Southern cannon. "Treason" was the word on many lips. But the Union would survive, for the most dedicated patriot of his time was in command.

Abraham Lincoln: First Inaugural Address (March 4, 1861)

Fellow-citizens of the United States:

—In compliance with a custom as old as the Government itself, I appear before you to address you briefly, and to take in your presence the oath prescribed by the Constitution of the United States to be taken by the President "before he enters on the execution of his office.". . .

Apprehension seems to exist among the people of the Southern States that by the accession of a Republican administration their property and their peace and personal security are to be endangered. There has never been any reasonable cause for such apprehension. Indeed, the most ample evidence to the contrary has all the while existed and been open to their inspection. It is found in nearly all the published speeches of him who now addresses you. I do but quote from one of those speeches when I declare that "I have no purpose, directly or indirectly, to interfere with the institution of slavery in the States where it exists. I believe I have no lawful right to do so, and I have no inclination to do so.". . .

I now reiterate these sentiments; and, in doing so, I only press upon the public attention the most conclusive evidence of which the case is susceptible, that the property, peace and security of no section are to be in any wise endangered by the now incoming administration.

Lincoln profile. A youthful hint of the greatness to come. This picture was made in Springfield, Illinois, on June 3, 1860.

This picture of **Lincoln** was made by Christopher S. German early in 1861. The beard seems to accent the tragic quality in the man's face.

A disruption of the Federal Union, heretofore only menaced, is now formidably attempted.

I hold that, in contemplation of universal law and of the Constitution, the Union of these States is perpetual. Perpetuity is implied, if not expressed, in the fundamental law of all national governments. It is safe to assert that no government proper ever had a provision in its organic law for its own termination. Continue to execute all the express provisions of our national Constitution, and the Union will endure forever—it being impossible to destroy it except by some action not provided for in the instrument itself. . . .

Descending from these general principles, we find the proposition that in legal comtemplation the Union is perpetual confirmed by the history of the Union itself. The Union is much older than the Constitution. It was formed, in fact, by the Articles of Association in 1774. It was matured and continued by the Declaration of Independence in 1776. It was further matured, and the faith of all the then thirteen States expressly plighted and engaged that it should be perpetual, by the Articles of Confederation in 1778. And, finally, in 1787 one of the declared objects for ordaining and establishing the Constitution was "to form a more perfect Union."

But if the destruction of the Union by one or by a part only of the States be lawfully possible, the Union is less perfect than before the Constitution, having lost the vital element of perpetuity.

It follows from these views that no State upon its own mere notion can lawfully get out of the Union; that resolves and ordinances to that effect are legally void; and that acts of violence, within any State or States, against the authority of the United States, are insurrectionary or revolutionary, according to circumstances.

I therefore consider that, in view of the Constitution and the laws, the Union is unbroken and to the extent of my ability I shall take care, as the Constitution itself expressly enjoins upon me, that the laws of the Union be faithfully executed in all the States. Doing this I deem to be only a simple duty on my part; and I shall perform it so far as practicable, unless my rightful masters, the American people, shall withhold the requisite means, or in some authoritative manner direct the contrary. I trust this will not be regarded as a menace, but only as the declared purpose of the Union that it will constitutionally defend and maintain itself.

97

In doing this there needs to be no bloodshed or violence; and there shall be none, unless it be forced upon the national authority. The power confided to me will be used to hold, occupy, and possess the property and places belonging to the Government, and to collect the duties and imposts; but beyond what may be necessary for these objects, there will be no invasion, no using of force against or among the people anywhere. . . .

The mails, unless repelled, will continue to be furnished in all parts of the Union. So far as possible, the people everywhere shall have that sense of perfect security which is most favorable to calm thought and reflection. . . .

That there are persons in one section or another who seek to destroy the Union at all events, and are glad of any pretext to do it, I will neither affirm nor deny; but if there be such, I need address no word to them. To those, however, who really love the Union may I not speak?

Before entering upon so grave a matter as the destruction of our national fabric, with all its benefits, its memories, and its hopes, would it not be wise to ascertain precisely why we do it? Will you hazard so desperate a step while there is any possibility that any portion of the ills you fly from have no real existence? Will you, while the certain ills you fly to are greater than all the real ones you fly from—will you risk the commission of so fearful a mistake? . . .

May Congress prohibit slavery in the Territories? The Constitution does not expressly say. *Must* Congress protect slavery in the Territories? The Constitution does not expressly say.

From questions of this class spring all our constitutional controversies, and we divide upon them into majorities and minorities. If the minority will not acquiesce, the majority must, or the Government must cease. There is no other alternative; for continuing the Government is acquiescence on one side or the other.

The inauguration of President Abraham Lincoln, March 1861.

If a minority in such case will secede rather than acquiesce, they make a precedent which in turn will divide and ruin them; for a minority of their own will secede from them whenever a majority refuses to be controlled by such minority. . . .

One section of our country believes slavery is right, and ought to be extended, while the other believes it is wrong, and ought not to be extended. This is the only substantial dispute. The fugitive slave clause of the Constitution and the law for the suppression of the foreign slave trade are each as well enforced, perhaps, as any law can ever be in a community where the moral sense of the people imperfectly supports the law itself. . . .

Physically speaking, we cannot separate. We cannot remove our respective sections from each other, nor build an impassable wall between them. A husband and wife may be divorced and go out of the presence and beyond the reach of each other; but the different parts of our country cannot do this. They cannot but remain face to face, and intercourse, either amicable or hostile, must continue between them. Is it possible, then, to make that intercourse more advantageous or more satisfactory after separation then before? Can aliens make treaties easier than friends can make laws? Can treaties be more faithfully enforced between aliens than laws can among friends? Suppose you go to war, you cannot fight always; and when, after much loss on both sides, and no gain on either, you cease fighting, the identical old questions as to terms of intercourse are again upon you.

This country, with its institutions, belongs to the people who inhabit it. Whenever they shall grow weary of the existing government, they can exercise their constitutional right of amending it, or their revolutionary right to dismember or overthrow it. I cannot be ignorant of the fact that many worthy and patriotic citizens are desirous of having the national Constitution amended. While I make no recommendation of amendments, I fully recognize the rightful authority of the people over the whole subject, to be exercised in either of the modes prescribed in the instrument itself, and I should, under existing circumstances, favor rather than oppose a fair opportunity being afforded the people to act upon it. . . .

Why should there not be a patient confidence in the ultimate justice of the people? Is there any better or equal hope in the world? In our present differences is either party without faith of being in the right? If the Almighty Ruler of nations, with His eternal truth and justice, be on your side of the North, or on yours of the South, that truth and that justice will surely prevail by the judgment of this great tribunal of the American people.

By the frame of the government under which we live, this same people have wisely given their public servants but little power for mischief; and have, with equal wisdom, provided for the return of that little to their own hands at very short intervals. While the people retain their virtue and vigilance, no administration, by any extreme of wickedness or folly, can very seriously injure the government in the short space of four years.

My countrymen, one and all, think calmly and well upon this whole subject. Nothing valuable can be lost by taking time. If there be an object to hurry any of you in hot haste to a step which you would never take deliberately, that object will be frustrated by taking time; but no good object can be frustrated by it. . . .

In your hands, my dissatisfied fellow-countrymen, and not in mine, is the momentous issue of civil war. The government will not assail you. You can have no conflict without being yourselves the aggressors. You have no oath registered in heaven to destroy the government, while I shall have the most solemn one to "preserve, protect, and defend" it.

I am loathe to close. We are not enemies, but friends. We must not be enemies. Though passion may have strained, it must not break our bonds of affection. The mystic chords of memory, stretching from every battle-field and patriot grave to every living heart and hearthstone all over this broad land, will yet swell the chorus of the Union when again touched, as surely they will be, by the better angels of our nature.

31. Two American Heroes

The events surrounding the Civil War produced many heroes, but two in particular caught the popular imagination, and both were quickly taken up as the subject of legend. The true facts of their lives, however, have been of less importance than the fact that for generations of schoolchildren they stood for commitment and courage, two of the staples of the patriotic spirit.

John Brown

John Brown provided the flint that fired the Civil War. For many years, Brown, an ardent Abolitionist, and his five sons ran a station on the Underground Railway, which spirited runaway slaves to freedom. In 1855, he became captain of an anti-slavery colony on the Osawatomie River in disputed Kansas territory. The sack of Lawrence, Kansas, by pro-slavers led Brown to counterattack, and in 1856 he and his sons deliberately murdered five pro-slavers on the banks of the Pottawatomie.

That episode brought John Brown a wave of national publicity, and he soon developed a plan to establish a "free state" between Virginia and Maryland that would give refuge to fugitive slaves and give them a center for organizing to wage war on the slave owners. In 1859 he rented a farm near Harpers Ferry, Virginia, and collected followers and arms. On the night of October 16, with twenty-one men behind him, he crossed the Potomac and captured a U.S. arsenal. He also took possession of the town, killing the mayor.

Expecting help from black recruits, Brown waited at the arsenal for two days. No one came. Finally the government acted, sending in a group of U.S. Marines under the command of Colonel Robert E. Lee. They assaulted the raiders defending the locomotive roundhouse of the arsenal, killing ten of Brown's men and wounding Brown.

John Brown's trial started eight days later. The verdict was a foregone conclusion: criminal conspiracy and treason.

On December 2, 1859, John Brown, together with six followers, was hanged. History seems to say that he stepped down from the gallows into immortality.

The Last Moments of John Brown, by artist Thomas Hovenden, painted in 1884, depicts the Abolitionist pausing on his way to the gallows to kiss a black child. This incident was later discovered to have been, at least in part, a newspaper reporter's invention, but the dramatic image has remained a part of our national consciousness.

This painting recalling the saga of **Barbara Frietchie** was done by the great illustrator N. C. Wyeth (1882–1945).

Barbara Frietchie

In the year 1862, Barbara Frietchie, the ninety-seven-year-old widow of a glove maker, lived in Frederick, Maryland. She had been in her teens during the Revolution, and love of country was deeply rooted in her. When the advance troops of the Confederacy moved through Frederick that September, most of the citizens removed their Union flags and locked up their homes and businesses. But, defiantly, Mrs. Frietchie went to the top of her house, leaned far out of her attic window, and waved the Stars and Stripes. Shots broke the flagstaff, but Mrs. Frietchie rescued the broken pole and continued to wave the colors. The Southern troops did not fire again, and the flag remained in its place until the Union troops retook the town.

The poem "Barbara Frietchie," by John Greenleaf Whittier (1807–92), together with Walt Whitman's "O Captain! My Captain!" is remembered as one of the durable expressions of the thoughts and emotions of the Civil War period.

BARBARA FRIETCHIE (September 13, 1862)

Up from the meadows rich with corn,
Clear in the cool September morn,

The clustered spires of Frederick stand
Green-walled by the hills of Maryland.

Round about them orchards sweep,
Apple and peach tree fruited deep,

Fair as the garden of the Lord
To the eyes of the famished rebel horde,

On that pleasant morn of the early fall
When Lee marched over the mountain-wall;

Over the mountains winding down,
Horse and foot, into Frederick town.

Forty flags with their silver stars,
Forty flags with their crimson bars,

Flapped in the morning wind: the sun
Of noon looked down, and saw not one.

Up rose old Barbara Frietchie then,
Bowed with her fourscore years and ten;

Bravest of all in Frederick town,
She took up the flag the men hauled down;

In her attic window tbe staff she set,
To show that one heart was loyal yet.

Up the street came the rebel tread,
Stonewall Jackson riding ahead.

Under his slouched hat left and right
He glanced; the old flag met his sight.

"Halt!"—the dust-brown ranks stood fast.
"Fire!"—out blazed the rifle-blast.

It shivered the window, pane and sash;
It rent the banner with seam and gash.

Quick, as it fell, from the broken staff
Dame Barbara snatched the silken scarf.

She leaned far out on the window-sill,
And shook it forth with a royal will.

"Shoot, if you must, this old gray head,
But spare your country's flag," she said.

A shade of sadness, a blush of shame,
Over the face of the leader came;

The nobler nature within him stirred
To life at that woman's deed and word;

"Who touches a hair of yon gray head
Dies like a dog! March on!" he said.

All day long through Frederick street
Sounded the tread of marching feet:

All day long that free flag tost
Over the heads of the rebel host.

Ever its torn folds rose and fell
On the loyal winds that loved it well;

And through the hill-gaps sunset light
Shone over it with a warm good-night.

Barbara Frietchie's work is o'er,
And the Rebel rides on his raids no more

Honor to her! and let a tear
Fall, for her sake, on Stonewall's bier.

Over Barbara Frietchie's grave,
Flag of Freedom and Union, wave!

Peace and order and beauty draw
Round thy symbol of light and law;

And ever the stars above look down
On the stars below in Frederick town!

JOHN GREENLEAF WHITTIER

32. A Nation Torn Asunder

The conflict of ideas, the clash of opinion, and the bitterness of debate was, in the end, reduced to battlefield confrontation. The argument was finished; the guns spoke.

For four violent years the nation fought with itself as cotton challenged cannon and sectionalism and moral indignation dissolved into a single issue: could this Union survive?

The loss of life on the battlegrounds was monumental: casualties for the North 140,414; for the South 74,524. Property loss has never been estimated.

Not until the meeting in those hot July days at Gettysburg in 1863 was there some indication of a probable outcome. The conflict had ranged over a broad front, east and west, along the Mississippi, and finally into the Pennsylvania heartland and across the Georgia plantations, before the weight of Northern power and its superior naval forces proved the difference. Out of the holocaust the issue seemed to be settled: it was to be, indeed, one nation, indivisible. Lincoln had been vindicated; Father Abraham and national unity. On April 9, 1865, Lee surrendered his army. The Confederacy was history.

"Burnt district" of Richmond, 1865

This **Mathew Brady photograph of Lincoln and his generals** was taken October 1, 1862, after Antietam. They are: Colonel Delos B. Sackett, Major Montieth, General N. B. Sweitzer, General G. W. Morrell, unidentified (possibly Andrew A. Humphreys), General George B. McClellan, Scout Adams, Colonel Alexander S. Webb, General G. A. Custer (?), President Lincoln, General Lewis C. Hunt, General Fitz John Porter, Allan Pinkerton, Colonel Fred Locke, Surgeon Letterman, and Colonel Bachelder.

The mystic chords of memory, stretching from every battle-field and patriot grave to every living heart and hearthstone all over this broad land, will yet swell the chorus of the Union when again touched, as surely they will be, by the better angels of our nature.

ABRAHAM LINCOLN,
First Inaugural Address,
March 4, 1861

William Tecumseh Sherman

William Tecumseh Sherman (1820–91) had served in the Mexican War and proved himself a capable corps commander. He wore his clothes carelessly, in the manner of General Grant, and sported a short red beard. Sherman grasped the uses of surprise and mobility and appreciated the value of "total war." He was named a major general in 1862 and was responsible for the "march to the sea" that resulted in the capture of Atlanta and Savannah.

George B. McClellan

George B. McClellan (1826–85), a West Point graduate in the class of 1846, had served in the Mexican War. He was a good organizer with a methodical mind. McClellan revamped the Army of the Potomac after the defeat of the Union forces at Bull Run and was given command of the troops in Washington. He was named major general in 1861. McClellan was known as "Little Mac" but preferred the label of "Young Napoleon." Lee counted him as the ablest of his opponents.

George Gordon Meade

George Gordon Meade (1815–72) was a tough, loyal army officer who rose to command from the ranks of the Army Engineers. In private life he had been a civil engineer and surveyor for railroads and had served the Army in the Mexican War. He had seen action at Bull Run, at Antietam, and at Fredericksburg before Lincoln chose him to command the Army of the Potomac in June 1863. Meade's mission was to check General Lee's invasion of the North. That mission was accomplished in the field at Gettysburg.

Ulysses S. Grant

Ulysses S. Grant (1822–85) had no affection for war and was not especially attuned to the business of the Army. A West Point graduate, he had served with distinction in the Mexican War as a lieutenant. At the start of the Civil War he earned a brigadier's commission in Missouri and brought notice to himself when he took the enemy camp at Fort Donelson in February 1861. It was on that occasion that he became known as "Unconditional Surrender" Grant. In July 1863 his forces took the enemy stronghold at Vicksburg, and at the village of Appomattox Court House, on April 9, 1865, it was he who received the surrender from General Lee.

33. Words to Stir a Nation

THE REPUBLIC FROM "THE BUILDING OF THE SHIP"

Thou, too, sail on, O Ship of State!
Sail on, O Union, strong and great!
Humanity with all its fears,
With all the hopes of future years,
Is hanging breathless on thy fate!
We know what Master laid thy keel,
What Workmen wrought thy ribs of steel,
Who made each mast, and sail, and rope,
What anvils rang, what hammers beat,
In what a forge and what a heat
Were shaped the anchors of thy hope!
Fear not each sudden sound and shock,

'Tis of the wave and not the rock;
'Tis but the flapping of the sail,
And not a rent made by the gale!
In spite of rock and tempest's roar,
In spite of false lights on the shore,
Sail on, nor fear to breast the sea!
Our hearts, our hopes, are all with thee,
Our hearts, our hopes, our prayers, our tears,
Our faith triumphant o'er our fears,
Are all with thee,—are all with thee!

HENRY WADSWORTH LONGFELLOW

Henry Ward Beecher: The National Flag
(From an Address Given May 1861)

From the earliest periods nations seem to have gone forth to war under some banner. Sometimes it has been merely the pennon of a leader, and was only a rallying signal. So, doubtless, began the habit of carrying banners, to direct men in the confusion of conflict, that the leader might gather his followers around him when he himself was liable to be lost out of their sight.

Later in the history of nations the banner acquired other uses and peculiar significance from the parties, the orders, the houses, or governments, that adopted it. At length, as consolidated governments drank up into themselves all these lesser independent authorities, banners became significant chiefly of national authority. And thus in our day every people has its peculiar flag. There is no civilized nation without its banner.

A thoughtful mind, when it sees a nation's flag, sees not the flag, but the nation itself. And whatever may be its symbols, its insignia, he reads chiefly in the flag the government, the principles, the truths, the history, that belong to the nation that sets it forth. When the French tricolor rolls out to the wind, we see France. When the new-found Italian flag is unfurled, we see resurrected Italy. When the other three-colored Hungarian flag shall be lifted to the wind, we shall see in it the long buried, but never dead, principles of Hungarian liberty. When the united crosses of St. Andrew and St. George, on a fiery ground, set forth the banner of Old England, we see not the cloth merely; there rises up before the mind the idea of that great monarchy.

This nation has a banner, too, and . . . wherever it [has] streamed abroad men saw day break bursting on their eyes. For . . . the American flag has been a symbol of Liberty, and men rejoiced in it. Not another flag on the globe had such an errand, or went forth upon the sea carrying everywhere, the world around, such hope to the captive, and such glorious tidings. The stars upon it

Henry Wadsworth Longfellow has been called "democracy's favorite poet." In 1849 he wrote "The Seaside and the Fireside," including the peroration "The Building of the Ship," an ode describing the construction and launching of a great sailing ship. It concludes with a hymn of praise to the federal Union, which begins, "Thou, too, sail on, O Ship of State!" Few lines had greater effect in creating devotion to the Union.

were to the pining nations like the bright morning stars of God, and the stripes upon it were beams of morning light. As at early dawn the stars shine forth even while it grows light, and then as the sun advances that light breaks into banks and streaming lines of color, the glowing red and intense white striving together, and ribbing the horizon with bars effulgent, so, on the American flag, stars and beams of many-colored light shine out together. And wherever this flag comes, and men behold it, they see in its sacred emblazonry no ramping lion, and no fierce eagle; no embattled castles, or insignia of imperial authority; they see the symbols of light. It is the banner of dawn. It means Liberty; and the galley-slave, the poor oppressed conscript, the trodden-down creature of foreign despotism, sees in the American flag that very promise and prediction of God,—"The people which sat in darkness saw a great light; and to them which sat in the region and shadow of death light is sprung up."

Is there a mere fancy? On the 4th of July, 1776, the Declaration of American Independence was confirmed and promulgated. Already for more than a year the colonies had been at war with the mother country. But until this time there had been no American flag. The flag of the mother country covered us during all our colonial period; and each state that chose had a separate and significant state banner.

In 1777, within a few days of one year after the Declaration of Independence, and two years and more after the war began, upon the 14th of June, the Congress of the colonies, or the confederated states, assembled, and ordained this glorious national flag which now we hold and defend, and advanced it full high before God and all men as the flag of Liberty. It was no holiday flag, gorgeously emblazoned for gaiety or vanity. It was a solemn national signal. When that banner first unrolled to the sun, it was the symbol of all those holy truths and purposes which brought together the colonial American Congress.

Consider the men who devised and set forth this banner. The Rutledges, the Pickneys, the Jays, the Franklins, the Hamiltons, the Jeffersons, the Adamses,—these men were all either officially connected with it or consulted concerning it. They were men that had taken their lives in their hands, and consecrated all their worldly possessions—for what? For the doctrines, and for the personal fact, of liberty,—for the right of all men to liberty. They had just given forth to the world a Declaration of Facts and Faiths out of which sprung the Constitution, and on which they now planted this new-devised flag of our Union.

If one, then, asks me the meaning of our flag, I say to him, It means just what Concord and Lexington meant, what Bunker Hill meant; it means the whole glorious Revolutionary War, which was, in short, the rising up of a valiant young people against an old tyranny, to establish the most momentous doctrine that the world had ever known, or has since known,—the right of men to their own selves and to their liberties.

In solemn conclave our fathers had issued to the world that glorious manifesto, the Declaration of Independence. A little later, that the fundamental principles of liberty might have the best organization, they gave to this land our imperishable Constitution. Our flag means, then, all that our fathers meant in the Revolutionary War; all that the Declaration of Independence meant; it means all that the Constitution of our people, organizing for justice, for liberty, and for happiness, meant. Our flag carries American ideas, American history and American feelings. Beginning with the colonies, and coming down to our time, in its sacred heraldry, in its glorious insignia, it has gathered and stored chiefly this supreme idea: Divine right of liberty in man. Every color means liberty; every thread means liberty; every form of star and beam or stripe of light means liberty; not lawlessness, not license; but organized, institutional liberty,—liberty through law, and laws for liberty!

This American flag was the safeguard of liberty. Not an atom of crown was allowed to go into its insigna. Not a symbol of authority in the ruler was permitted to go into it. It was an ordinance of liberty by the people for the people. That it meant, that it means, and, by the blessings of God, that it shall mean to the end of time!

A Beecher family group *(left to right):* Harriet Beecher Stowe Stowe, her father, Lyman Beecher, Presbyterian minister, and her brother Henry Ward Beecher, noted Congregational minister and lecturer—dominant figures in the thinking of their period.

34. Songs of War

Never before the Civil War were the sounds of battle, the thunder of artillery, and the rattle of rifle fire as close to the average citizen, or on so wide a scale. Never had so great a force of citizen-soldiers been assembled. As never before, the Civil War immersed an entire country in conflict.

At stake was the nation itself, and the conflict bared every citizen's love of the land, whether it was for the Union or for the Confederacy. It was a war that reached into every village crossroads of the country. And with the efforts of artists, writers, and musicians, the sentiments of war, on both sides, were being expressed in a literal barrage. Patriotic expression had become a weapon.

Folk songs, religious songs, and parlor songs were adapted with fresh words for immediate wartime use. Thus, ''John Brown's Body'' emerged as the ''Battle Hymn of the Republic'' and ''We'll All Take a Ride'' became ''The Union Wagon.'' Some songs found favor on both the Northern and Southern sides. ''Tenting on the Old Camp Ground'' and ''Just Before the Battle, Mother'' were among these. The South had a choice of tunes, which included ''Dixie,'' ''Goober Peas,'' ''The Bonnie Blue Flag,'' and ''The Rebel Soldier,'' while the Union forces sang ''We're Coming Father Abraham'' and ''Tramp, Tramp, Tramp, the Boys are Marching.''

A picture of **a sharpshooter of the Army of the Potomac** perched in a pine tree is one of the memorable impressions of the great wartime artist Winslow Homer. The intensity of the lone figure epitomized the struggle of the armies that had gathered to settle the issue on a dozen battlefields. In 1861 Homer was sent to the battlefields as a correspondent for *Harper's Weekly* where he produced some of the most durable scenic reporting of the war.

Battle Hymn of the Republic

In times of war popular songs often emerge through which a nation expresses its hopes and its goals. If, during the Civil War, the people of the North needed a new expression of spirit, they found it in an old song set to new words. The song "Glory, Hallelujah" had been copyrighted in 1858 under the title "Say, Brothers, Will You Meet Us?" It was a Methodist hymn with a solid singable tune. As early as 1861, it became a jocular Union marching song under the title "John Brown." The John Brown of the song was, interestingly, a Massachusetts recruiting sergeant, not related to the Abolitionist martyr.

On a visit to Washington in 1861, Julia Ward Howe heard the troops singing the tune under the "John Brown" title. A clergyman, James Freeman Clark, asked Mrs. Howe if she could save the hymn from ribaldry by giving it a new verse. That night, at Willard's Hotel, she began to compose the poem, and she finished it on November 19. Mrs. Howe's inspiring words first appeared in print in the *New York Daily Tribune* in January 1862 and were later published in the *Atlantic Monthly.*

Julia Ward Howe, poet, Abolitionist, and reformer (1819–1910) was a leader of women's suffrage and peace movements and the first woman to be invited into the American Academy of Arts and Letters.

Originally written as a poem in 1861 by Baltimorean James Ryder Randall. It attacked the North: "The despot's heel is on thy shore."

Subtitled "The Prisoner's Hope," it consoled the captured soldiers with the thought that "beneath the starry flag we shall breathe the air again."

It was adapted to the popular melody "Glory Hallelujah."

The Battle Cry of Freedom

George Frederick Root, a Chicago composer, wrote many of the popular songs that lifted American spirits during the Civil War.

Shortly after the end of the Civil War, a Confederate officer, socializing with Union brass while the band played, is reported to have said: "Gentlemen, if we had your songs, we would have licked you out of your boots."

For all the rebel yells, the North had the clear advantage in stirring, singable music. Much of this was the work of composer George Frederick Root (1820–95), a teacher who wrote gospel songs and sentimental ballads and then, when war broke out, turned his attention to martial tunes. Right at the start, there was something called "Fort Sumter Quick Step." Then came "Tramp, Tramp, Tramp" and "Just Before the Battle, Mother," both of which swept the North.

Root's major triumph was his "Battle Cry of Freedom," written about 1861, when Lincoln issued his second call for troops. It was first sung at a rally directly from manuscript copy. It caught on instantly and was soon being heard around the country. By order of William Starke Rosecrans, commanding general of the Army of the Cumberland, the soldiers sang "Battle Cry" when going into action.

35. "Slavery Must Die That the Nation Might Live"

Though such a document had been under discussion at the White House, it was not until September 1862, after the Battle of Antietam, with the victory in hand, that President Lincoln issued his "Emancipation Proclamation." The Union had needed a victory to make those words meaningful.

At Antietam, after terrible casualties on both sides, the Southern forces, exhausted, had been denied an advance into the Northern heartland and had retreated into Virginia. A week later, with adroit timing, Lincoln issued his proclamation, based on his constitutional powers as commander in chief.

By the declaration, which was to take effect as of January 1, 1863, all slaves in the rebellious states were declared free. Those in loyal or conquered states were to be set free by other legislation.

The proclamation was, in effect, a reaffirmation of Lincoln's policies, later to be reinforced by the Thirteenth Amendment. The announcement, warmly received abroad, was credited with bringing liberal world opinion to Lincoln's side, and helped stave off British recognition of the Confederacy, which was being contemplated in Parliament. President Lincoln had succeeded in transforming the conflict from a civil war into a crusade.

"Emancipation Proclamation"
By the President of the United States of America:
A Proclamation (January 1, 1863)

Whereas, on the twenty-second day of September, in the year of our Lord one thousand eight hundred and sixty-two, a proclamation was issued by the President of the United States, containing, among other things, the following, to wit:

"That on the first day of January, in the year of our Lord one thousand eight hundred and sixty-three, all persons held as slaves within any State, or designated part of a State, the people whereof shall then be in rebellion against the United States, shall be then, thenceforward, and forever free; and the Executive Government of the United States, including the military and naval authority thereof, will recognize and maintain the freedom of such persons, and will do no act or acts to repress such persons, or any of them, in any efforts they may make for their actual freedom.

"That the Executive will, on the first day of January aforesaid, by proclamation, designate the States and part of States, if any, in which the people thereof respectively shall then be in rebellion against the United States; and the fact that any State, or the people thereof, shall on that day be in good faith represented in the Congress of the United States by members chosen thereto at elections wherein a majority of the qualified voters of such State shall have participated, shall in the absence of strong countervailing testimony be deemed conclusive evidence that such State and the people thereof are not then in rebellion against the United States."

Now, therefore, I, Abraham Lincoln, President of the United States, by virtue of the power in me vested as commander in chief of the army and navy of the United States, in time of actual armed rebellion against the authority and government of the United States, and as a fit and necessary war measure for suppressing said rebellion, do, on this first day of January, in the year of our Lord one thousand eight hundred and sixty-three, and in accordance with my

This unusual calligraphic version of **the Emancipation Proclamation** was the work of artist William Burford. Such presentations of the historic document were mass-produced at the time and framed for display in the home.

purpose so to do, publicly proclaimed for the full period of 100 days from the day first above mentioned, order and designate as the States and parts of States wherein the people thereof, respectively, are this day in rebellion against the United States, the following, to wit:

Arkansas, Texas, Louisiana (except the parishes of St. Bernard, Plaquemines, Jefferson, St. John, St. Charles, St. James, Ascension, Assumption, Terre Bonne, Lafourche, St. Mary, St. Martin, and Orleans, including the city of New Orleans), Mississippi, Alabama, Florida, Georgia, South Carolina, North Carolina, and Virginia (except the forty-eight counties designated as West Virginia, and also the counties of Berkeley, Accomac, Northampton, Elizabeth City, York, Princess Ann, and Norfolk, including the cities of Norfolk and Portsmouth), and which excepted parts are for the present left precisely as if this proclamation were not issued.

And by virtue of the power and for the purpose aforesaid, I do order and declare that all persons held as slaves within said designated States and parts of States are, and henceforward shall be, free; and that the Executive Government of the United States, including the military and naval authorities thereof, will recognize and maintain the freedom of said persons.

And I hereby enjoin upon the people so declared to be free to abstain from all violence, unless in necessary self-defense; and I recommend to them that, in all cases when allowed, they labor faithfully for reasonable wages.

And I further declare and make known that such persons of suitable condition will be received into the armed service of the United States to garrison forts, positions, stations, and other places, and to man vessels of all sorts in said service.

And upon this act, sincerely believed to be an act of justice, warranted by the Constitution upon military necessity, I invoke the considerate judgment of mankind and the gracious favor of Almighty God.

In witness whereof, I have hereunto set my hand, and caused the seal of the United States to be affixed.

Done at the city of Washington, this first day of January, in the year of our Lord one thousand eight hundred and sixty-three, and of the independence of the United States of America the eighty-seventh.

President Lincoln reading the first draft of the Emancipation Proclamation to his Cabinet, July 22, 1862. *From left to right:* Edwin M. Stanton, secretary of war; Salmon P. Chase, secretary of the treasury; the President; Gideon Welles, secretary of the navy; Caleb B. Smith, secretary of the interior; William H. Seward, secretary of state (*seated*); Montgomery Blair, postmaster general; Edward Bates, attorney general. The painting by Francis Bicknell was executed in 1864 from photographs of the individuals present. It was widely reproduced.

36. Gettysburg: A Fusion in Blood

The internecine bloodletting came to a peak in the early days of July 1863 near the lazy Pennsylvania country town of Gettysburg. Here, quite by chance, was fought the greatest battle of the Civil War. Neither command wanted a confrontation at that point.

General Lee, brilliant and tenacious, had decided on a bold move. He wanted to march into Pennsylvania and cut Union communications at Harrisburg, separating East from West. He also needed supplies, chiefly boots and shoes, for his operating force of 76,000 men. He might find those supplies for his advance force and his 190,000 backup troops in Gettysburg and Harrisburg.

General George Meade, new commander for the North, had a good eye for tactics and terrain. And there were many civilians who were suddenly aware of the crisis. They were ready for action.

Intermittent action marked the first two days of July. The Union had set up defenses on a ridge near the town. Meade was determined to hold his heaviest guns, 172 of them, at a position directed on the center, facing open country.

Then, on July 3, Lee decided to order an attack on the center. Under Major General George E. Pickett, 15,000 Confederates moved across the open field. The Union guns poured out a deadly fire, but the Gray attacks reached the first Union line and the Confederate flag was hoisted on the ridge. Union forces moved in to swallow the attackers, and for twenty minutes the outcome hung in the balance. Southern losses were tremendous as Union defenders closed ranks. A retreat was ordered for Pickett's troops. The Civil War had crested. The next day Lee retreated and Meade did not follow. Word followed that Vicksburg had fallen to General Ulysses S. Grant.

On July 3, 1863, in the midst of a terrific artillery exchange, came a **climactic charge by the Southern troops led by Major General George E. Pickett** against the Union troops defending Cemetery Ridge. Barely reaching their objective, the Gray attackers were finally turned back by devastating fire.

37. A New Birth of Freedom

On the morning of November 19, 1863, a little more than four months after the terrible battle at Gettysburg, a military cemetery was to be dedicated on the battleground site. President Lincoln himself was scheduled to appear, though not as the featured speaker.

Edward Everett, former president of Harvard University and a noted public speaker, was chosen to deliver the principal speech for the occasion. Everett made a lengthy address. Lincoln had seen a copy of this speech about eleven days earlier and remarked to a reporter at that time that he was thinking of saying something "short, short, short."

Lincoln rose after the applause for Everett had ended and spoke for less than five minutes—just ten sentences. Though he himself thought it was a "flat failure," his speech was to become one of the key expressions of American democracy. Everett expressed what generations have felt since that November day: "I should be glad if I could flatter myself that I came as near the central idea of the occasion in two hours as you did in two minutes."

Of all of Lincoln's speeches and writings, more than a million words, the fewer than three hundred words of the Gettysburg Address have the ageless echo. They comprise one of our most eloquent expressions of patriotism.

President Lincoln delivering his immortal address dedicating the Gettysburg National Cemetery on November 19, 1863.

Abraham Lincoln: The Gettysburg Address
(November 19, 1863)

Fourscore and seven years ago our fathers brought forth, on this continent, a new nation, conceived in Liberty, and dedicated to the proposition that all men are created equal.

Now we are engaged in a great civil war, testing whether that nation, or any nation so conceived, and so dedicated, can long endure. We are met on a great battlefield of that war. We have come to dedicate a portion of that field, as a final resting-place for those who have given their lives, that that nation might live. It is altogether fitting and proper that we should do this.

But, in a larger sense, we can not dedicate—we can not consecrate—we can not hallow—this ground. The brave men, living and dead, who struggled here, have consecrated it far above our poor power to add or detract. The world will little note, nor long remember what we say here, but it can never forget what they did here. It is for us the living, rather, to be dedicated here to the unfinished work which they who fought here have thus far so nobly advanced. It is rather for us to be here dedicated to the great task remaining before us— that from these honored dead we take increased devotion to that cause for which they here gave the last full measure of devotion—that we here highly resolve that these dead shall not have died in vain—that this nation, under God, shall have a new birth of freedom—and that government of the people, by the people, for the people, shall not perish from the earth.

Abraham Lincoln: Letter to Mrs. Bixby
(November 21, 1864)

Mrs. Bixby, Boston, Massachusetts.

Dear Madam: I have been shown in the files of the War Department a statement of the Adjutant-General of Massachusetts that you are the mother of five sons who have died gloriously on the field of battle. I feel how weak and fruitless must be any words of mine which should attempt to beguile you from the grief of a loss so overwhelming. But I cannot refrain from tendering to you the consolation that may be found in the thanks of the Republic they died to save. I pray that our heavenly Father may assuage the anguish of your bereavement, and leave you only the cherished memory of the loved and lost, and the solemn pride that must be yours to have laid so costly a sacrifice upon the altar of freedom.

Yours very sincerely and respectfully,
Abraham Lincoln

Lincoln's "Letter to Mrs. Bixby" reflects his unique ability to pin down the emotions of the moment. It stands as a monument in American literature. At the request of the Governor of Massachusetts, the President wrote a note of condolence to a Boston mother who had lost five sons in combat. Through Mrs. Bixby, Lincoln reached all those who in the years of bitter struggle had lost loved ones. The letter was delivered to Mrs. Bixby on November 25, 1864. Later research revealed that she had not lost that many offspring, but the message remains, nonetheless, a valued expression of love of country.

THE BLUE AND THE GRAY (1867)

Perhaps the rows of crosses that marked the battle sites, and the casualty figures that finally translated into family loss, cooled sectional feelings. It was hardly more than two years after the final battles that the Civil War became a tortured national memory and the animosity began to fade. In those locations where the graves of Northern soldiers touched upon the graves of Southern troops, the mourners came to decorate each marker without regard to the side represented. In this spirit Francis Miles Finch, a prominent lawyer, judge, and poet, as well as professor of law at Cornell's College of Law, wrote his memorable tribute, "The Blue and the Gray," which was published posthumously in 1867.

By the flow of the inland river,
Whence the fleets of iron have fled,
Where the blades of the grave-grass quiver,
Asleep are the ranks of the dead:
Under the sod and the dew,
Waiting the judgment-day;
Under the one, the Blue,
Under the other, the Gray.

These in the robings of glory,
Those in the gloom of defeat,
All with the battle-blood gory,
In the dusk of eternity meet:
Under the sod and the dew,
Waiting the judgment-day;
Under the laurel, the Blue,
Under the willow, the Gray.

From the silence of sorrowful hours
The desolate mourners go,
Lovingly laden with flowers
Alike for the friend and the foe:
Under the sod and the dew,
Waiting the judgment-day;
Under the roses, the Blue,
Under the lilies, the Gray.

So with an equal splendor,
The morning sun-rays fall,
With a touch impartially tender,
On the blossoms blooming for all:
Under the sod and the dew,
Waiting the judgment-day;
Broidered with gold, the Blue,
Mellowed with gold, the Gray.

So, when the summer calleth,
On forest and field of grain,
With an equal murmur falleth
The cooling drip of the rain:
Under the sod and the dew,
Waiting the judgment-day;
Wet with the rain, the Blue,
Wet with the rain, the Gray.

Sadly, but not with upbraiding,
The generous deed was done,
In the storm of the years that are fading
No braver battle was won:
Under the sod and the dew,
Waiting the judgment-day;
Under the blossoms, the Blue,
Under the garlands, the Gray.

No more shall the war cry sever,
Or the winding rivers be red;
They banish our anger forever
When they laurel the graves of our dead!
Under the sod and the dew,
Waiting the judgment-day;
Love and tears for the Blue,
Tears and love for the Gray.

FRANCIS MILES FINCH

38. With Malice Toward None

March 4, 1865, was a dismal, windy day in Washington. The new dome on the Capitol building stood out against the surrounding gloom. At times the sun appeared ready to break through the overcast. A faithful crowd had gathered at the East Portico to witness the ceremony as Abraham Lincoln took the presidential oath for the second time. He had won 2, 216,067 popular votes against his opponent, General George B. McClellan, who had 1,808,725.

The previous four years, Lincoln's first term, had marked the nation's bloodiest ordeal. More than 214,000 lives had been sacrificed. Though the struggle had been bitter, the end was now in sight. The Confederacy was trying to ward off the final blows by Union forces under Grant and Sherman, but Confederate desertions were high and food shortages gripped the cities of the South. In February, peace commissioners from both sides had met, and the South, despite its desperate situation, was still pressing for independence. Lincoln stuck to his demand that the Union be restored. Still, there was no trace of hatred in Lincoln's measured words. Even now, what he sought was reconciliation.

Abraham Lincoln taking the presidential oath for the second time on March 4, 1865. This sketch is from a photograph by Alexander Gardner.

President Lincoln: Second Inaugural Address
(March 4, 1865)

Fellow-countrymen:

At this second appearing to take the oath of the presidential office, there is less occasion for an extended address than there was at the first. Then a statement, somewhat in detail, of a course to be pursued, seemed fitting and proper. Now, at the expiration of four years, during which public declarations have been constantly called forth on every point and phase of the great contest which still absorbs the attention and engrosses the energies of the nation, little that is new could be presented. The progress of our arms, upon which all else chiefly depends, is as well known to the public as to myself; and it is, I trust, reasonably satisfactory and encouraging to all. With high hope for the future, no prediction in regard to it is ventured.

On the occasion corresponding to this four years ago, all thoughts were anxiously directed to an impending civil war. All dreaded it—all sought to avert it. While the inaugural address was being delivered from this place, devoted altogether to saving the Union without war, insurgent agents were in the city seeking to destroy it without war—seeking to dissolve the Union, and divide effects, by negotiation. Both parties deprecated war; but one of them would make war rather than let the nation survive; and the other would accept war rather than let it perish. And the war came.

One-eighth of the whole population were colored slaves, not distributed generally over the Union, but localized in the Southern part of it. These slaves constituted a peculiar and powerful interest. All knew that this interest was, somehow, the cause of the war. To strengthen, perpetuate, and extend this interest was the object for which the insurgents would rend the Union, even by war; while the government claimed no right to do more than to restrict the territorial enlargement of it.

Neither party expected for the war the magnitude or the duration which it has already attained. Neither anticipated that the cause of the conflict might cease with, or even before, the conflict itself should cease. Each looked for an easier triumph, and a result less fundamental and astounding. Both read the same Bible, and pray to the same God; and each invokes His aid against the other. It may seem strange that any men should dare to ask a just God's assistance in wringing their bread from the sweat of other men's faces; but let us judge not, that we be not judged. The prayers of both could not be answered—that of neither has been answered fully.

The Almighty has His own purposes. "Woe unto the world because of offences! for it must needs be that offences come; but woe to that man by whom the offence cometh." If we shall suppose that American slavery is one of those offences which, in the providence of God, must needs come, but which, having continued through His appointed time, He now wills to remove, and that he gives to both North and South this terrible war, as the woe due to those by whom the offence came, shall we discern therein any departure from those divine attributes which the believers in a living God always ascribe to Him? Fondly do we hope—fervently do we pray—that this mighty scourge of war may speedily pass away. Yet, if God wills that it continue until all the wealth piled by the bondmen's two hundred and fifty years of unrequited toil shall be sunk, and until every drop of blood drawn with the lash shall be paid by another drawn with the sword, as was said three thousand years ago, so still it must be said, "The judgments of the Lord are true and righteous altogether."

With malice toward none; with charity for all; with firmness in the right, as God gives us to see the right, let us strive on to finish the work we are in; to bind up the nation's wounds; to care for him who shall have borne the battle, and for his widow, and his orphan—to do all which may achieve and cherish a just and lasting peace among ourselves, and with all nations.

39. Surrender at Appomattox

It was an afternoon of peace, Palm Sunday, April 9, 1865. Two generals, their long and bloody struggle over, were meeting in the living room of the Wilmer MacLean farmhouse in the tiny Virginia village called Appomattox Court House.

Union General Ulysses S. Grant, forty-three years old, wore his usual nondescript field uniform, only the shoulder straps indicating his high rank. Fifty-five-year-old Confederate General Robert E. Lee, at top command for only about two months, was attired in a new full-dress uniform, complete with sash and a jeweled sword. Grant was attended by his staff and his principal officers; Lee only by his military secretary, Colonel Charles Marshall.

At first there was casual talk about those years at West Point, about life in the army, about experiences in Mexico. Then the conference got down to business, and General Grant began to write the surrender terms in his own hand. Officers could retain their sidearms . . . their luggage . . . their mounts. They must agree that they would no longer try to fight. An allotment of Union Army rations would be turned over to the Confederates.

Lee surrendering to Grant. On April 9, 1865, General Robert E. Lee of the Confederacy surrendered to General Ulysses S. Grant of the Union at Appomattox Court House in Virginia. This painting was done by Louis M. D. Guillaume.

General Lee needed his spectacles to read Grant's words. His eyes relaxed when he finished. The terms were generous. There was dignity in the surrender. It was to be an honorable peace, an appearance, at least, of reconciliation rather than victory.

When the conference was ended, General Lee strode to the front door and hesitated as he gazed out over the Union troops drawn up at attention. Three times he struck his fist into his gauntleted hand. Then he quickly walked to his horse. A spontaneous cheer spread out over the Union forces. It reached the ears of Grant, who ordered that it be halted immediately. There was to be no celebration. "The war is over," said the general, "the rebels are our countrymen again."

General Lee in his full dress Confederate uniform, a photograph said to have been taken for Queen Victoria.

General R. E. Lee's Farewell to His Army at Headquarters, Army of Northern Virginia (April 10, 1865)

After four years of arduous service, marked by unsurpassed courage and fortitude, the Army of Northern Virginia has been compelled to yield to overwhelming numbers and resources. I need not tell the survivors of so many hard-fought battles, who have remained steadfast to the last, that I have consented to this result from no distrust of them; but, feeling that valor and devotion could accomplish nothing that could compensate for the loss that would have attended the continuation of the contest, I have determined to avoid the useless sacrifice of those whose past services have endeared them to their countrymen. By the terms of the agreement, officers and men can return to their homes and remain there until exchanged. You will take with you the satisfaction that proceeds from the consciousness of duty faithfully performed; and I earnestly pray that a merciful God will extend to you His blessing and protection. With an increasing admiration of your constancy and devotion to your country, and a grateful remembrance of your kind and generous consideration of myself, I bid you an affectionate farewell.

Robert E. Lee (1807–70) did not approve of secession and regarded the Civil War as a tragedy. But when called on for leadership, he served gallantly, an inspiration to his men, who were absolutely devoted to him.

Lee's father died when Robert was only eleven, and his devoted mother had a deep influence on the boy. He was generally regarded as courteous and kindhearted, and as a person who preferred to keep his own counsel. At eighteen Lee became a cadet at West Point, but he was not a traditional "man's man"; he did not smoke or drink. He did love horses, however, especially his mount Traveller.

During the Civil War Lee proved himself an inspiring leader equal to any assignment. What he lacked in supplies and manpower he made up in swiftness and surprise.

After Appomattox, General Lee applied for official amnesty. It was never granted. Later he became president of Washington College, which eventually would become Washington and Lee University, and for the rest of his life he urged the South to help in restoring a united country. Historians now seem to emphasize that it was Lee's abilities that kept the South alive during those bitter war years. He has truly achieved the status of American hero.

40. To Live and Die for Dixie

The Confederate States of America was born in the caldron of war. South Carolina was the first state to break the Union bond, seceding on December 20, 1860, and by February 8, 1861, about a month before Abraham Lincoln was inaugurated, the Confederate States of America already had a provisional constitution. On March 4, 1861, the very day Lincoln took the oath of office, the Confederacy unfurled its own flag, the Stars and Bars, making itself a nation within a nation.

The Confederacy was a reality. Whenever it gained a new member the alliance was greeted with joy and celebration. In the eyes of Southern patriots it was just and holy, with the same right to live as any nation. In the four grim years of its existence, it put massive armies in the field, found capable commanders, supplied its soldiers as best it could, tried to establish itself in the family of nations. It sought and gained the loyalty and hope of its citizens as a new federal government that found its way into every facet of life.

Ultimately about 258,000 Johnny Rebs died for their country, 133,821 right on the battlefield. They were as committed to their cause as any Billy Yank from Ohio, Massachusetts, or Indiana. They gave the last full measure of devotion.

Jefferson Davis: Last Message to the People of the Confederacy (April 4, 1865)

To the People of the Confederate States of America:

The General in Chief of our Army has found it necessary to make such movements of the troops as to uncover the capital and thus involve the withdrawal of the Government from the city of Richmond.

It would be unwise, even were it possible, to conceal the great moral as well as material injury to our cause that must result from the occupation of Richmond by the enemy. It is equally unwise and unworthy of us, as patriots engaged in a most sacred cause, to allow our energies to falter, our spirits to grow faint, or our efforts to become relaxed under reverses, however, calamitous. . . . For many months the largest and finest army of the Confederacy, under the command of a leader whose presence inspires equal confidence in the troops and the people, has been greatly trammeled by the necessity of keeping constant watch over the approaches to the capital, and has thus been forced to forego more than one opportunity for promising enterprise. The hopes and confidence of the enemy have been constantly excited by the belief that their possession of Richmond would be the signal for our submission to their rule, and relieve them from the burden of war, as their failing resources admonish them it must be abandoned if not speedily brought to a successful close. It is for us, my countrymen, to show by our bearing under reverses how wretched has been the self-deception of those who have believed us less able to endure misfortune with fortitude than to encounter danger with courage. We have now entered upon a new phase of a struggle the memory of which is to endure for all ages and to shed an increasing luster upon our country. . . .

Animated by the confidence in your spirit and fortitude, which never yet has failed me, I announce to you, fellow-countrymen, that it is my purpose to maintain your cause with my whole heart and soul; that I will never consent to abandon to the enemy one foot of the soil of any one of the States of the Confederacy. . . . If by stress of numbers we should ever be compelled to a temporary withdrawal from her limits, or those of any other border State, again and again we will return, until the baffled and exhausted enemy shall abandon in despair his endless and impossible task of making slaves of a people resolved to be free.

Let us not, then, despond, my countrymen; but relying on the never-failing mercies and protecting care of our God, let us meet the foe with fresh defiance, with unconquered and unconquerable hearts.

Jefferson Davis

Although history and hindsight have raised questions about Jefferson Davis's sense of strategy, there has been little doubt about his fitness for office. He had come to politics as a successful Mississippi planter and he had developed into a strong voice for the South before the Civil War. When he was sworn in as President of the Confederate States of America, Davis also assumed responsibility as commander in chief of the Confederate forces. He considered himself a man of the people and was respected for his undeniable devotion to the Southern cause. A conservative in military affairs, he had a real talent for selecting able men to command his forces, and he backed them in the face of pressure.

Toward the close of the war Jefferson Davis was hoping for some miracle that would save the South. He slipped out of Richmond at the last moment but was captured on May 10, 1865, and charged with treason and involvement in the Lincoln assassination. Davis was never brought to trial. He died in 1889 at the age of eighty-one.

Dixie

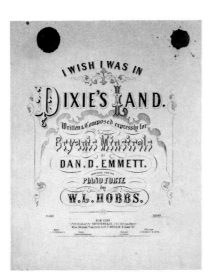

"Dixie" was composed by a Northerner, Daniel Decatur Emmett, who wrote songs for minstrel shows, but it became the national anthem of the Confederacy. Originally called "Dixie's Land," it was first performed by Bryant's Minstrels at Mechanic's Hall in New York City, on April 4, 1859. It was announced as a "plantation song and dance."

Eventually, the term "Dixie" came to be synonymous with the territory below the Mason-Dixon line and was used by the Confederates as a term for the South. The song was played at Jefferson Davis's inauguration, and later the composer, a Union sympathizer, said, "If I had known to what use they were going to put my song, I'll be damned if I'd have written it."

On the day after Appomattox, when he was serenaded with band music outside the White House, President Lincoln took a long step in restoring "Dixie" as a national song. He said, "I had heard that our adversaries over the way had attempted to appropriate it. I insisted yesterday that we had fairly captured it. . . . I presented the question to the Attorney-General and he gave his opinion that it is our lawful prize. . . . I asked the band to give us a good turn upon it."

And the band played "Dixie."

Jefferson Davis. This mezzotint portrait by William Sartain (1843–1924) was done after a photograph by Mathew Brady.

41. A Leader Is Lost, but the Nation Survives

On Good Friday morning, April 14, 1865, only five days after Appomattox, the President met with his cabinet. "Blood cannot restore blood," he cautioned as he asked his closest aides to work for peace without revenge. After four years of bitter warfare, he was ready to lift the Union blockade of the South, and he did not want Washington to run the state governments in the former Confederacy. Let the South do that job.

That evening, Lincoln, with his wife and two friends, attended Ford's Theatre, where Laura Keene was appearing in the play *Our American Cousin.* At 10:13, a flamboyant actor, John Wilkes Booth, a Southern sympathizer and plotter, deranged by the turn of military events and seeking revenge, slipped into the presidential box and fired his pistol into Lincoln's head.

Booth leaped to the stage, paused in a gesture of defiance, shouted in Latin, *"Sic Semper Tyrannis"* (Thus always with tyrants), and rushed out through a rear door, where a horse was waiting. He was tracked down and eventually trapped and shot in a burning barn.

The President died the next morning, at 7:22. News of the assassination at the high tide of victory plunged the nation into bewildered grief, followed by angry cries for revenge and accusations that Southern leadership had been involved in Booth's mad act. President Lincoln had asked for charity for all and malice toward none. But the wounds were not easy to forget, especially that moment when tragedy took over at Ford's Theatre.

Lincoln's funeral train cortege wound its tragic and lonely way back to his home town, Springfield, Illinois. The country found what consolation it could in Secretary Stanton's words over a dead Lincoln: "Now he belongs to the ages."

Of the scores of monuments that grace Washington, D.C., none is dearer to Americans than the majestic Lincoln Memorial, set in 164 acres of the capital's Potomac Park. At the west end of the Mall, facing the Capitol, it stands in isolated splendor, a symbol of the man who acted so firmly and so successfully to preserve the Union. Since it was dedicated in 1922, with Robert Todd Lincoln, son of the President, in attendance, it has become the city's most revered shrine, open day and night, attracting more visitors than any other building in Washington.

Discussions began on a Lincoln memorial shortly after his death, with some planners favoring an obelisk to match the Washington monument. The building finally erected after nearly sixty years was designed by architect Henry Bacon. Its peristyle of thirty-six Doric columns represents the states in the Union at the close of the Civil War, and its forty-eight bas-relief festoons inside represent the states at the time of dedication. The inner walls are inscribed with texts from Lincoln's Gettysburg Speech and his Second Inaugural Address, and with murals by artist Jules Guerin.

The heroic statue of Lincoln, seated but strangely alert, is the crowning work of Daniel Chester French (1850–1931), a sculptor who left a legacy of hundreds of works around the nation, including the famous *Minute Man of Concord.* His heroic Lincoln, superbly adapted to the architecture that surrounds it, is gentle but firm, with a look that leaves a special and lasting imprint on each person who comes to pay homage. Around this great shrine the inscription reads: "In this temple, as in the hearts of the people for whom he saved the Union, the memory of Abraham Lincoln is enshrined forever."

Overleaf:
Lincoln Memorial,
Washington, D.C.

O CAPTAIN! MY CAPTAIN! (April 14, 1865)

O Captain! my Captain! our fearful trip is done,
The ship has weather'd every rack, the prize we sought is won,
The port is near, the bells I hear, the people all exulting,
While follow eyes the steady keel, the vessel grim and daring;
But O heart! heart! heart!
O the bleeding drops of red,
Where on the deck my Captain lies,
Fallen cold and dead.

O Captain! my Captain! rise up and hear the bells;
Rise up—for you the flag is flung—for you the bugle trills,
For you bouquets and ribbon'd wreaths—for you the shores a-crowding,
For you they call, the swaying mass, their eager faces turning;
Here Captain! dear father!
This arm beneath your head!
It is some dream that on the deck,
You've fallen cold and dead.

My Captain does not answer, his lips are pale and still,
My father does not feel my arm, he has no pulse nor will,
The ship is anchor'd safe and sound, its voyage closed and done,
From fearful trip the victor ship comes in with object won;
Exult O shores, and ring O bells!
But I with mournful tread,
Walk the deck my Captain lies,
Fallen cold and dead.

42. "I Will Bear True Faith to the United States"

"There's bread and work for all, and the sun always shines."

That was the American dream for millions of immigrants who came to America in the late nineteenth and early twentieth centuries. Some called it the "Land of the Ever-Young," others believed the streets were paved with gold. They came to this promised land with great hope and fervor. They seemed to absorb the land itself, even as America absorbed them.

In the early 1800s, tales of this new, exciting nation reached the downtrodden of Europe, first filtering into the villages of Ireland and Germany, then to Scandinavia and the isolated settlements of Central Europe, Poland, and Russia, the scattered towns of the Austro-Hungarian Empire, and the Italian peninsula. The Continent was in revolt against centuries of misrule, against pogroms and military conscription. Recurring crop failures, economic injustices, and years of starvation also helped bring about vast shifts of population. The United States provided an attractive haven.

The immigration flood started as a trickle in 1820, when 8,385 new arrivals were counted. In the next ten years the number grew to 143,439. But even that was only the first hint of an enormous tide that was to reach 8,795,386 in the decade from 1901 to 1910. In a single day in 1907, a record 12,000 immigrants poured into the country. Between 1820 and 1979, the total came to an astounding 49,125,413 newcomers.

For many millions of these travelers the passage had been a nightmare. They came in steerage in the abysmal holds of slow-moving vessels, known as "coffin ships," where, by law, they were allotted space amounting to six feet by eighteen inches. They did their own cooking. The price of a ticket varied from twelve to thirty dollars, and one counted oneself lucky merely to have survived the miserable experience.

It was not until 1855 that the federal government took steps to control this massive tide of humanity. First there were literacy, then medical and mental tests, close questioning and proof of the immigrant's fiscal status (would someone vouch for him or her so that he or she would not become a state charge?), and finally a set of national quotas was imposed. These quotas were not lifted until 1965.

The earliest immigrants were channeled through a refitted Army facility on Manhattan called Castle Garden. In 1890 that facility was deemed inadequate and its operations were transferred to Ellis Island, where the millions out of steerage were tested to determine whether they were fit to land. Many with odd-sounding, hard-to-spell European names emerged to a new land, a new life, and often, courtesy of an immigration officer, a new name.

Once in this country they scattered to the city neighborhoods and the distant states—the Irish to Boston, Germans to Milwaukee, Swedes to Minnesota, Jews to New York—where they could be with others in their ethnic group, where they could find their own houses of worship and the foods they loved.

The America to which the immigrants had turned was expanding; their muscle and skills were needed. They became miners and railroad workers, tailors and peddlers, farmhands and lumberjacks. They opened their own little shops or found their way to the factories.

The melting pot was bubbling. In one Lawrence, Massachusetts, mill no fewer than forty-five languages were represented. If you worked in the competitive atmosphere of the needle trades in New York, you had to put in ninety hours of work for a fifteen-dollar paycheck, but at least you had a start. Within the "native" population there was resentment against the immigrants with their strange ways. They were believed to be responsible for the low wage levels, and this was especially true of the workers along the West Coast, who resented the Chinese immigrants. Finally, in fact, laws were passed that cut off Chinese immigration.

Despite those early struggles, most of the immigrants, for all the obstacles, found their way into the American mainstream. They learned English, managed to raise families; often they prospered. Their children attended schools where every day they pledged allegiance to the Stars and Stripes and sang with conviction of America as the land where "our fathers died." The first newcomers were content to remain in the isolated ethnic communities that had welcomed them, but their children, and their children's children, were quick to assimilate. It was all a part of the peopling of America.

For most immigrants there came, at last, that day of days when, having shown five years of residency, a good character, and an understanding of the English language and the fundamentals of American history and government, they swore this oath before a judge:

"I hereby declare on oath, that I absolutely and entirely renounce and abjure all allegiance and fidelity to any foreign prince, potentate, state or sovereignty, to whom or which I have heretofore been a subject or citizen; that I will support America against all enemies, foreign and domestic; that I will bear true faith and allegiance to the same; that I will bear arms on behalf of the United States when required by the law; that I will perform noncombatant service in the armed forces of the United States when required by the law; that I will perform work of national importance under civilian direction when required by the law; and that I take this obligation freely without any mental reservation or purpose of evasion; so help me God."

Chinese immigrants are instructed in the English language during their first weeks in this country.

ARRIVAL AT CASTLE GARDEN

REGISTER EMIGRANTS

PASSING THE INSPECTING PHYSICIAN

Irish immigrants, taking their first steps on American soil, move toward the admittance quarters at Castle Garden. The year is 1866, about ten years after the U.S. government passed the first laws covering immigration. The signs were generally in both English and German, reflecting the post-1848 wave of immigration.

At **Castle Garden in New York,** where immigrants were first received, newcomers gather at the registration desk.

Immigrants on their arrival at Castle Garden in New York pass through the line of inspecting physicians.

133

43. America Flexes Its Muscles

For more than four heady decades, from 1870 to 1914, America, robust and confident, found reasons to celebrate itself. There was a vibrant and contagious spirit in the nation, reborn after its bitter Civil War. It was reflected in the extravagant new World's Fairs, such as those in St. Louis, Philadelphia, and Chicago. It showed in the larger cities under the hands of imaginative architects, and the American skyscraper changed skylines around the nation. America's railroads reached out to all corners of the country, and new bridges spanned its rivers.

Great museums were founded. Artists devoted themselves to celebrating the life of the people, to recording scenes of the Far West, to dramatic American landscapes, and even, for the first time, to exciting moments in sports. Currier and Ives poured out the prints that found their way to millions of home walls, and such sculptors as Daniel Chester French and Augustus Saint-Gaudens

The National Chorus,
the cover of *Life* magazine for
July 4, 1912.

contributed to heroic sculpture. In music, orchestras were organized in New York, Chicago, Boston, and Philadelphia. Walt Whitman, Mark Twain, Henry Wadsworth Longfellow, John Greenleaf Whittier, and Oliver Wendell Holmes gave America its own style of literature. Theater fostered its own group of native actors and actresses. Popular education grew, especially higher education.

All of these developments were expressions of a special national pride and confidence. It was a period of unabashed optimism, of proud, confident Fourth of July speeches. It was a time of enthusiastic patriotism for a great, growing America.

I HEAR AMERICA SINGING

I hear America singing, the varied carols I hear,
Those of mechanics, each one singing his as it should be blithe and strong,
The carpenter singing his as he measures his plank or beam,
The mason singing his as he makes ready for work, or leaves off work,
The boatman singing what belongs to him in his boat, the deckhand
*   singing on the steamboat deck,*
The shoemaker singing as he sits on his bench, the hatter singing as he
*   stands,*
The wood-cutter's song, the ploughboy's on his way in the morning, or at
*   noon intermission or at sundown,*
The delicious singing of the mother, or of the young wife at work, or of the
*   girl sewing or washing,*
Each singing what belongs to him or her and to none else,
The day what belongs to the day—at night the party of young fellows,
*   robust, friendly,*
Singing with open mouths their strong melodious songs.

WALT WHITMAN

Walt Whitman

In midyear of 1855, shortly after *Leaves of Grass* appeared, no less a critic than Ralph Waldo Emerson was stirred enough to write: "I find it the most extraordinary piece of wit and wisdom that America has yet contributed." To the poet, Walt Whitman, he added: "I greet you at the beginning of a great career, which you must have had a long foreground somewhere, for such a start." Emerson was right. Whitman had been a printer, teacher, and journalist. Later he was to work as an editor and a volunteer hospital nurse.

As a poet, considered by many the greatest of all American poets, he sang of freedom, of individual dignity, of democracy and the brotherhood of man. His *Leaves of Grass* comprises some of the most influential poetry in the whole spectrum of American literature.

In later life the "good gray poet" was often short-tempered, but he managed to appear congenial and contemplative. He liked to move among working people and counted friends among railroad and farm workers and sailors. Whitman is regarded as the poet who most ardently wrote of American democracy and progress. His poem "I Hear America Singing," published in 1860, reflects the manner in which Whitman wrote of his country.

44. Stars and Stripes Forever

Certainly, among the resounding sounds of patriotism American-style, none were more stirring than the marches of John Philip Sousa (1854–1932). Across the nation, bands of every degree had a repertory of Sousa marches. "The Stars and Stripes Forever" rivaled "The Star-spangled Banner" as the favorite national song. And there were also "Semper Fidelis" and "El Capitan" not far behind.

The bands in the parades, the bands in the park shells, the bands at every high school and college game provided an unending stream of Sousa music. And the sound seemed appropriately American, expressing in vigorous tempo the national heartbeat, the national pride.

Sousa, composer and bandmaster, started as a classical composer of serious music, then conducted the U.S. Marine Corps band (of which his father had been a member) from 1880 to 1892. He organized his own band in 1892.

Sousa composed "Semper Fidelis" in 1888, "El Capitan" in 1896, and "The Stars and Stripes Forever" in 1897.

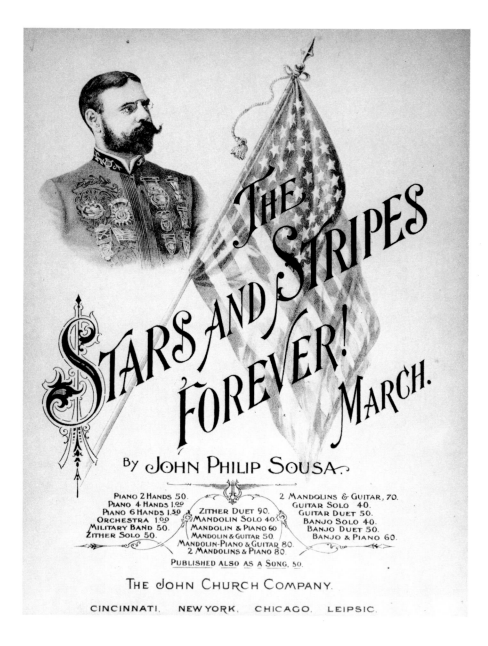

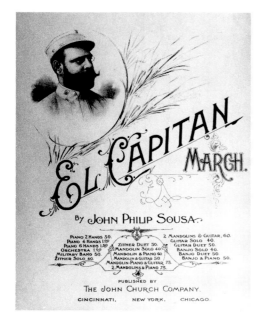

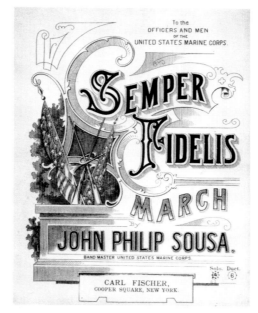

THE FLAG GOES BY

Hats off!
Along the street there comes
A blare of bugles, a ruffle of drums,
A flash of color beneath the sky:
Hats off!
The flag is passing by!

Blue and crimson and white it shines,
Over the steel-tipped, ordered lines.
Hats off!
The colors before us fly;
But more than the flag is passing by.

Sea-fights and land-fights, grim and great,
Fought to make and to save the State:
Weary marches and sinking ships;
Cheers of victory on dying lips;

Days of plenty and years of peace;
March of a strong land's swift increase;
Equal justice, right, and law,
Stately honor and reverend awe;

Sign of a nation, great and strong
Toward her people from foreign wrong:
Pride and glory and honor,—all
Live in the colours to stand or fall.

Hats off!
Along the street there comes
A blare of bugles, a ruffle of drums;
And loyal hearts are beating high:
Hats off!
The flag is passing by!

Henry Holcomb Bennett was born in Chillicothe, Ohio, in 1863. He devoted himself to ornithology, book illustration, and writing short stories mainly about Army life. His well-remembered and widely anthologized poem "The Flag Goes By" was published in 1904.

HENRY HOLCOMB BENNETT

America's largest flag, set against the New York skyline.

45. "Meet Me at the Fair..."

Modern "world's fairs" were an outgrowth of medieval trade fairs, where, at a caravan crossroads or resting place, merchants might display their wares from Asia, Africa, or the far-off Indies.

Beginning in the nineteenth century, such "expositions" began to take on a patriotic complexion, reflecting technological progress and celebrating national achievements.

For Americans, the massive displays, many heralding new inventions, provided a vision of better times ahead, a message of national momentum they could spread when they went back to their home towns.

The great expositions dramatized the America that could be and, indeed, would be. In glittering settings, its displays brought to life so much of the American dream, the lifestyle of the future: the inventions that would make living more comfortable, the innovations that would make human labor easier and more productive, the giant machines that would replace man's muscles—and the side attractions that made living a little less humdrum.

These were shows that touched the imagination, drawing thousands of families from distant farms, cities, and villages. A trip to the fair was an experience to be planned to the smallest detail and to be savored for years. You came home bursting with the excitement you had known, and you spoke of it to every relative and friend who would listen. And somewhere in some secret chest drawer you kept a personal memento of that happy time.

In 1804 the first U.S. agricultural fair was held in Washington, D.C. By 1810 there was a cattle show in Pittsfield, Massachusetts, which developed into the first permanent agricultural association.

The so-called international fairs, stressing cultural progress or technological innovation, with displays of industrial and artistic products, originated in London in 1851 with the Crystal Palace exhibit. New York followed suit in 1853, but the roof of its exhibition hall leaked, and the displays were reported too "foreign" for American tastes.

In 1876, on the occasion of the nation's hundredth birthday, a vast Centennial Exposition was held in Philadephia's Fairmount Park. On May 10, 1876, President Ulysses S. Grant opened the show by starting the massive Corliss steam engine that powered many of the exhibits. There were 299 structures on 285 acres. The summer was the hottest in sixty years, but, still, in a period of six months, 10 million visitors poured into the Exposition. The show was a massive success and set the trend in American expositions for the next century.

Benjamin Franklin's own manually operated printing press was on view at the exposition, as was a pair of George Washington's trousers. But the accent was on inventive genius and the world ahead. There was a new writing machine called a typewriter, and a new power lift called an elevator. There was a self-binding reaper, a railway air brake, a refrigerator car, and a printing press that printed on a continuous roll of paper. There was also Alexander Graham Bell's new "talking instrument," which astounded the emperor of Brazil.

Also on display was a great new patriotic painting by Archibald M. Willard called *The Spirit of '76*, and the torch hand of the new Statue of Liberty, then being built.

On July 4, 1876, General William Tecumseh Sherman reviewed the parade in front of Independence Hall; the ceremonies were interrupted by a women's rights demonstration led by Susan B. Anthony.

Opposite page:
The nation celebrates its one hundredth birthday with this midnight parade in front of Independence Hall in Philadelphia.

Splendid facades, statuary, and promenades were among the many attractive and memorable features of the gigantic **Chicago World's Fair,** an exposition that stressed the growth of the nation.

Eight years later New Orleans had the opportunity to show its hospitality with the World's Industrial and Cotton Centennial, featuring the world's largest greenhouse and emphasizing crop cultivation rather than industry.

To mark the four hundredth anniversary of the discovery of America by Columbus, Chicago staged its memorable Columbian Exposition in 1893. Despite the fact that the show was a year late, the display was a true spellbinder. Three of the greatest architects of the time—Louis Sullivan, Daniel Burnham, and Frederic Law Olmsted—combined their talents in this sprawling fantasy of canals, lagoons, and great structures, in what came to be known as "White City," a wonderland of city planning.

In addition to the vistas that promised great city planning for the future, there were displayed such marvels as the phonograph, the Linotype typesetting machine, and the Pullman car, as well as George Ferris's giant 250-foot wheel. There was a spread of artificial ice for midsummer skating, and a mile-long Midway where "Little Egypt" entranced the onlookers with a distinctive kind of dancing that came to be known as the "hootchy-kootchy." Buffalo Bill was there, the first zipper was there, and there was a big gun sent by the Germans that could fire a shell sixteen miles. At night, the grounds were an electrical extravaganza. A total of 27 million visitors relished these displays.

In 1901 Buffalo took the spotlight with its Pan American Exposition, in which the use of electricity transformed the 350-acre spread into a city of the future. This show was the unhappy site of the assassination of President McKinley.

To mark the centenary of Thomas Jefferson's real estate deal with France, St. Louis put on the 1904 Louisiana Purchase Exposition, a vast spread of statuary and water shows that outstripped its predecessors in terms of cost and left tuneful recollections about meeting at the fair in St. Louis. It was here that the American automobile made its smashing debut, together with a big roller coaster, ice cream cones, iced tea, and hamburgers.

The era of the modern fair or exposition began in 1939 and 1940, when San Francisco, at one side of the country, celebrated the opening of the San Francisco–Oakland and Golden Gate Bridges with a show on a man-made island in the bay, visited by 17 million people.

And at the other side of America there was New York's World's Fair, a "World of Tomorrow" in which sixty-three countries and thirty-three states participated. It marked the one hundred fiftieth anniversary of the inauguration of George Washington as the first President. Besides the soaring trylon pyramid and the perisphere; the superhighways and space rockets, there were displays of the new fabric called nylon, air conditioning, and television.

In the 1960s, there was another World's Fair in New York, with its symbolic unisphere dedicated to peace through understanding and a massive model of the earth. Michelangelo's *Pietà*, sent on loan from the Vatican, proved a highlight of the show. In 1974 the city of Spokane accented the history of the American Indian and stressed environmental concerns with its supershow.

With all the variations over a century and a half, each planned to amaze, astound, and amuse, the big shows, wherever held and for whatever reason, have served to lend some of that patriotic feeling, that touch of self-confidence, that marks our pride as a people. They have served to confirm our past and illuminate our future.

President Grant Opens the Philadelphia Centennial (1876)

My Countrymen:

It has been thought appropriate, upon this Centennial occasion, to bring together in Philadelphia, for popular inspection, specimens of our attainments in the industrial and fine arts, and in literature, science, and philosophy, as well as in the great business of agriculture and of commerce.

That we may the more thoroughly appreciate the excellences and deficiencies of our achievements, and also give emphatic expression to our earnest desire to cultivate the friendship of our fellow members of this great family of nations, the enlightened agricultural, commercial, and manufacturing people of the world have been invited to send hither corresponding specimens of their skills to exhibit on equal terms and friendly competition with our own. To this invitation they have generously responded. For so doing we render them our hearty thanks.

The beauty and utility of the contributions will this day be submitted to your inspection by the managers of this exhibition. We are glad to know that a view of specimens of the skill of all nations will afford to you unalloyed pleasure as well as yield to you a valuable, practical knowledge of so many of the remarkable results of the wonderful skill existing in enlightened communities.

One hundred years ago our country was new and but partially settled. Our necessities have compelled us to chiefly expend our means and time in felling forests, subduing prairies, building dwellings, factories, ships, docks, warehouses, roads, canals, machinery, etc. Most of our schools, churches, libraries, and asylums have been established within a hundred years. Burdened by these great primal works of necessity, which could not be delayed, we yet may have done what this exhibition will show in the direction of rivaling older and more advanced nations in law, medicine, and theology; in science, literature, philosophy, and the fine arts. While proud of what we have done, we regret that we have not done more. Our achievements have not been great enough, however, to make it easy for our people to acknowledge superior merit wherever found.

And now, fellow-citizens, I hope a careful examination of what is about to be exhibited to you will not only inspire you with a profound respect for the skill and taste of our friends from other nations, but also satisfy you with the attainments made by our own people during the past one hundred years. I invoke your generous cooperation with the worthy Commissioner to secure a brilliant success to this International Exhibition, and to make the stay of our foreign visitors—to whom we extend a hearty welcome—both profitable and pleasant to them.

I declare the International Exhibition now open.

Opposite page:
One of the many wonders of **the Centennial in Philadelphia** was the exhibit of the new Corliss engine, which was started up in a ceremony presided over by President Grant of the United States and Dom Pedro of Brazil. This is a copy of a wood engraving after a sketch by Theodore C. Davis in *Harper's Weekly.*

The 1904 fair in St. Louis, officially known as the Louisiana Purchase Exposition, had the required statuary and fountains, but it also served to introduce the hamburger and ice cream cone, while featuring a massive exhibit of the new automobile.

46. "I Lift My Lamp Beside the Golden Door"

Of all the symbols of American patriotism, the Statue of Liberty has become a special favorite. She is the focus of our patriotic warmth. Holding her torch and her tablet, stern and yet benign, she regards us with that unwavering look that makes us remember that as Americans we stand for special ideas and ideals.

Once the statue carried the very formal name *Liberty Enlightening the World.* Then it became simply the "Statue of Liberty," the lady with the torch in her right hand and the tablet (inscribed July 4, 1776, in roman numerals) in her left hand.

Her story begins at a dinner table in France near the town of Versailles, in the year 1865, at the home of the eminent jurist and historian Edouard de Laboulaye. De Laboulaye, a great admirer of the United States who wrote a three-volume history of our country, was entertaining a group of friends, among them a young Alsatian sculptor, Frédéric Auguste Bartholdi. The conversation turned to the friendship between France and the United States, and it was proposed that a society be formed to properly commemorate a century of American independence, which had been achieved with French help, perhaps with a centennial gift such as a statue. The Franco-American Union was born, and Bartholdi was deeply interested in the idea.

Bartholdi, an energetic young man, was quite aware of the popularity of massive statues commemorating people or events, which were in fashion at the time. A couple of years later he was in Egypt, where he was deeply impressed by the ancient colossi and tried to persuade the ruling authorities to commission him for a large statue to grace the entrance of the new Suez Canal. When war broke out between France and Prussia, Bartholdi was in uniform as a French officer. France's defeat was a bitter pill.

The Versailles dinner table ideas never slipped Bartholdi's mind. In 1871, during the first of several trips to America, Bartholdi worked on the idea of a giant statue for the harbor at New York, a giant monument to be built in an era of giant monuments.

Bartholdi's plans took fifteen years to achieve fruition and ten years to build, but he was a determined and persuasive man. This statue of Liberty would be 152 feet high, weigh 225 tons, and be constructed of copper sheets, about 300 separate pieces. The French nation would pay for the statue itself; the American people would pay for the pedestal. French contributions poured in from the start. Composer Charles Gounod wrote a cantata to mark the project; a Paris department store held a lottery. A total of $400,000 was raised.

"Liberty" took shape as the sculptor put his ideas to work in copper. He was a passionate patriot and the statue became a personal statement. Even his mother was drawn into the work. She was the model for "Liberty's" face. Classical concepts, with a Greco-Roman flourish, brought into being the dignified draped lady, with a broken chain on her feet to tell of her victory over tyranny. The torch arm rose forty-two feet, the hand itself sixteen feet.

In a kind of piecemeal preview, the torch arm was on view at the Philadelphia Centennial in 1876, and the head, ten feet ear to ear, could be seen at the Paris Fair of 1878, complete with a seven-spiked tiara symbolizing the seven seas.

The entire figure took ten years to assemble. Bartholdi used an ancient method of sculpting a hammered copper sheet to accommodate the huge size. Gustave Eiffel, the noted French engineer who had built railroad bridges and who would build the spectacular Eiffel Tower, was called upon to construct the vital armature or core of the statue on four iron posts.

Opposite page:
The 152-foot-high **Statue of Liberty** dominates the harbor at New York.

While the project moved forward rapidly in France, this was not true in America. It took a last-minute, all-out newspaper campaign by the *New York World* and its publisher, Joseph Pulitzer, a Hungarian immigrant who had fought for the Union in the Civil War, to raise enough funds for Richard Hunt's massive concrete pedestal. The *World* printed the name of every individual contributor, no matter how small the donation.

Hunt's pedestal required 11,680 cubic yards of concrete, the largest mass of such building material assembled up to that time. In 1903 a plaque bearing the words of the poem ''The New Colossus'' by Emma Lazarus, a renowned poet, was placed on the pedestal.

''Liberty'' herself was shipped to the United States aboard a French warship.

On August 5, 1884, the cornerstone of the pedestal was placed. The site, chosen by Bartholdi himself, was on Bedloe's Island in the upper bay, ideal for moving spectators, who could see the 302-foot image placed at an angle that seemed to pivot with the viewer who watched as his ship moved by. The whole monument was placed on an eleven-point star in what had formerly served as Fort Wood, an Army base. Bedloe's Island was renamed Liberty Island in 1956.

On October 28, 1886, *Liberty Enlightening the World* was dedicated by President Grover Cleveland. In the torch, Bartholdi himself, a bit ahead of cue, pulled the cord that removed France's tricolor flag from ''Liberty's'' face. For a period of thirteen years ''Liberty'' reigned as the tallest structure in the area, until the commercial buildings in lower Manhattan reached higher and higher into the clouds. But for decades the statue, which had at first served as a lighthouse with 168 steps to the top, dominated the bay.

Since 1924, the statue, standing so majestically on Liberty Island, has been classed as a national monument, with a million visitors annually.

By the 1930s, with the vast ethnic changes brought on by immigration, the Statue of Liberty, initial sight for the newcomer, came to be the image indelibly associated with the New World.

THE NEW COLOSSUS

Not like the brazen giant of Greek fame,
With conquering limbs astride from land to land;
Here at our sea-washed, sunset gates shall stand
A mighty woman with a torch, whose flame
Is the imprisoned lightning, and her name
Mother of Exiles. From her beacon-hand
Glows world-wide welcome; her mild eyes command
The air-bridged harbor that twin cities frame.
"Keep, ancient lands, your storied pomp!" cries she
With silent lips. "Give me your tired, your poor,
Your huddled masses yearning to breathe free,
The wretched refuse of your teeming shore.
Send these, the homeless, tempest-tost to me,
I lift my lamp beside the golden door!"

EMMA LAZARUS

Newcomers to America get their first glimpse of the Statue of Liberty in the New York Harbor.

Commodore Dewey on the Bridge of the Flagship* Olympia *at the Battle of Manila Bay,
was painted by Rufus Zogbaum. George Dewey had graduated from Annapolis in 1858 and he saw active
duty in the Civil War. In 1897, with the rank of commodore, he was appointed by President McKinley to
command the U.S. Asiatic squadron. On May 1, 1898, about six weeks after the U.S. battleship *Maine*
had been destroyed in Havana Harbor, helping to precipitate the Spanish-American War, Dewey, under
secret orders, entered Manila harbor after midnight, confronted the Spanish fleet, and destroyed
eight Spanish ships. Only eight Americans were wounded. In 1899 George Dewey was appointed to
the rank of admiral, and he retired a hero.

47. "A Splendid Little War"

It was a two-front war that lasted only 112 days. In ten weeks a four hundred-year-old empire was destroyed. And out of it the United States of America, a young stripling of a nation little more than a century old and just emerging from a bloody Civil War, climbed to a leading position in the affairs of Latin America and the Far East. We have come to call it the Spanish-American War, and it did serve, in a brief, hectic period, to allow us to flex our muscles for conflicts to come and to remind us that war is far more than battlefield glory.

For years at the end of the century, the nearby island of Cuba, torn by insurrection and suffering under brutal Spanish military rule, had been winning national notice. Atrocity stories from the unhappy island filled the press. Intervention seemed only a matter of time.

For the same period, there were unrestrained signs of an expansionist mood in the United States. Our writers, and especially our journalists, were boasting of a certain "consciousness of strength," of a "manifest destiny," and of the "joy of fighting." Imperialism was still in fashion, and so was the responsibility for colonizing "backward" regions of the world. The tide of chauvinism was high.

But there were other, more practical considerations as well. Our growing navy needed coaling and harbor facilities, and because we were thinking of the possibility of a canal through the Isthmus of Panama, we were looking for ways to be sure that we could protect that canal.

Actually, Spain was in a better position for war than the U.S. There were more than two hundred thousand troops in Cuba, and the Spanish Navy was well equipped with armored cruisers and torpedo craft. But it was the United States that had the hankering to fight.

Two incidents served, finally, to light the fuse. The contents of a private letter from the Spanish ambassador to the United States, casting slurs on President McKinley, was published. It was seen as a national insult, and the diplomat went home. Then, on February 15, 1898, the U.S. battleship *Maine*, sent to protect American life and property, was blown up in the harbor of Havana, with a loss of 260 men. The cause was not determined, but the incident provided a slogan: "Remember the *Maine*."

By April 25, 1898, after some international exchanges and peace feelers, with a certain vacillation on both sides, war was at last declared by both parties.

Most of the action took place at sea or in Spanish territory. On May 1, 1898, Admiral George Dewey, warned well in advance to be ready for action, entered Manila Bay in the Philippine Islands and destroyed the Spanish fleet of ten ships and 381 men. Only 8 Americans were wounded. It was here that Dewey informed the captain of his flagship *Olympia,* "You may fire when ready, Gridley." Dewey completed the job by 12:30 P.M. of the same day, after about seven hours of fighting.

Then, two months later, on July 3, in the action at Cuba's Santiago Bay, American fire killed 180 Spaniards, and the Americans captured 1,800. The U.S. lost one man and sustained one wounded. It was here that Captain John W. Philip of the battleship *Texas* called out as a Spanish cruiser turned ashore in flames: "Don't cheer, boys, the poor devils are dying."

In land battles on the previous day, a brash young lieutenant colonel, Teddy Roosevelt, lead his First Volunteer Cavalry, known as the "Rough Riders," in a charge up Cuba's San Juan Hill to help secure that victory.

The war was a genuinely popular one, as politicians and the press continually whipped up public sentiment. The war reportage of Richard Harding Davis, a veteran journalist, provided many of the colorful and dramatic stories that kept people's interest at fever pitch.

You may fire when ready, Gridley.

To the captain of Admiral Dewey's flagship *Olympia* at the Battle of Manila Bay, May 1, 1898

W. G. Read

In 1898, shortly after the outbreak of the Spanish-American War, Theodore Roosevelt resigned his position as assistant secretary of the Navy and organized a group of U.S. Cavalry volunteers for service in the conflict. The regiment won fame as Roosevelt's "Rough Riders." **This print is in the spirit of the Rough Riders' charge up San Juan Hill on July 2, 1898,** but it is, in fact, historic fiction, since the terrain would not have allowed this kind of operation. Nonetheless, Theodore Roosevelt's charge became a cherished part of America's historic legend. This chromolithograph is by George S. Harris and Son from a watercolor by W. G. Read.

By August a peace protocol was ready, and a treaty was signed in December. Spain withdrew from Cuba, and ceded Guam, Puerto Rico, and the Philippines to the United States, which made a $20 million payment for the Philippines.

During the conflict it became clear that we were not ready for war, that disease took a higher toll (2,161) than did enemy bullets (385), and that our war department was inadequate. Still, we had tested ourselves; we had a fresh sense of our own strength. We had new slogans and new heroes in our pantheon.

For the same period, there were unrestrained signs of an expansionist mood in the United States. Our writers, and especially our journalists, were boasting of a certain "consciousness of strength," of a "manifest destiny," and of the "joy of fighting." Imperialism was still in fashion, and so was the responsibility for colonizing "backward" regions of the world. The tide of chauvinism was high. John Hay, President McKinley's secretary of state, called the Spanish-American conflict "a splendid little war."

48. "God Shed His Grace on Thee . . ."

The patriotic hymn "America the Beautiful," expressing our love of the land, provides a lyrical tribute to the American scene. The words were written by Katherine Lee Bates (1859–1929), who was a professor of English at Wellesley College and wrote books on scholarly subjects and stories for children. After standing on the summit of Pikes Peak in Colorado, Bates, deeply moved by the scope of her view from that 14,000-foot vantage point, wrote her poem. It was first printed in 1895 in the *Congregationalist* magazine and was set to music by Samuel A. Ward.

AMERICA, THE BEAUTIFUL

O beautiful for spacious skies,
For amber waves of grain,
For purple mountain majesties
Above the fruited plain.
America! America! God shed His grace on thee
And crown thy good with brotherhood
From sea to shining sea!

O beautiful for pilgrim feet,
Whose stern, impassioned stress
A thoroughfare of freedom beat
Across the wilderness!
America! America! God mend thine every flaw,
Confirm thy soul in self control,
Thy liberty in law!

O beautiful for heroes proved
In liberating strife,
Who more than self their country loved,
And mercy more than life!
America! America! May God thy gold refine,
Till all success be nobleness,
And every gain divine!

O beautiful for patriot dream
That sees beyond the years
Thine alabaster cities gleam
Undimmed by human tears!
America! America! God shed His grace on thee,
And crown thy good with brotherhood
From sea to shining sea!

KATHERINE LEE BATES

The Grand Canyon, with its majestic vistas, has attracted artists for decades. This painting was done in 1893 by Thomas Moran.

The spectacular **Niagara Falls** was painted in 1835 by John Vanderlyn.

157

America the beautiful—
a sampling includes the Acadia
country of Louisiana, with its
bayous and Spanish-moss-
covered trees; fields of ripened
grain in Iowa; orange groves of
California.

159

49. Cowboy!

The cowboy image remains a durable part of American nostalgia, its love of broad unfenced spaces, its patriotic feeling.

In books and songs, in movies and television serials, the eternal struggle between the cleanshaven lads in the white hats and the black-hatted ones with the week-old stubble remains to be resolved on dusty village streets.

Long ago the hard-worked horse largely gave way to the frisky pickup truck, but the bowlegged drifter with the lovable drawl and the mythical machismo left his impact on music and fashion and on the younger fry, who still ask for cowboy suits and six-shooter cap guns. The heyday of the cowboy breed lasted about three decades, but that was enough to give the cowboys a solid niche in the gallery of Americana. They were enshrined in the fiction of Zane Grey, Ned Buntline, and Owen Wister; in the art of Frederic Remington and Charles M. Russell; in the songs of Daniel Kelley and the wit of Will Rogers; in the films of William S. Hart, Tom Mix, and Harry Carey; and in the movie, radio, and television serials of Roy Rogers, Gene Autry, and the Lone Ranger.

The men who worked with the massive cattle herds and followed the hazardous trail from the Texas ranges to the Kansas railheads had to be ready for storm and stampede, heat and hostile Indians. In the roundup it was the cowpokes' job to count the animals and brand the new calves. They had to know how to shoot and ride. They had to exist on a meager diet and be satisfied with pay of about a hundred dollars or less for driving two thousand longhorns up the trail for three months, at ten to twenty miles per day. The greatest threat was stampede, which started in an unpredictable split second, roared ahead blindly for three or four miles, and had to be turned into a vast circle so its speed could be controlled. On the trail, at the start or at the finish, the buckaroos would sometimes take over a town where there was only a solitary two-gun sheriff, who tried his best to keep the peace. It was an authentic part of the American scene.

In the entire repertory of American folk music, few songs have achieved greater popularity than "Home on the Range," evoking as it does the sense of boundless freedom in the so-called wide-open spaces. This tribute to playful deer and antelope has the charm of folklore, but is also a revealing expression of American ideals and self-confidence. It is a kind of patriotic anthem.

This vigorous oil on canvas by Frederic Remington (1861–1909), titled **The Cowpuncher,** carries the vibrant action that marks this artist's feeling for Western material. Remington drew on his own life in the West for his superb cowboys, Indians, horses, and cattle.

The words and music for the song we call **"Home on the Range,"** originally called An Arizona Home, were probably written in the early 1870s. The song has become a standard of folklore repertory, popular for country-western sing-alongs and campfire cookouts.

Buffalo Bill

William Frederick Cody was folklore in the flesh. As ''Buffalo Bill'' he brought to rousing life the hard-riding sharp-shooting Western hero, dear to the heart of America, forever ennobled as the good guy in the white hat. He created a legend and kept it alive.

Iowa-born Cody was all the heroes rolled into one—Civil War scout and trooper, pony express rider, Indian fighter. He was a hunter who supplied meat for railroad crews working in the West, and he gained his nickname in a buffalo-killing contest in the 1870s.

In 1883 he began a show business career that lasted more than three decades, starring in his own Wild West Show that toured the byways of America, bringing the thrills of the early West to every isolated American community within reach, and to Europe.

Into that show Cody brought such attractions as sharp-shooting Annie Oakley, who could split a playing card edgewise at thirty paces, and the Sioux chief, Sitting Bull, who took part in a dramatic attack on a stagecoach. Buffalo Bill was one of the major Midway attractions at the Chicago World's Fair. His show grew to a point where he was using six hundred riders to astound his audience. His fame grew into legend in the dime novels of Ned Buntline.

50. The Simple Life: This Land Is Our Land

American patriotism is deeply rooted in American soil. Once the overwhelming majority of us lived on farms, or in small towns, and we viewed ourselves as an agricultural people. Now most of us live in towns and cities, but we are still swayed by images of the simple life. Our closeness to the land, our ownership of the land, our historic identity with it, are vital ingredients of our patriotic spirit. The Minuteman held a rifle, but at his side was a plow. Nearly all those who fought in the American Revolution were farmers. Our favorite national seer, Ralph Waldo Emerson, spoke of the "embattled farmer" as the embodiment of the patriotic spirit. The pioneers who crossed the plains were mainly farm families.

Much of our patriotic ritual is rural in concept: the county fair, the rural schoolhouse, the small-town parade on July 4, the frame church. When we became mainly a nation of city dwellers, our nostalgia still flavored our patriotism and the land continued to pull us. It is not as easy to feel patriotic about a high-rise apartment, a skyscraper, or a six-lane highway.

Fourth of July,
by Grandma Moses

Grandma Moses Going to the Big City, by Grandma Moses

Thanksgiving Turkey, by Grandma Moses

Grandma Moses

Her full name was Anna Mary Robertson Moses, but even in those later years when she had achieved international fame, she was affectionately known as "Grandma Moses." "Grandma" was born in 1860 in rural New York state and spent most of her life at the arduous tasks of the typical farm wife of her time. Then, in her seventies, she taught herself to paint, concentrating on the simple scenes of life in the village and on the farm and bringing a special primitive charm to her work. At the age of one hundred she was still at work. She died at the age of one hundred and one.

165

51. Making the World Safe for Democracy

At first the sound of guns was only a distant echo. The war in Europe seemed to be fought on another planet. After all, what did we have to do with the assassination of an archduke and his wife on a street in a distant Balkan town, the name of which we couldn't even pronounce? The choosing of sides was accomplished in a few days. Austria went to war against Serbia . . . Germany joined Austria, Russia marched with Serbia, France joined Russia, and England joined the anti-German forces. Why worry about those air raids on Paris? And the British tank battles. What, indeed, were tanks?

The war ground along for three years, and suddenly we were involved. The German army had crushed Belgium in ruthless fashion, and on May 7, 1915, the unarmed British liner *Lusitania*, bound from New York for Liverpool, was sunk by German submarines, and 128 Americans lost their lives. The tides of American feeling swung against the Central Powers.

In January 1917 Germany, in order to cut England's import lines and end the war quickly, decided on a policy of unrestricted submarine warfare. Six American vessels went down in two months, with 48 lives lost. Moreover, German diplomatic interchange indicated the possible involvement of Mexico on the German side.

On April 2, 1917, President Wilson asked for a declaration of war; on April 6, the Congress gave it to him.

In a brief year and a half, America was transformed into a fighting machine. The entire economy was mobilized, under five thousand federal agencies. Four million men went into the Army, six hundred thousand into the Navy. At the Philadelphia Naval Yard alone, there were twenty-three thousand laborers.

There were Liberty Loan drives that eventually collected $21 billion; there were parades and rallies and the proud display of flags. The minds of Americans were also mobilized to "Kick the Kaiser" and "Crush the Hun" and "Give till it Hurts."

Anti-German fervor rose to amusing heights. Sauerkraut became "liberty cabbage," dachshunds "liberty pups," and hamburger "Salisbury steak."

We were all singing "Over There" and declaring that the "Yanks are coming." Never had our patriotic fervor been stirred so deeply. The call to arms had become a crusade.

When the vanguard of the American Expeditionary Forces, under General "Black Jack" Pershing, arrived in Europe, there was on July 4, 1917, a ceremony at the grave of a French patriot. An American officer was able to say "Lafayette, we are here."

On the night of April 2, 1917, a spring rain settled over the city of Washington. The President had come to the Capitol to ask for war. Before the assembled Congress, President Wilson delivered a noble speech that defined the American purpose. The world, he said, must be made safe for democracy. Armed imperialism had no place. Four days later Wilson had the authority to go to war.

American intervention was a direct reply to German depredation on the seas. The land war was deadlocked. The Germans announced a policy of unrestricted submarine warfare to break British control of the sea lanes. The U.S. broke off diplomatic relations. Then came our entry into World War I, or the Great War, as it has come to be called.

President Wilson: War Against Germany (April 2, 1917)

I have called the Congress into extraordinary session because there are serious, very serious, choices of policy to be made, and made immediately, which it was neither right nor constitutionally permissible that I should assume the responsibility of making.

On the third of February last I officially laid before you the extraordinary announcement of the imperial German government that on and after the first day of February it was its purpose to put aside all restraints of law or of humanity and use its submarines to sink every vessel that sought to approach either the ports of Great Britain or Ireland or the western coasts of Europe or any of the ports controlled by the enemies of Germany within the Mediterranean. That had seemed to be the object of the German submarine warfare earlier in the war, but since April of last year the imperial government had somewhat restrained the commanders of its undersea craft in conformity with its promise then given to us that passenger boats should not be sunk and that due warning would be given to all other vessels which its submarines might seek to destroy, when no resistance was offered or escape attempted, and care taken that their crews were given at least a fair chance to save their lives in their open boats. The precautions taken were meager and haphazard enough, as was proved in distressing instance after instance in the progress of the cruel and unmanly business, but a certain degree of restraint was observed. The new policy has swept every restriction aside. Vessels of every kind, whatever their flag, their character, their cargo, their destination, their errand, have been ruthlessly sent to the bottom without warning and without thought of help or mercy for those on board, the vessels of friendly neutrals along with those of belligerents.

It is a war against all nations. American ships have been sunk, American lives taken, in ways which it has stirred us very deeply to learn of, but the ships and people of other neutral and friendly nations have been sunk and overwhelmed in the waters in the same way. There has been no discrimination. The challenge is to all mankind. Each nation must decide for itself how it will meet it. The choice we make for ourselves must be made with a moderation of counsel and a temperateness of judgment befitting our character and our motives as a nation. We must put excited feeling away. Our motive will not be revenge or the victorious assertion of the physical might of the nation, but only the vindication of right, of human right, of which we are only a single champion.

When I addressed the Congress on the twenty-sixth of February last I thought that it would suffice to assert our neutral rights with arms, our right to use the seas against unlawful interference, our right to keep our people safe against unlawful violence. But armed neutrality, it now appears, is impracticable. Because submarines are in effect outlaws when used as the German submarines have been used against merchant shipping, it is impossible to defend ships against their attacks as the law of nations has assumed that merchantmen would defend themselves against privateers or cruisers, visible craft giving chase upon the open sea. It is common prudence in such circumstances, grim necessity indeed, to endeavor to destroy them before they have shown their own intention. They must be dealt with upon sight, if dealt with at all.

With a profound sense of the solemn and even tragical character of the step I am taking and of the grave responsibilities which it involves, but in unhesitating obedience to what I deem my constitutional duty, I advise that the Congress declare the recent course of the imperial German government to be in fact nothing less than war against the government and people of the United States; that it formally accept the status of belligerent which has thus been thrust upon it; and that it take immediate steps not only to put the country in a more thorough state of defense, but also to exert all its power and employ all its resources to bring the government of the German empire to terms and end the war.

What this will involve is clear. It will involve the utmost practicable co-operation in counsel and action with the governments now at war with Germany, and, as incident to that, the extension to those governments of the most liberal financial credits, in order that our resources may so far as possible be added to theirs. It will involve the organization and mobilization of all the material resources of the country to supply the materials of war and serve the incidental needs of the nation in the most abundant and yet the most economical and efficient way possible. It will involve the immediate full equipment of

To fight thus for the ultimate peace of the world and for the liberation of its peoples, the German peoples included: for the rights of nations great and small and the privilege of men everywhere to choose their way of life and of obedience. The world must be made safe for democracy.

WOODROW WILSON,
address to Congress,
April 2, 1917

Woodrow Wilson,
by F. Graham Coates

the navy in all respects but particularly in supplying it with the best means of dealing with the enemy's submarines. It will involve the immediate addition to the armed forces of the United States already provided for by law in case of war at least five hundred thousand men, who should, in my opinion, be chosen upon the principle of universal liability to service, and also the authorization of subsequent additional increments of equal force so soon as they may be needed and can be handled in training. It will involve also, of course, the granting of adequate credits to the government, sustained, I hope, so far as they can equitably be sustained by the present generation, by well-conceived taxation. . . .

We have no quarrel with the German people. We have no feeling toward them but one of sympathy and friendship. It was not upon their impulse that their government acted in entering this war. It was not with their previous knowledge or approval. It was a war determined upon as wars used to be determined upon in the old, unhappy days when peoples were nowhere consulted by their rulers and wars were provoked and waged in the interest of dynasties or of little groups of ambitious men who were accustomed to use their fellow men as pawns and tools. Self-governed nations do not fill their neighbor states with spies or set the course of intrigue to bring about some critical posture of affairs which will give them an opportunity to strike and make conquest. Such designs can be successfully worked out only under cover and where no one has the right to ask questions. Cunningly contrived plans of deception or aggression, carried, it may be, from generation to generation, can be worked out and kept from the light only within the privacy of courts or behind the carefully guarded confidences of a narrow and privileged class. They are happily impossible where public opinion commands and insists upon full information concerning all the nation's affairs. . . .

One of the things that has served to convince us that the Prussian autocracy was not and could never be our friend is that from the very outset of the present war it has filled our unsuspecting communities and even our offices of government with spies and set criminal intrigues everywhere afoot against our national unity of counsel, our peace within and without, our industries, and our commerce. Indeed, it is now evident that its spies were here even before the war began; and it is unhappily not a matter of conjecture but a fact proved in our courts of justice that the intrigues which have more than once come perilously near to disturbing the peace and dislocating the industries of the country have been carried on at the instigation, with the support, and even under the personal direction of official agents of the imperial government accredited to the government of the United States. Even in checking these things and trying to extirpate them we have sought to put the most generous interpretation possible upon them because we knew that their source lay not in any hostile feeling or purpose of the German people towards us (who were no doubt as ignorant of them as we ourselves were), but only in the selfish designs of a government that did what it pleased and told its people nothing. But they have played their part in serving to convince us at last that that government entertains no real friendship for us and means to act against our peace and security at its convenience. That it means to stir up enemies against us at our very doors the intercepted note to the German minister at Mexico City is eloquent evidence.

We are accepting this challenge of hostile purpose because we know that in such a government, following such methods, we can never have a friend; and that in the presence of its organized power, always lying in wait to accomplish we know not what purpose, there can be no assured security for the democratic governments of the world. We are now about to accept the gage of battle with this natural foe to liberty and shall, if necessary, spend the whole force of the nation to check and nullify its pretensions and its power. We are glad, now that we see the facts with no veil of false pretense about them, to fight thus for the ultimate peace of the world and for the liberation of its peoples, the German peoples included: for the rights of nations great and small and the privilege of men everywhere to choose their way of life and of obedience. The world must be made safe for democracy.

It is a distressing and oppressive duty, gentlemen of the Congress, which I have performed in thus addressing you. There are, it may be, many months of fiery trial and sacrifice ahead of us. It is a fearful thing to lead this great peaceful people into war, into the most terrible and disastrous of all wars, civilization itself seeming to be in the balance. But the right is more precious than peace, and we shall fight for the things which we have always carried nearest our hearts—for democracy, for the right of those who submit to authority to have a voice in their own governments, for the dominion of right by such a concert of free peoples as shall bring peace and safety to all nations and make the world itself at last free. To such a task we can dedicate our lives and our fortunes, everything that we are and everything that we have, with the pride of those who know that the day has come when America is privileged to spend her blood and her might for the principles that gave her birth and happiness and the peace which she has treasured. God helping her, she can do no other.

52. A Great Nation in a Great War

By 1915, about 140 years after independence, the United States stood at the threshold of world power.

With a population of close to 100 million and an immigration rate that had been averaging about 8,800,000 per year, Americans could view the vast reaches of more than 3 million square miles with a sense of strength and a feeling for manifest destiny. The future, surely, was safe.

Unfortunately, we had not yet fully grasped the global commitment that went with global power. Our songs, our poetry, our art looked inward. There was talk about a big war in Europe, but these were tired opponents engaged in tired wars. It took a studious college president who wore high stiff collars, who had promised to keep us out of war, to take us into it. We had to expand our sense of commitment, to recognize friend and foe, and to grapple with the idea that if human liberty was in danger anywhere, it was in jeopardy here at home.

In April 1917 the U.S. entered World War I and the scope of American patriotism took on a broader meaning. If we were intent on a place in the world, as a power to be reckoned with, we had to fight for what we believed. And the more than 11 million immigrants and new citizens admitted since the turn of the century might now, in a tangible way, show their gratitude by adding their strength to the force of native-born soldiers.

"I Believe in the United States of America . . ."

I believe in the United States of America as a Government of the people, by the people, for the people; whose just powers are derived from the consent of the governed; a democracy in a republic, a sovereign Nation of many sovereign States; a perfect Union one and inseparable; established upon those principles of freedom, equality, justice and humanity for which American patriots sacrificed their lives and fortunes. I therefore believe it is my duty to my country to love it, to support its Constitution, to obey its laws, to respect its flag, and to defend it against all enemies.

WILLIAM TYLER PAGE
"The American Creed," 1918

New York City children salute the flag at school. Such classroom exercises were vital in Americanizing newcomers and instilling patriotic values.

I AM AN AMERICAN

I am an American.
My father belongs to the Sons of the Revolution;
My mother, to the Colonial Dames.
One of my ancestors pitched tea overboard in Boston Harbor;
Another stood his ground with Warren;
Another hungered with Washington at Valley Forge.
My forefathers were America in the making:
They spoke in her council halls;
They died on her battle-fields;
They commanded her ships;
They cleared her forests.
Dawns reddened and paled.
Staunch hearts of mine beat fast at each new star
In the nation's flag.
Keen eyes of mine foresaw her greater glory:
The sweep of her seas,
The plenty of her plains,
The man-hives in her billion-wired cities.
Every drop of blood in me holds a heritage of patriotism.
I am proud of my past.
I am an American.

I am an American.
My father was an atom of dust,
My mother a straw in the wind,
To His Serene Majesty.
One of my ancestors died in the mines of Siberia;
Another was crippled for life by twenty blows of the knout;
Another was killed defending his home during the massacres.
The history of my ancestors is a trail of blood
To the palace-gate of the Great White Czar.
But then the dream came—
The dream of America.
In the light of the Liberty torch
The atom of dust became a man
And the straw in the wind became a woman
For the first time.
"See," said my father, pointing to the flag that fluttered near,
"That flag of stars and stripes is yours;
It is the emblem of the promised land.
It means, my son, the hope of humanity.
Live for it . . . die for it!"
Under the open sky of my new country I swore to do so;
And every drop of blood in me will keep that vow.
I am proud of my future.
I am an American.

ELIAS LIEBERMAN

Elias Lieberman came to America from Russia when he was eight years old. He was educated in New York City public schools and colleges and became an English teacher as well as a recognized poet and magazine editor. His books include Hand Organ Man, Poems for Enjoyment, and Man in the Shadows. His stirring poem "I Am an American" first appeared in Everybody's Weekly in July 1916.

53. The General and the Sergeant

Among the 4,700,000 men who served in American uniform in World War I, there were two in particular who managed to personify valor and patriotism to the public back home. One was a noted West Point graduate and career officer; the other an unknown sharpshooting farm boy from Tennessee who believed for a time he was a conscientious objector, then decided to fight, and ended up doing a historic job of soldiering.

John Joseph Pershing was born in Missouri and graduated from the Point in 1886. He served as a cavalry officer in campaigns against the Indians and against the Moros in the Philippines. He had led the punitive expedition against the raiders under Pancho Villa from Mexico. In 1917 he was named commander in chief of the American Expeditionary Forces in France.

General Pershing,
by (Stephen Arnold)
Douglas Volk

It was John Joseph Pershing who was assigned the huge job of molding untried doughboys into combat units. The Allies wanted simply to bring the fresh Americans into the tiring ranks of the European Allies. Wilson and Pershing would not agree, insisting on holding the Americans together in their own groups and using these as fighting units. Under Pershing in France the Americans distinguished themselves at Saint-Mihiel and the Meuse-Argonne drive. Pershing achieved a reputation in and out of the Army for his austerity, toughness, and the skills he brought to his assignments.

Pershing, in his trim general's uniform and with his ability to speak for all American fighting men, quickly assumed the role of national hero. He later served as Permanent General of the Armies of the United States and then as chief of staff.

Alvin Cullum York was a hero for the common man. In October 1918 York killed 25 Germans, captured 132 others, and, by himself, took a hill in the Argonne operations. He was a one-man army. York received the highest decorations of the American and French governments. Then he went back to his beloved Tennessee and founded a school. He had become an authentic American hero.

Sergeant Alvin C. York

54. From the Halls of Montezuma

In 1847, during the war with Mexico, an unknown poet of the Marine Corps, inspired by the history surrounding him, particularly the ruins from the time of Montezuma, set the first lyrics of the "Marines' Hymn" to the music of a popular French opera by Jacques Offenbach. But there are musicologists who hear the echoes of an old Spanish folk tune.

The years rolled by and there were alterations in the lyrics generally credited to L. Z. Smith, Colonel Henry C. Davis, and General Charles Doyen. The first sheet music was published in 1918.

Since it was written, the "Marines' Hymn" has been sung around the world by U.S. Marines on their far-flung missions and has been generally adopted by the civilian population as one of our favorite patriotic songs.

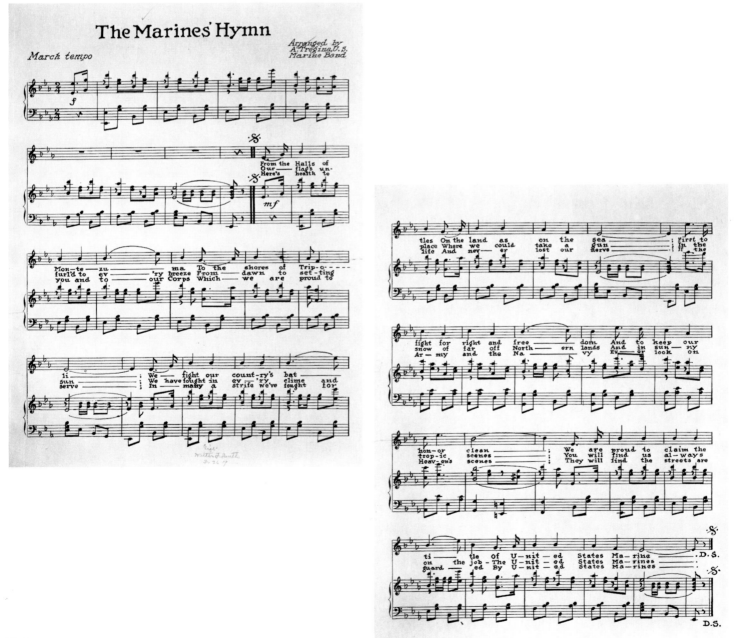

55. The Yankee Doodle Dandy

Few entertainers, no matter how beloved, could match the high level of patriotic fervor that was generated by George M. Cohan (1878–1942).

Born into a stage family, Cohan had his early training as a trouper in his family's vaudeville act, "The Four Cohans." In 1891 he made his stage debut in Peck's Bad Boy, and from then on, over a period of a half century, he dominated Broadway. He wrote twenty musicals in his own quick-tempo style. He danced, he wrote music, he adapted plays, he wrote plays, he acted, he directed.

When he embraced a patriotic theme, Cohan was inimitable, an exuberant one-of-a-kind. Even though he was actually born on July 3 (1878), in his song "Yankee Doodle Dandy" he insisted he was born on the fourth of July, and no one dared argue with him. His "Over There" was widely sung in two world wars and has now become the classic American war song.

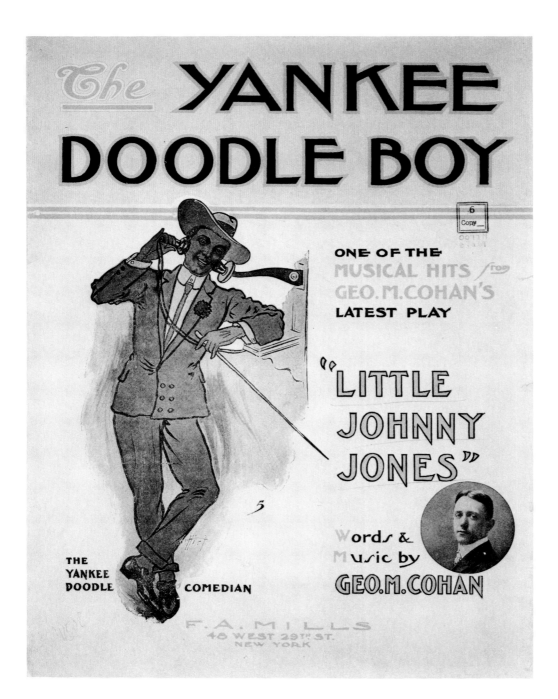

56. America Gets Back on Normalcy Track

Today it remains a distant yet distinct decade, that flamboyant period between 1919 and 1929, between the Senate's rejection of the Versailles Treaty and the stock market crash. Rowdy and rollicking in the eyes of some observers, they called it the Roaring Twenties, though it is not quite clear who did the roaring. Others, some literary perhaps, viewed the time as the Ballyhoo Years, or the Jazz Age, and still others as the Era of Nonsense.

That time period has been endowed with a hearty assortment of historic labels, including the businesslike stamp of "back to normalcy." There was a problem about what was normalcy, for in the five years from 1914 to 1919, when the war had its greatest impact on the economy, a quart of milk went from 9 to 15 cents, a pound of sirloin from 27 to 42 cents, a pound of butter from 32 to 61 cents, and a dozen eggs from 34 to 62 cents.

Whatever the label, whatever the price of food, this was a watershed period. We were changing.

Something of the patriotic fervor generated by the war years remained during those Roaring Twenties. Business and leisure progressed at a higher gear. Our sports champions were transformed into demigods; our Wall Street wizards were endowed with money magic. We lived at a faster pace than ever before. This could happen only in our land.

The war had left some open wounds, some uncounted casualties. Perhaps the greatest of these was President Woodrow Wilson himself. Despite his extraordinary personal effort, dedication, and fervor, the agreements he had helped to fashion went down to defeat in November 1919 and that left him a very sick and embittered man.

The idealism for international peace was evaporating. The nation, confused and uncertain, withdrew from its natural stance of leadership, and isolationism became the philosophy of the day.

But as we turned to ourselves after the war years, what we saw we liked. As a world power we had come through the rites of passage, and there was a certain ardent nationalism afloat. We had known an exhilarating period of parades and rallies and broad community effort, and all of this left its stamp. The Liberty Loan drives had taught us lessons of cooperation we could apply in many ways. A free spirit, a laissez-faire attitude, permeated our society. And the flag itself had taken on fresh meaning.

For a period of a dozen years there was Republican leadership in the White House: Warren G. Harding from a small Ohio town, Calvin Coolidge from the hills of Vermont, and Herbert Hoover, an engineer from Iowa. They steered one course: "the business of America is business." High-level government scandals were accepted as part of the scene.

There were some disarmament efforts and some long-distance peace plans, but the nation was determined to tend its own shop. We were not quite ready to assume the role of international leadership. That was still in the hands of a restless Europe, suffering from its postwar wounds.

Though the changes in American politics were few, the changes in American society were many.

Techniques learned under the stress of war demand were quickly applied to peacetime uses. The automobile and the radio helped to lead the way. Auto output was less than 7 million cars in 1919, but by 1929 it had zoomed to 33 million. And if you needed it, there was this new plan called installment buying.

American exports, too, were reaching international markets on an unprecedented scale. Business was booming, and land became a hot item, particularly, for a period, in Florida. Then the acquisitive urge shifted to the stock market and, in an orgy of speculation, stocks drove upward as if prosperity would never end. There were 75 millionaires in 1924; by 1927 there were 283.

Meantime, there were radical changes in the manners and morals of the nation. The overseas experience had shown some of those in uniform that the entire world did not live by one social code. Women, too, tried a different lifestyle. In 1920 the Nineteenth Amendment had admitted them to the voting booth. They had national suffrage after a long fight.

The so-called flappers set the pace. Their prototype was the movie star Clara Bow. Skirts were higher; dancers danced closer. Women started to smoke, and they even invaded bars for more than a sip of beer. This "permissiveness" penetrated deeply into the social fabric, and conservative groups howled for restrictions. Only so many inches above the ankles, and that was that. In Philadelphia, a "moral" gown was designed that rose seven and a half inches above the shoe bottom.

Much of this change in public attitude was reflected in the movies we viewed and the books we read. We were reading Sinclair Lewis's *Main Street* and *Babbitt*, John Dos Passos's *Manhattan Transfer*, Theodore Dreiser's *An American Tragedy*, and Carl Sandburg's *Chicago Poems*. At the movie palaces we enjoyed Harold Lloyd in *Grandma's Boy*, Mary Pickford in *The Little Princess*, and Charlie Chaplin in *The Gold Rush*.

After a thirteen-hour debate in Congress, we had a Prohibition law that produced bootlegging mobs, speak-easies, and a Chicago gangster who could claim $105 million as income in a single year.

Ratification of the Nineteenth Amendment, on August 26, 1920, allowing women to vote. The National Women's Party had reason to celebrate.

Commander Richard E. Byrd, the man who sought a "frozen continent" at the North Pole. Big Bill Tilden reigned supreme on the tennis courts of the world. Jack Dempsey ruled as heavyweight king from 1919 to 1926.

178

Colonel Charles A. Lindbergh poses in front of his monoplane, *Spirit of St. Louis*, just before his history-making flight across the Atlantic on May 21, 1927.

The decade has been frequently called the golden era of sports. Sports heroes were in the spotlight: Jack Dempsey in professional boxing; Babe Ruth in baseball; Red Grange in football; Bobby Jones in golf; and Bill Tilden in tennis. Gertrude Ederle swam the English Channel.

Mah-jongg was the parlor-game sensation of the time, with its bamboos, flowers, and South Winds. "Charleston" was the dance craze, and for those who preferred a somewhat more sedate diversion there was the new crossword puzzle that was catching newspaper readers' fancy.

Many will argue that the most significant date of the entire decade was May 21, 1927, when a twenty-seven-year-old former airmail pilot, Charles Augustus Lindbergh, flew a single-engine plane nonstop from New York to Paris. He landed at 10:30 P.M. after 33½ hours in the air.

Lindbergh's remarkable feat had a strong impact on American pride and American patriotism. Here was an American, young and handsome, out of the heartland, who had accomplished this, a history-making trip, all by himself against enormous odds. He personified American courage and resourcefulness. All America came to love him.

Then came October 29, 1929, when the New York stock market, after repeated signs of weakness, collapsed in an avalanche of selling. A dizzy decade came to a grinding halt.

179

57. The American Spirit in Crisis: FDR

History writes its own labels. For instance, Thursday, October 24, 1929, is now called "Black Thursday." On that date America went through a sea change. The euphoria of the twenties, those soaring Roaring Twenties, collapsed. The Jazz Age evaporated. The vaunted American prosperity and those years of frenzied finance and paper profits came to a shattering halt. The national vision of endless good living, primed by overproduction and jeopardized by a fragile banking structure, faded in the light of reality. There had been cautious warnings from many quarters, signs of disaster in Europe, but the momentum here was too great and the warnings went unheeded.

On that "Black Thursday," an avalanche of selling hit the New York Stock Exchange. From the opening bell, it was sell, sell, sell. A total of 16,400,000 shares, incredible for that time, inundated the exchange floor, the ticker ran far behind, while 40 points were shaved from the averages. That was the signal. From that day on, for almost three dismal years, the trend was downward.

By 1932 there were 12 million unemployed, one third of the labor force. Five thousand banks had failed. Pullman trains were completing their runs without a single passenger. Apple sellers appeared on city streets, and the soup lines grew longer. Shantytowns, built of old boxes and discarded lumber, sprouted in city lots. They were called "Hoovervilles." The economic stress was compounded by a series of dust storms that ripped off the topsoil from vast agricultural areas of the Midwest and deposited the dust over large sections of the countryside. Working farms were abandoned for some far-western Utopia.

History applied another label, the "Great Depression." The national lament was "Brother, can you spare a dime?"

The statistics were only a distorted mirror of the country's temper. In the face of national suffering, there remained a certain basic optimism. Outrage and bafflement, yes, but loss of faith, no. The American spirit that had brought us through a war for independence and a bloody fratricidal conflict was being tested in a dark crucible. The outlook was bleak.

Then came the election of 1932 and a change of leadership.

Franklin Delano Roosevelt: First Inaugural Address
(March 4, 1933)

President Hoover, Mr. Chief Justice, my friends:

This is a day of national consecration, and I am certain that my fellow-Americans expect that on my induction into the Presidency I will address them with a candor and a decision which the present situation of our nation impels.

This is pre-eminently the time to speak the truth, the whole truth, frankly and boldly. Nor need we shrink from honestly facing conditions in our country today. This great nation will endure as it has endured, will revive and will prosper.

So first of all let me assert my firm belief that the only thing we have to fear is fear itself—nameless, unreasoning, unjustified terror which paralyzes needed efforts to convert retreat into advance.

In every dark hour of our national life a leadership of frankness and vigor has met with that understanding and support of the people themselves which is essential to victory. I am convinced that you will again give that support to leadership in these critical days.

In such a spirit on my part and on yours we face our common difficulties. They concern, thank God, only material things. Values have shrunken to fantastic levels; taxes have risen; our ability to pay has fallen; government of all

In the presidential election of 1932, a fear-ridden nation went to the polls to elect the thirty-second President. Hoover's opponent was Franklin Delano Roosevelt, fifth cousin of former President Theodore Roosevelt, twice governor of New York, a former assistant secretary of the Navy and vice-presidential candidate.

Roosevelt was a dynamic man, with remarkable oratorical ability, great charm and personality, and a flair for the dramatic. In 1905 he married a niece of former President Roosevelt. In the summer of 1921 he was stricken with poliomyelitis, which left him with useless legs. For the rest of his life he had to use crutches, braces, and a wheelchair.

In 1932 Roosevelt, having won the Democratic presidential nomination, conducted a vigorous campaign, stumping the country, making full use of his stirring voice on the radio. Losing only six states, the Roosevelt ticket swept the country.

On March 4, 1933, a raw, dark, and cloudy day, he stood bareheaded on the east front of the Capitol when he was sworn into office.

kinds is faced by serious curtailment of income; the means of exchange are frozen in the currents of trade; the withered leaves of industrial enterprise lie on every side; farmers find no markets for their produce; the savings of many years in thousands of families are gone.

More important, a host of unemployed citizens face the grim problem of existence, and an equally great number toil with little return. Only a foolish optimist can deny the dark realities of the moment.

Yet our distress comes from no failure of substance. We are stricken by no plague of locusts. Compared with the perils which our forefathers conquered because they believed and were not afraid, we have still much to be thankful for. Nature still offers her bounty and human efforts have multiplied it. Plenty is at our doorstep, but a generous use of it languishes in the very sight of the supply.

Primarily, this is because the rulers of the exchange of mankind's goods have failed through their own stubbornness and their own incompetence, have admitted their failure and abdicated. . . .

The money changers have fled from their high seats in the temple of our civilization. We may now restore that temple to the ancient truths.

The measure of the restoration lies in the extent to which we apply social values more noble than mere monetary profit.

Happiness lies not in the mere possession of money; it lies in the joy of achievement, in the thrill of creative effort. . . .

Small wonder that confidence languishes, for it thrives only on honesty, on honor, on the sacredness of obligations, on faithful protection, on unselfish performance. Without them it cannot live.

Restoration calls, however, not for changes in ethics alone. This nation asks for action, and action now.

Our greatest primary task is to put people to work. This is no unsolvable problem if we face it wisely and courageously.

181

It can be accomplished in part by direct recruiting by the government itself, treating the task as we would treat the emergency of a war, but at the same time, through this employment, accomplishing greatly needed projects to stimulate and reorganize the use of our natural resources. . . .

It can be helped by preventing realistically the tragedy of the growing loss, through foreclosure, of our small homes and our farms.

It can be helped by insistence that the Federal, State and local governments act forthwith on the demand that their cost be drastically reduced. . . .

There are many ways in which it can be helped, but it can never be helped merely by talking about it. We must act, and act quickly.

Finally, in our progress toward a resumption of work we require two safeguards against a return of the evils of the old order; there must be a strict supervision of all banking and credits and investments; there must be an end to speculation with other people's money, and there must be provision for an adequate but sound currency.

These are the lines of attack. I shall presently urge upon a new Congress in special session detailed measures for their fulfillment, and I shall seek the immediate assistance of the several States.

Through this program of action we address ourselves to putting our own national house in order and making income balance outgo. . . .

In the field of world policy I would dedicate this nation to the policy of the good neighbor—the neighbor who resolutely respects himself and, because he does so, respects the rights of others—the neighbor who respects his obligations and respects the sanctity of his agreements in and with a world of neighbors.

If I read the temper of our people correctly, we now realize as we have never before, our interdependence on each other; that we cannot merely take, but we must give as well; that if we are to go forward we must move as a trained and loyal army willing to sacrifice for the good of a common discipline, because, without such discipline, no progress is made, no leadership becomes effective.

We are, I know, ready and willing to submit our lives and property to such discipline because it makes possible a leadership which aims at a larger good.

This I propose to offer, pledging that the larger purposes will bind upon us all as a sacred obligation with a unity of duty hitherto evoked only in time of armed strife.

With this pledge taken, I assume unhesitatingly the leadership of this great army of our people, dedicated to a disciplined attack upon our common problems.

Action in this image and to this end is feasible under the form of government which we have inherited from our ancestors.

Our Constitution is so simple and practical that it is possible always to meet extraordinary needs by changes in emphasis and arrangement without loss of essential form.

That is why our constitutional system has proved itself the most superbly enduring political mechanism the modern world has produced. It has met every stress of vast expansion of territory, of foreign wars, of bitter internal strife, of world relations.

It is to be hoped that the normal balance of executive and legislative authority may be wholly adequate to meet the unprecedented task before us. But it may be that an unprecedented demand and need for undelayed action may call for temporary departure from that normal balance of public procedure.

I am prepared under my constitutional duty to recommend the measures that a stricken nation in the midst of a stricken world may require.

These measures, or such other measures as the Congress may build out of its experience and wisdom, I shall seek, within my constitutional authority, to bring to speedy adoption.

But in the event that the Congress shall fail to take one of these two courses, and in the event that the national emergency is still critical, I shall not evade the clear course of duty that will then confront me.

I shall ask the Congress for the one remaining instrument to meet the crisis—broad executive power to wage a war against the emergency as great as the power that would be given me if we were in fact invaded by a foreign foe.

For the trust reposed in me I will return the courage and the devotion that befit the time. I can do no less.

We face the arduous days that lie before us in the warm courage of national unity; with the clear consciousness of seeking old and precious moral values; with the clear satisfaction that comes from the stern performance of duty by old and young alike.

We aim at the assurance of a rounded and permanent national life.

We do not distrust the future of essential democracy. The people of the United States have not failed. In their need they have registered a mandate that they want direct, vigorous action.

They have asked for discipline and direction under leadership. They have made me the present instrument of their wishes. In the spirit of the gift I take it.

In this dedication of a nation we humbly ask the blessing of God. May He protect each and every one of us! May He guide me in the days to come!

✻   ✻   ✻

President Roosevelt
showing his famous smile and his equally famous cigarette holder, chats with reporters from his automobile in Warm Springs, Georgia.

Franklin Delano Roosevelt was a master of the media, notably the radio microphone. His easy humor and unflappable charm were new to White House press relations. And his "fireside chats" succeeded in bringing a maximum Sunday night radio audience into the Oval Office itself. The "chats," which served as a sounding board for his plans, generated a unique intimacy.

More than any President in American history, Roosevelt gave the individual citizen a feeling of participation and reflected a self-confidence that was needed at that time. They helped restore our sense of direction.

From President Roosevelt's First Fireside Chat (March 12, 1933)

I want to talk for a few minutes with the people of the United States about banking—with the comparatively few who understand the mechanics of banking, but more particularly with the overwhelming majority who use banks for the making of deposits and the drawing of checks. I want to tell you what has been done in the last few days, why it was done, and what the next steps are going to be. I recognize that the many proclamations from state capitols and from Washington, the legislation, the Treasury regulations, etc., couched for the most part in banking and legal terms, should be explained for the benefit of the average citizen. I owe this in particular because of the fortitude and good temper with which everybody has accepted the inconvenience and hardships of the banking holiday. I know that when you understand what we in Washington have been about I shall continue to have your cooperation as fully as I have had your sympathy and help during the past week.

First of all, let me state the simple fact that when you deposit money in a bank the bank does not put the money into a safe-deposit vault. It invests your money in many different forms of credit—bonds, commercial paper, mortgages, and many other kinds of loans. In other words, the bank puts your money to work to keep the wheels of industry and of agriculture turning around. A comparatively small part of the money you put into the bank is kept in currency—an amount which in normal times is wholly sufficient to cover the cash needs of the average citizen. In other words, the total amount of all currency in the country is only a small fraction of the total deposits in all of the banks.

What, then, happened during the last few days of February and the first few days of March? Because of undermined confidence on the part of the public, there was a general rush by a large portion of our population to turn bank deposits into currency or gold—a rush so great that the soundest banks could not get enough currency to meet the demand. . . .

By the afternoon of March 3 scarcely a bank in the country was open to do business. Proclamations temporarily closing them in whole or in part had been issued by the governors in almost all the states.

It was then that I issued the proclamation providing for the nationwide bank holiday, and this was the first step in the government's reconstruction of our financial and economic fabric.

The second step was the legislation promptly and patriotically passed by the Congress confirming my proclamation and broadening my powers so that it became possible in view of the requirement of time to extend the holiday and lift the ban of the holiday gradually. This law also gave authority to develop a program of rehabilitation of our banking facilities. I want to tell our citizens in every part of the nation that the national Congress—Republicans and Democrats alike—showed by this action a devotion to public welfare and a realization of the emergency and the necessity for speed that it is difficult to match in our history.

The third stage has been the series of regulations permitting the banks to continue their functions to take care of the distribution of food and household necessities and the payment of payrolls.

This bank holiday, while resulting in many cases in great inconvenience, is affording us the opportunity to supply the currency necessary to meet the situation. No sound bank is a dollar worse off than it was when it closed its doors last Monday. Neither is any bank which may turn out not to be in a position for immediate opening. . . .

We start tomorrow, Monday, with the opening of banks in the twelve Federal Reserve Bank cities—those banks which on first examination by the Treasury have already been found to be all right. This will be followed on Tuesday by the resumption of all their functions by banks already found to be sound in cities where there are recognized clearinghouses. That means about 250 cities of the United States.

On Wednesday and succeeding days banks in smaller places all through the country will resume business, subject, of course, to the government's physical ability to complete its survey. It is necessary that the reopening of banks be extended over a period in order to permit the banks to make applications for necessary loans, to obtain currency needed to meet their requirements, and to enable the government to make common-sense checkups. . . .

The success of our whole great national program depends, of course, upon the cooperation of the public—on its intelligent support and use of a reliable system.

Remember that the essential accomplishment of the new legislation is that it makes it possible for banks more readily to convert their assets into cash than was the case before. More liberal provision has been made for banks to borrow on these assets at the Reserve Banks and more liberal provision has also been made for issuing currency on the security of these good assets. . . .

I hope you can see from this elemental recital of what your government is doing that there is nothing complex, or radical, in the process. . . .

It has been wonderful for me to catch the note of confidence from all over the country. I can never be sufficiently grateful to the people for the loyal support they have given me in their acceptance of the judgment that has dictated our course, even though all our processes may not have seemed clear to them.

After all, there is an element in the readjustment of our financial system more important than currency, more important than gold, and that is the confidence of the people. Confidence and courage are the essentials of success in carrying out our plan. You people must have faith; you must not be stampeded by rumors or guesses. Let us unite in banishing fear. We have provided the machinery to restore our financial system; it is up to you to support and make it work.

It is your problem no less than it is mine. Together we cannot fail.

58. The Struggle for National Regeneration

It was called a "New Deal." After years of fixed policies and winters of discontent, there was an innovative quality in the air and a sense of experimentation. A government that once claimed it could do nothing was now doing everything, penetrating every sector of the national life. It was a frontal attack on the country's malaise, and the cards for this New Deal were being dealt out with the greatest rapidity.

During his first one hundred days in office Roosevelt made ten speeches and delivered fifteen messages to Congress. Twice a week the Washington press corps was called into conference. Always there was that serene, confident, and reassuring air.

Despair had stalked the land, and now there was an avalanche of acronyms. A prostrate nation had asked for action, and now the stream of legislation was bewildering.

First came the moves to shore up the financial system, an emergency banking act, a broadening of Federal Reserve control over the stock market, insurance to protect bank deposits against losses, dollar devaluation to lift prices, Social Security to provide pensions for retired workers, insurance for the unemployed, for the aged and handicapped, plans for generating hydroelectric power.

A stream of ideas was fed into the legislative mill, and a rush of agencies poured out—AAA, CCC, FDIC, NRA, SEC, TVA, WPA. It seemed endless.

The Agricultural Administration was paying farmers to slaughter hogs or to plow under the cotton crop, in the hope of decreasing supplies and raising prices.

The Civilian Conservation Corps was offering the nation's youth the opportunity to work on the land, to build firebreaks, dig ditches, plant trees. A total of 600 airports were built, 100,000 bridges, 500,000 sewers.

The National Recovery Administration, with its Blue Eagle symbol, set minimum wages and maximum hours but permitted industry itself to fix prices and devise rules for competition.

The Works Program was a direct attack on unemployment, putting employable men and women to work in a score of areas. Ten thousand theater people were put to work to produce live theater, old and new. Artists in every medium were engaged at their crafts, and writers at theirs.

The overall program was designed to bail out failing business, put money into empty pockets, restore economic health. There were those who saw it as a daring adventure in social and economic welfare, and there were reversals at the Supreme Court level. Conservatives denounced the whole process, and no fewer than twelve New Deal statutes were voided on the grounds they invaded states' rights.

Though it took massive defense production with the threat of war to finally solve the basic problem of unemployment, it was clear that the federal government had assumed responsibility for the economic well-being of the citizenry. In its way, the New Deal had restored the country's faith in its future.

The Arts in the Service of National Recovery

The spirit of optimistic struggle that characterized the recovery years affected particularly the artists and writers of America. Because they were among those most severely affected by the devastation of the Depression, they received unusual support from the government, which created projects to give them work on various public arts projects. Most turned their energies to the problems of bolstering national energies to face and master their massive crises. *One Third of a Nation*, a play about housing, was staged by the Federal Theatre Project, a government-subsidized production, during the thirties. *Composition* by Stuart Davis (1935) shows a relationship between art and American industry and agriculture.

This land is your land
This land is my land
From California to the New York Island
From the redwood forest
To the gulfstream waters
This land was made for you and me.

WOODY GUTHRIE

59. The Growing Shadow of War

Appeasement had failed, and in 1939 Germany, under the rule of Adolf Hitler and his Nazi party, marched on Poland. World War II was under way. Within two years the German armies overran nearly all of Europe.

As France fell before the Germans and England was subjected to merciless blitz bombing by the Luftwaffe, America watched in stunned disbelief. For months there was violent debate on the extent to which this country should become involved.

There were those who felt the struggle was none of our concern: let Europe settle its own problems. There were others who felt that Hitler, after he finished off England, would attack us on the way to world domination.

On January 6, 1941, in his annual message to Congress, Roosevelt made his stand. He urged that America become an arsenal of democracy by helping to arm all nations fighting the totalitarian juggernaut. He proposed that all peoples be guaranteed four freedoms: freedom from want, freedom of speech, freedom of worship, and freedom from fear.

It was America's call to the future, a cornerstone for the world to be.

Four days later the lend-lease bill proposed making American war materials available to fighting democracies.

Roosevelt: "Four Freedoms" Speech (January 6, 1941)

To the Congress of the United States:

I address you, the Members of the Seventy-Seventh Congress, at a moment unprecedented in the history of the Union. I use the word "unprecedented" because at no previous time has American security been as seriously threatened from without as it is today. . . .

It is true that prior to 1914 the United States often had been disturbed by events in other Continents. We had even engaged in two wars with European nations and in a number of undeclared wars in the West Indies, in the Mediterranean and in the Pacific for the maintenance of American rights and for the principles of peaceful commerce. In no case, however, had a serious threat been raised against our national safety or our independence.

What I seek to convey is the historic truth that the United States as a nation has at all times maintained opposition to any attempt to lock us in behind an ancient Chinese wall while the procession of civilization went past. Today, thinking of our children and their children, we oppose enforced isolation for ourselves or for any part of the Americas. . . .

Every realist knows that the democratic way of life is at this moment being directly assailed in every part of the world—assailed either by arms, or by secret spreading of poisonous propaganda by those who seek to destroy unity and promote discord in nations still at peace. During sixteen months this assault has blotted out the whole pattern of democratic life in an appalling number of independent nations, great and small. The assailants are still on the march, threatening other nations, great and small.

Therefore, as your President, performing my constitutional duty to "give to the Congress information of the state of the Union," I find it necessary to report that the future and the safety of our country and of our democracy are overwhelmingly involved in events far beyond our borders. . . .

In times like these it is immature—and incidentally untrue—for anybody to brag that an unprepared America, single-handed, and with one hand tied behind its back, can hold off the whole world. . . .

I have recently pointed out how quickly the tempo of modern warfare could bring into our very midst the physical attack which we must expect if the dictator nations win this war. . . .

As long as the aggressor nations maintain the offensive, they—not we—will choose the time and the place and the method of their attack. That is why the future of all American Republics is today in serious danger. That is why this Annual Message to the Congress is unique in our history. That is why every member of the Executive branch of the government and every member of the Congress face great responsibility—and great accountability.

The need of the moment is that our actions and our policy should be devoted primarily—almost exclusively—to meeting this foreign peril. For all our domestic problems are now a part of the great emergency. . . .

Our national policy is this.

First, by an impressive expression of the public will and without regard to partisanship, we are committed to all-inclusive national defense.

Second, by an impressive expression of the public will and without regard to partisanship, we are committed to full support of all those resolute peoples, everywhere, who are resisting aggression and are thereby keeping war away from our Hemisphere. . . .

Third, by an impressive expression of the public will and without regard to partisanship we are committed to the proposition that principles of morality and considerations for our own security will never permit us to acquiesce in a peace dictated by aggressors and sponsored by appeasers. We know that enduring peace cannot be bought at the cost of other people's freedom. . . .

Today, it is abundantly evident that American citizens everywhere are demanding and supporting speedy and complete action in recognition of obvious danger. Therefore, the immediate need is a swift and driving increase in our armament production. . . .

Our most useful and immediate rule is to act as an arsenal for them as well as for ourselves. They do not need man power. They do need billions of dollars worth of the weapons of defense. . . .

The happiness of future generations of Americans may well depend upon how effective and how immediate we can make our aid felt. No one can tell the exact character of the emergency situations that we may be called upon to meet. The Nation's hands must not be tied when the Nation's life is in danger. . . .

There is nothing mysterious about the foundations of a healthy and strong democracy. The basic things expected by our people of their political and economic systems are simple. They are: equality of opportunity for youth and for others; jobs for those who can work; security for those who need it; the ending of special privileges for the few; the preservation of civil liberties for all; the enjoyment of the fruits of scientific progress in a wider and constantly rising standard of living.

These are the simple and basic things that must never be lost sight of in the turmoil and unbelievable complexity of our modern world. The inner and abiding strength of our economic and political systems is dependent upon the degree to which they fulfill these expectations.

Many subjects connected with our social economy call for immediate improvement. As examples: We should bring more citizens under the coverage of old age pensions and unemployment insurance. We should widen the opportunities for adequate medical care. We should plan a better system by which persons deserving or needing gainful employment may obtain it.

I have called for personal sacrifice. I am assured of the willingness of almost all Americans to respond to that call. . . .

In the future days, which we seek to make secure, we look forward to a world founded upon four essential human freedoms.

Four Freedoms stamp

The first is freedom of speech and expression—everywhere in the world.

The second is freedom of every person to worship God in his own way—everywhere in the world.

The third is freedom from want—which, translated into world terms, means economic understandings which will secure to every nation a healthy peace time life for its inhabitants—everywhere in the world.

The fourth is freedom from fear—which, translated into world terms, means a worldwide reduction of armaments to such a point and in such a

Freedom of Speech

Artist Norman Rockwell
painted this set of illustrations
to dramatize the Four Freedoms.

Freedom of Worship

190

thorough fashion that no nation will be in a position to commit an act of physical aggression against any neighbor—anywhere in the world.

This nation has placed its destiny in the hands and heads and hearts of its millions of free men and women; and its faith in freedom under the guidance of God. Freedom means the supremacy of human rights everywhere. Our support goes to those who struggle to gain those rights or keep them. Our strength is in our unity of purpose.

To that high concept there can be no end save victory.

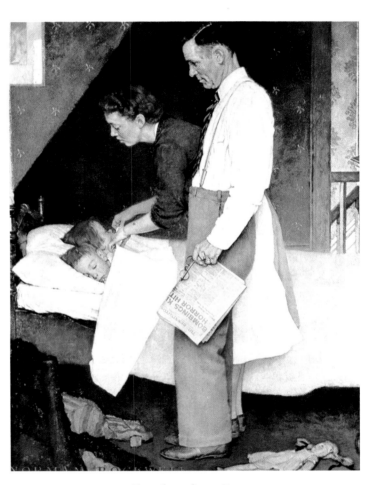

Freedom from Fear

Freedom from Want

60. Remember Pearl Harbor

While the Japanese attack at Pearl Harbor on December 7, 1941, crippled the U.S. Navy, it also served to arouse the total energy of the nation to the demands of war.

No longer was the conflict confined to the approaches to Moscow, the jungles of Indochina, or the sea lanes of the Mediterranean and the Atlantic. The Japanese had brought the war to our doorstep. Carrier-based Japanese planes hitting the American Pacific fleet anchored at Pearl Harbor in Hawaii sank 19 vessels, destroyed 188 planes, and killed 2,280 men. It was a Sunday morning nightmare, and it took weeks for the public to absorb it. Nothing comparable had ever been perpetrated before, especially at a time when negotiations were taking place.

On the following day the President, addressing a joint meeting of the Congress, asked for a declaration of war.

For five years the nation had mustered its strength, pouring out armament to help its friends. Now the Japanese had struck at the jugular and had provoked a sleeping giant. All talk of isolationism ceased; peace parties folded. We had been wounded, but not fatally. A new and lofty level of national purpose was needed. United, our strength and resources would now be directed to one objective. We were inspired as never before. Victory was the only answer.

The **USS _Shaw_** explodes in a shower of flame, smoke, and debris during the Japanese raid on Pearl Harbor.

President Franklin D. Roosevelt signs the declaration of war against Japan on December 8, 1941.

President Roosevelt Asks for War Against Japan
(December 8, 1941)

Yesterday, December 7, 1941—a date which will live in infamy—the United States of America was suddenly and deliberately attacked by naval and air forces of the Empire of Japan.

The United States was at peace with that nation and, at the solicitation of Japan, was still in conversation with its Government and its Emperor looking toward the maintenance of peace in the Pacific. Indeed, one hour after Japanese air squadrons had commenced bombing in Oahu, the Japanese Ambassador to the United States and his colleague delivered to the Secretary of State a formal reply to a recent American message. While this reply stated that it seemed useless to continue the existing diplomatic negotiations, it contained no threat or hint of war or armed attack.

It will be recorded that the distance of Hawaii from Japan makes it obvious that the attack was deliberately planned many days or even weeks ago. During the intervening time the Japanese Government has deliberately sought to deceive the United States by false statements and expressions of hope for continued peace.

193

The **USS *Arizona* memorial** in Pearl Harbor stands as a reminder of the events of December 7, 1941.

The attack yesterday on the Hawaiian Islands has caused severe damage to American naval and military forces. Very many American lives have been lost. In addition American ships have been reported torpedoed on the high seas between San Francisco and Honolulu.

Yesterday the Japanese Government also launched an attack against Malaya. Last night Japanese forces attacked Hong Kong. Last night Japanese forces attacked the Philippine Islands. Last night the Japanese attacked Wake Island. This morning the Japanese attacked Midway Island.

Japan has, therefore, undertaken a surprise offensive extending throughout the Pacific area. The facts of yesterday speak for themselves. The people of the United States have already formed their opinions and well understand the implications to the very life and safety of our nation.

As Commander-in-Chief of the Army and Navy, I have directed that all measures be taken for our defense.

Always will we remember the character of the onslaught against us.

No matter how long it may take us to overcome this premeditated invasion, the American people in their righteous might will win through to absolute victory.

I believe I interpret the will of the Congress and of the people when I assert that we will not only defend ourselves to the uttermost but will make very certain that this form of treachery shall never endanger us again.

Hostilities exist. There is no blinking out the fact that our people, our territory and our interests are in grave danger.

With confidence in our armed forces—with the unbounded determination of our people—we will gain the inevitable triumph—so help us God.

I ask that the Congress declare that since the unprovoked and dastardly attack by Japan on Sunday, December seventh, a state of war has existed between the United States and the Japanese Empire.

61. The Nation's Leaders in War

In World War II, as in major wars of the past, America produced the quality of leadership it needed in a crisis. This was a coalition war, conducted on a global scale, and from the very start it demanded broad-scale thinking to cope with the enormous problems in manpower, supply, logistics, and strategy. The scope of military planning and the needs of recruitment and supply had no precedent in all the annals of warfare.

Pearl Harbor might have been a knockout blow for America, but when the initial shock was over, when the nightmare had dissipated, when the size of the challenge had been defined, a corps of leaders emerged. They were supported by the firm resolution that could only spell victory.

Here were men of distinct personality. Some were colorful and dynamic, inclined to flamboyant display of braid and other accouterments of command; others were quiet and retiring. Some were congenial and self-confident; others were remote and austere. Some had a flair for strategy with modern weaponry; others were mainly managers of people, highly skilled at reconciling differences. Some were field commanders, always ready to lead the charge; others, whose talents rested in training and supply, never set foot on a battlefield. All of them fitted into the massive team effort.

Whether with their broad grins, their braided caps, their corncob pipes, or their pearl-handled pistols, each in his own fashion spurred all of us—in and out of uniform—to the national effort. They found their way into national consciousness, grew large as legend, and remain in our memory.

General Dwight David Eisenhower

General Dwight David Eisenhower (1890–1969), a genial but magnetic Midwesterner from Kansas, possessed a remarkable talent for arbitration that enabled him to forge the Allied military commanders into a fighting team. To the nation he was "Ike," whether it was during his term as Supreme Allied Commander in Western Europe, or chief of staff, or even when he became president of Columbia University on his retirement from the Army. In 1952 he was elected the thirty-fourth President of the United States. During the war his special ability to inspire confidence was an essential element in his charisma. After the war, his image in the White House brought a sense of stability to a nation emerging from a long period of testing.

General Douglas MacArthur

General Douglas MacArthur (1880–1964) was a military leader who symbolized America's resilience in World War II. Raised in an Army family, he was a West Point graduate and had served in World War I. In the early weeks of World War II he had held Corregidor against the Japanese until ordered to retreat to Australia. But he carried out his promise to return to the Philippines, and it was MacArthur, as Supreme Commander of the Allied Forces in the South Pacific, who accepted the surrender of Japan on September 8, 1945. For millions of Americans, in and out of uniform, he was the top American military hero; and the heavily braided cap, corncob pipe, and sunglasses were his special trademarks. With a voice that was made for command and a flair for the ringing phrase, he helped America muster its energies.

General George Smith Patton, Jr.

General George Smith Patton, Jr. (1885–1945), was a larger-than-life image of the fighting general. After graduating from West Point in 1909, he served in World War I and was wounded while commanding a tank brigade in France. In World War II Patton fought in North Africa, Sicily, and France. In March 1945 he raced with his Third Army troops across southern Germany and into Czechoslovakia. Patton, with his riding breeches and pearl-handled revolvers, with his talents as a military strategist, became a legend even before he was fatally injured in an automobile accident in Germany at the close of the war.

Admiral William Frederick Halsey

Admiral William Frederick Halsey (1882–1959)—better known under the nickname "Bull"—gained fame as head of the U.S. Third Fleet in the Pacific in World War II. In October 1944, he directed naval action in the Philippines that led to the bombardment of Japan. Though he was a Navy man, bred in the tradition of ship against ship, Halsey recognized the full value of air power based on carriers, and this was his trump card. It was on his flagship, the USS *Missouri*, that the Japanese surrender was signed. "Bull" Halsey rests securely in the pantheon of naval heroes along with John Paul Jones, Stephen Decatur, and Oliver Hazard Perry.

Admiral Ernest Joseph King

Admiral Ernest Joseph King (1878–1956) was a master of naval logistics. He was old Navy, having been commissioned in 1903. In 1941, shortly after Pearl Harbor, he was named commander in chief of the U.S. Fleet, and then chief of naval operations, a unique combination of authority in the hands of one man. It was King strategy that helped destroy the Japanese naval power in the Pacific. King's attention was focused on the area rather than the European theater, which he believed called for land and air forces. Though he was starchy, exacting, and remote, he had the authentic aura of a Navy hero.

Admiral Chester William Nimitz

Admiral Chester William Nimitz (1885–1966) was a brilliant, highly respected, and somewhat reserved Navy officer. He spent many of his early years in the submarine service. Shortly after Pearl Harbor, Nimitz was put in command of the U.S. Pacific Fleet. The subsequent "island hopping" plan of Pacific strategy was, in effect, a melding of his own ideas with the overall plans of Admiral King and General MacArthur. At first Nimitz had to wait for naval construction to catch up, but by war's end he commanded a fleet of over 6,250 vessels.

General Jonathan Mayhew Wainwright

General Jonathan Mayhew Wainwright (1883–1953) was placed in command of the Philippine forces when General MacArthur was ordered to Australia. He bore the responsibility of defending Corregidor and Bataan from March to May 1942, when surrender to the Japanese took place. General Wainwright was a captive of the Japanese until he was released from a Manchurian prison camp in time to witness the Japanese surrender on Tokyo Bay. The wasted figure of this hero-soldier who had endured so much in the war against Japan caught the eye of all who saw pictures of the surrender ceremony. It was a sight to touch the heart of every American. Wainwright became one of the unforgettables of World War II.

General George Catlett Marshall

General George Catlett Marshall (1880–1959) served his nation in two capacities. In the military, he was chief of staff from 1939 to 1945, when he directed much of the overall war strategy, and was secretary of defense from 1950 to 1951. Marshall served also as secretary of state from 1947 to 1949. He possessed a broad feel for logistics, and during the war he helped, through recruitment, to build an 8-million-man Army and to supervise the development of new arms. He was able, even under stress, to get the job done. As secretary of state, Marshall formulated the so-called Marshall Plan for European economic recovery. In 1953 he was awarded the Nobel Peace Prize, an unusual honor for a professional soldier.

General Omar Nelson Bradley

General Omar Nelson Bradley (1893–1981) commanded the U.S. First Army in the bitter fighting at Utah and Omaha beaches during the Normandy invasion on June 6, 1944. In one area, German machine guns were only two hundred yards from the water's edge. It was Bradley's men who broke through the German lines on July 24, and it was Bradley's units that crossed the Rhine at Remagen on March 7, 1945, to close out the final days of fighting. An efficient, reticent man whose views carried weight, Omar Bradley was affectionately referred to as the "GI's general."

General Henry Harley "Hap" Arnold

General Henry Harley "Hap" Arnold (1886–1950) was the link that connected the Wright brothers with the U.S. Air Force in World War II. Arnold had learned how to fly from pioneer Orville Wright himself, and he became the tireless advocate of air power to implement strategy. When, in 1938, Arnold became Army Air Corps chief, he put into development his plan for airplane manufacturing and pilot training. He believed in the value of big bomber attacks, and by the end of the war the strike power of the U.S. air arm was the greatest in military history. "Hap" Arnold needs no more fitting tribute.

62. The Images of War

Suddenly, World War II was everywhere, and never quite as remote as those maps might indicate. The combat reached out from the isolated islands of the South Pacific to the deserts of North Africa, from the mountain passes of Italy to the beaches of France. There was action on the North and South Atlantic and the remote seas of the South Pacific. Pictures and news stories and voices from the remote places came to us on the hour, as newspapers and radio conveyed minute-by-minute reports. In the movie theaters the newsreels unfolded a vision of belching guns, darting jeeps, men in camouflage, battlecraft bursting in fury, airplanes zooming to engage the enemy.

In all of history no war had been so closely observed or so thoroughly reported. The names of the reporters and the radio commentators became as well known as those of the generals—Ernie Pyle, Edward R. Murrow, Bob Considine, Quentin Reynolds, Gabriel Heatter, Bill Mauldin, Floyd Gibbons, William Shirer. They wrote and spoke of what they saw, and we were part of the scene.

It is not enough to fight. It is the spirit which we bring to the fight that decides the issue. It is morale that wins the victory.

GEORGE C. MARSHALL

USS *Yorktown* under Japanese attack during the Battle of Midway, June 1942.

USS *Greer* in heavy seas on convoy duty in the North Atlantic, June 1943.

First U.S. Army men **crossing the bridge over the Rhine at Remagen,** Germany, March 1945.

USS Coast Guard landing craft at the Normandy landings, D-Day, June 1944.

An old German woman, standing in despair between advancing U.S. Seventh Army troops, surveys the wreckage of her home in Bensheim, Germany, March 1945.

The Iwo Jima flag raising, a dramatic symbol of struggle and victory, marked the climax of a grueling operation in the Pacific theater during the final months of World War II. The initial assault on the island, site of an important Japanese air base, took place on February 19, 1945. Iwo Jima was taken by March 16, and the flag was planted on top of the island's Mount Surabachi. The Japanese lost over 20,000 men; the United States 4,590.

"Nuts!"

This was General Anthony C. McAuliffe's defiant reply to German demands for surrender of the 101st Airborne Division during the Battle of Bastogne, December 23, 1944. McAuliffe's 101st liked to refer to themselves as the "battered bastards of Bastogne."

Bringing Down the Captain's Body

In this war I have known a lot of officers who were loved and respected by the soldiers under them. But never have I crossed the trail of any man as beloved as Captain Henry T. Waskow, of Belton, Texas.

Captain Waskow was a company commander in the Thirty-sixth Division. He had led his company since long before it left the States. He was very young, only in his middle twenties, but he carried in him a sincerity and a gentleness that made people want to be guided by him.

"After my father, he came next," a sergeant told me.

"He always looked after us," a soldier said. "He'd go to bat for us every time."

"I've never known him to do anything unfair," another said.

I was at the foot of the mule trail the night they brought Captain Waskow down. The moon was nearly full, and you could see far up the trail, and even partway across the valley below.

Dead men had been coming down the mountain all evening, lashed onto the backs of mules. They came lying belly-down across the wooden packsaddles, their heads hanging down on one side, their stiffened legs sticking out awkwardly from the other, bobbing up and down as the mules walked.

The Italian mule skinners were afraid to walk beside dead men, so Americans had to lead the mules down that night. Even the Americans were reluctant to unlash and lift off the bodies when they got to the bottom, so an officer had to do it himself and ask others to help.

I don't know who that first one was. You feel small in the presence of dead men, and you don't ask silly questions.

They slid him down from the mule, and stood him on his feet for a moment. In the half-light he might have been merely a sick man standing there leaning on the others. Then they laid him on the ground in the shadow of the stone wall alongside the road. We left him there beside the road, that first one, and we all went back into the cowshed and sat on water cans or lay on the straw, waiting for the next batch of mules.

Somebody said the dead soldier had been dead for four days and then nobody said anything more about it. We talked soldier talk for an hour or more; the dead man lay all alone, outside in the shadow of the wall.

Then a soldier came into the cowshed and said there were some more bodies outside. We went out into the road. Four mules stood there in the moonlight, in the road where the trail came down off the mountain. The soldiers who led them stood there waiting.

"This one is Captain Waskow," one of them said quietly.

Two men unlashed his body from the mule and lifted it off and laid it in the shadow beside the stone wall. Other men took the other bodies off. Finally, there were five lying end to end in a long row. You don't cover up dead men in the combat zones. They just lie there in the shadows until somebody comes after them.

The unburdened mules moved off to their olive grove. The men in the road seemed reluctant to leave. They stood around, and gradually I could sense them moving, one by one, close to Captain Waskow's body. Not so much to look, I think, as to say something in finality to him and to themselves. I stood close by and I could hear.

One soldier came and looked down, and he said out loud, "God damn it!"

That's all he said, and then he walked away.

Another one came, and he said, "God damn it to hell anyway!" He looked down for a few last moments and then turned and left.

Another man came. I think he was an officer. It was hard to tell officers from men in the dim light, for everybody was bearded and grimy. The man looked down into the dead captain's face and then spoke directly to him, as though he were alive, "I'm sorry, old man."

Then a soldier came and stood beside the officer and bent over, and he too spoke to his dead captain, not in a whisper but awfully tenderly, and he said, "I sure am sorry, sir."

Then the first man squatted down, and he reached down and took the captain's hand, and he sat there for a full five minutes holding the dead hand in his own and looking intently into the dead face. And he never uttered a sound all the time he sat there.

Finally he put the hand down. He reached over and gently straightened the points of the captain's shirt collar, and then he sort of rearranged the tattered edges of the uniform around the wound, and then he got up and walked away down the road in the moonlight, all alone.

The rest of us went back into the cowshed, leaving the five dead men lying in a line end to end in the shadow of the low stone wall. We lay down on the straw in the cowshed, and pretty soon we were all asleep.

ERNIE PYLE, *Brave Men*
(Henry Holt & Co., 1944)

"Kilroy was here."

This catchphrase spread throughout the world in 1945, wherever the American GI had set his foot. Kilroy is a kind of abstract conglomerate of all the gagsters in the U.S. Army. The phrase was scribbled on streets, billboards, and latrines throughout the world.

63. Patriotism on the Home Front

Rosie the Riveter, as Norman Rockwell captures her for *The Saturday Evening Post* in 1943.

Total war called for total effort, with every citizen, in and out of uniform, involved. This was patriotism at work.

This massive drive inevitably imposed its own imprint on the national lifestyle, as a nation of civilians was transformed into a nation of war workers.

Following a decade of depression, unemployment vanished. Women of all ages were needed to replace the men in uniform. Dressed in slacks and kerchiefs, equipped with lunch pails, they became welders and lathe operators, cleaned blast furnaces and greased locomotives. Some went off to war; others trained to become pilots, engineers, and chemists. Sex and race barriers crumbled before the need for manpower or womanpower. Rosie the Riveter became a national heroine.

The atmosphere was marked by cooperation and concern. Posters warned against loose talk. White-helmeted civilian defense wardens patrolled the neighborhoods; scrap drives brought willing responses; bond rallies went over the top. White-collar workers became blue-collar workers in their spare hours.

War savings stamps and war bonds found eager investors, and victory gardens graced millions of back yards and open lots. Gold-star flags, to mark a home that had sustained loss, began to appear.

Under the regulated economy, with controls on manpower, raw materials, labor, and prices, 1945 production was double that of 1939. Patriotism had found many expressions.

A group of women workers, under the eye of supervisors, turn out 37mm antitank shells at a Midwestern munitions plant.

Boy Scouts in Detroit, Michigan,
in July 1942, carry a solid line of
American flags at their meeting.

**Schoolchildren in San Juan Bautista,
California, parade** May 1942,
with the scrap metal they have collected
for the war effort.

The homecoming G.I. It was up to artist Norman Rockwell, whose illustrations so often caught the enchanted moment in American life, to record the return of the soldier boy gone to war.

64. "Praise the Lord and Pass the Ammunition"

As bombs from Japanese planes poured down on the USS *New Orleans*, anchored at Pearl Harbor on that Sunday morning, December 7, 1941, sailors at battle stations manned the cruiser's guns to answer the attack.

In that hour of trial a unique battle cry was born: "Praise the Lord and pass the ammunition!" It is credited to Chaplain Howell M. Forgy, who called out encouragement to his fighting shipmates.

In 1942, composer Frank Loesser, writer of many hit tunes and several Broadway shows, did a musical version of Forgy's stirring phrase that became extremely popular.

65. "Off We Go into the Wild Blue Yonder"

The official song of the U.S. Air Force, sometimes familiarly called "Wild Blue Yonder," was written by Robert McArthur Crawford, who offered it as an entry in a 1939 magazine competition to select an anthem for the Army Air Corps. The entry won the thousand-dollar first prize, and Major General Henry H. Arnold, chief of the Army Air Corps, approved "The Army Air Corps Song" as official for that service. Crawford, who flew in various capacities throughout the war, died in his native Alaska in 1961.

In 1947 the Army Air Corps became a separate service, the United States Air Force, and two years later a new title and appropriate new words were developed for the old song.

66. "Duty, Honor, Country"

Douglas MacArthur was the very model of a career military officer during the critical years when the armed forces spelled survival. He knew how to give orders—he had trouble taking them.

During World War II the name Douglas MacArthur symbolized the American fighting spirit. In the Pacific theater he had led the resistance against the Japanese invasion, the island-to-island counteroffensive, the dramatic return to the Philippines, and on September 2, 1945, it was MacArthur who accepted the Japanese surrender on board the USS *Missouri*.

In 1950, after the North Koreans invaded South Korea, MacArthur, now seventy, was placed in command of the United Nations forces opposing them. When the Chinese sent in two hundred thousand troops to aid the North Koreans, MacArthur wanted to make countermoves, including bombing the Chinese mainland. The bomb-China plan was vetoed by President Truman, and MacArthur, who decided to make public his disagreement with Washington, was relieved of his command. On April 19, 1951, MacArthur appeared before a joint session of the Congress to explain his stand. The "old soldier" has retained a firm place in the hearts of his countrymen.

On October 20, 1944, **General Douglas MacArthur** waded ashore on the island of Leyte to start the liberation of the Philippines. Splashing ashore from a landing craft, the general announced: "People of the Philippines, I have returned."

In May 1962 more than a decade after he had retired from active service with almost sixty years in the Army, General MacArthur returned to West Point to deliver a commencement address.

It was a moment of special significance for MacArthur, and he rose to the occasion.

For more than a century and a half the Point had been the home of the U.S. Military Academy. MacArthur was among the many military heroes who had received early training there and had left a mark on the nation's history. From 1919 to 1922, MacArthur had served as superintendent of the Point.

The eighty-two-year-old MacArthur delivered a memorable statement about the nature of American patriotism. His emphasis on duty, honor, and country summarized the code of the officer in the U.S. Army, but it also carried a message to every American citizen.

The general died in 1964, and his memory is appropriately marked by a statue on the grounds of his beloved West Point.

MacArthur at West Point (May 12, 1962)

As I was leaving the hotel this morning, a doorman asked me, "Where are you headed for, General?" And when I replied, "West Point," he remarked, "Beautiful place. Have you ever been there before?"

No human being could fail to be deeply moved by such a tribute as this. Coming from a profession I have served so long, and a people I have loved so well, it fills me with an emotion I cannot express. But this award is not intended primarily to honor a personality, but to symbolize a great moral code—the code of conduct and chivalry of those who guard this beloved land of culture and ancient descent. That is the meaning of this medallion. For all ages and for all time, it is an expression of the ethics of the American soldier. That I should be integrated in this way with so noble an ideal arouses a sense of pride and yet of humility which will be with me always. . . .

Duty-Honor-Country. Those three hallowed words reverently dictate what you ought to be, what you can be, what you will be. They are your rallying points; to build courage when courage seems to fail; to regain faith when there seems to be little cause for faith; to create hope when hope becomes forlorn. Unhappily, I possess neither that eloquence of diction, that poetry of imagination, nor that brilliance of metaphor to tell you all that they mean. The unbelievers will say they are but words, but a slogan, but a flamboyant phrase. Every pedant, every demagogue, every cynic, every hypocrite, every trouble-maker, and, I am sorry to say, some others of an entirely different character, will try to downgrade them even to the extent of mockery and ridicule.

But these are some of the things they do. They build your basic character; they mold you for your future roles as custodians of the nation's defense; they make you strong enough to know when you are weak, and brave enough to face yourself when you are afraid. They teach you to be proud and unbending in honest failure, but humble and gentle in success; not to substitute words for actions, not to seek the path of comfort, but to face the stress and spur of difficulty and challenge; to learn to stand up in the storm but to have compassion on those who fail; to master yourself before you seek to master others; to have a heart that is clean, a goal that is high; to learn to laugh yet never forget how to weep; to reach into the future yet never neglect the past; to be serious yet never to take yourself too seriously; to be modest so that you will remember the simplicity of true greatness, the open mind of true wisdom, the meekness of true strength. They give you a temper of the will, a quality of the imagination, a vigor of the emotions, a freshness of the deep springs of life, a temperamental predominance of courage over timidity, an appetite for adventure over love of

**Cadets marching at West
Point Military Academy**
carry the colors proudly.

210

ease. They create in your heart the sense of wonder, the unfailing hope of what next, and the joy and inspiration of life. They teach you in this way to be an officer and a gentleman.

And what sort of soldiers are those you are to lead? Are they reliable, are they brave, are they capable of victory? Their story is known to all of you; it is the story of the American man-at-arms. My estimate of him was formed on the battlefield many years ago, and has never changed. I regarded him then as I regard him now—as one of the world's noblest figures, not only as one of the finest military characters, but also as one of the most stainless. His name and fame are the birthright of every American citizen. In his youth and strength, his love and loyalty, he gave all that mortality can give. He needs no eulogy from me or from any other man. He has written his own history and written it in red on his enemy's breast. But when I think of his patience under adversity, of his courage under fire, and of his modesty in victory, I am filled with an emotion of admiration I cannot put into words. He belongs to history as furnishing one of the greatest examples of successful patriotism; he belongs to posterity as the instructor of future generations in the principles of liberty and freedom; he belongs to the present, to us, by his virtues and by his achievements. In twenty campaigns, on a hundred battlefields, around a thousand campfires, I have witnessed that enduring fortitude, that patriotic self-abnegation, and that invincible determination which have carved his status in the hearts of his people. From one end of the world to the other he has drained deep the chalice of courage.

As I listened to those songs of the glee club, in memory's eye I could see those staggering columns of the First World War, bending under soggy packs, on many a weary march from dripping dusk to drizzling dawn, slogging ankle deep through the mire of shell-shocked roads, to form grimly for the attack, blue-lipped, covered with sludge and mud, chilled by the wind and rain, driving home to their objective, and, for many, to the judgment seat of God. I do not know the dignity of their birth but I do know the glory of their death. They died unquestioning, uncomplaining, with faith in their hearts, and on their lips the hope that we would go on to victory. Always for them—Duty-Honor-Country; always their blood and sweat and tears as we sought the way and the light and the truth.

And twenty years after, on the other side of the globe, again the filth of murky foxholes, the stench of ghostly trenches, the slime of dripping dugouts; those broiling suns of relentless heat, those torrential rains of devastating storm, the loneliness and utter desolation of jungle trails, the bitterness of long separation from those they loved and cherished, the deadly pestilence of tropical disease, the horror of stricken areas of war; their resolute and determined defense, their swift and sure attack, their indomitable purpose, their complete and decisive victory—always victory—always through the bloody haze of their last reverberating shot, the vision of gaunt, ghastly men reverently following your password of Duty-Honor-Country.

You now face a new world—a world of change. The thrust into outer space of the satellites, spheres and missiles marked the beginning of another epoch in the long story of mankind—the chapter of the space age. In the five or more billions of years the scientists tell us it has taken to form the earth, in the three or more billion years of development of the human race, there has never been a greater, a more abrupt or staggering evolution. We deal now not with things of this world alone, but with the illimitable distance and as yet unfathomed mysteries of the universe. We are reaching out for a new and boundless frontier. We speak in strange terms: of harnessing the cosmic energy; of making winds and tides work for us; of creating unheard-of synthetic materials to supplement or even replace our old standard basics; of purifying sea water for our drink; of mining ocean floors for new fields of wealth and food; of disease preventatives to expand life into the hundreds of years; of controlling the weather for a more equitable distribution of heat and cold, of rain and shine; of space ships to the moon; of the primary target in war, no longer limited to the

Duty-Honor-Country. Those three hallowed words reverently dictate what you ought to be, what you can be, what you will be.

DOUGLAS MACARTHUR,
at West Point,
May 12, 1962

211

armed forces of an enemy, but instead to include his civil populations; of ultimate conflict between a united human race and the sinister forces of some other planetary galaxy; of such dreams and fantasies as to make life the most exciting of all time.

And through all this welter of change and development, your mission remains fixed, determined, inviolable—it is to win our wars. Everything else in your professional career is but a corollary to this vital dedication. All other public purposes, all other public projects, all other public needs, great or small, will find others for their accomplishment; but you are the ones who are trained to fight; yours is the profession of arms—the will to win, the sure knowledge that in war there is no substitute for victory; that if you lose, the nation will be destroyed; that the very obsession of your public service must be Duty-Honor-Country. Others will debate the controversial issues, national and international, which divide our minds; but serene, calm, aloof, you stand as the nation's war guardian, as guard from the raging tides of international conflict; as its gladiator in the arena of battle. For a century and a half, you have defended, guarded, and protected its hallowed traditions of liberty and freedom, of right and justice. Let civilian voices argue the merits or demerits of our processes of government; whether our strength is being sapped by deficit financing, indulged in too long; by federal paternalism grown too mighty; by power groups grown too arrogant; by politics grown too corrupt; by crime grown too rampant; by morals grown too low; by taxes grown too high; by extremists grown too violent; whether our personal liberties are as thorough and complete as they should be. These great national problems are not for your professional participation or military solution. Your guidepost stands out like a tenfold beacon in the night—Duty-Honor-Country.

You are the leaven which binds together the entire fabric of our national system of defense. From your ranks come the great captains who hold the nation's destiny in their hands the moment the war tocsin sounds. The Long Gray Line has never failed us. Were you to do so, a million ghosts in olive drab, in brown khaki, in blue and gray, would rise from their white crosses thundering those magic words—Duty-Honor-Country.

This does not mean that you are war mongers. On the contrary, the soldier, above all other people, prays for peace, for he must suffer and bear the deepest wounds and scars of war. But always in our ears rings the ominous words of Plato, that wisest of all philosophers, "Only the dead have seen the end of war."

The shadows are lengthening for me. The twilight is here. My days of old have vanished tone and tint; they have gone glimmering through the dreams of things that were. Their memory is one of wondrous beauty, watered by tears, and coaxed and caressed by the smiles of yesterday. I listen vainly, but with thirsty ear, for the witching melody of faint bugles blowing reveille, of far drums beating the long roll. In my dreams I hear again the crash of guns, the rattle of musketry, the strange mournful mutter of the battlefield. But in the evening of my memory, always I come back to West Point. Always there echoes and re-echoes in my ears—Duty-Honor-Country.

Today marks my final roll call with you. But I want you to know that when I cross the river my last conscious thoughts will be of the Corps—and the Corps—and the Corps.

I bid you farewell.

Opposite page:
This **statue of General MacArthur** on the grounds at West Point commemorates his stirring speech at commencement on May 12, 1962.

67. Eloquence in the Service of Patriotism: Stevenson

Adlai Ewing Stevenson, grandson of a former U.S. Vice-President, governor of Illinois, newspaper editor, and Chicago lawyer, had an enormous gift of words. He had done much groundwork on the founding of the United Nations and had served in the administration of Franklin D. Roosevelt. In 1952, and again in 1956, Stevenson opposed Dwight Eisenhower for the presidency and was defeated both times, his fluency and wit lost in the wave of Eisenhower's popularity. In 1961 President John Kennedy named him special ambassador to the United Nations. Stevenson died in London in July 1965, but his patriotic eloquence still echoes in the hearts of Americans.

The Words of Adlai E. Stevenson

What do we mean by patriotism in the context of our times? . . . A patriotism that puts country ahead of self; a patriotism which is not short, frenzied outbursts of emotion, but the tranquil and steady dedication of a lifetime. There are words that are easy to utter, but this is a mighty assignment. For it is often easier to fight for principles than to live up to them. . . .

When an American says that he loves his country, he means not only that he loves the New England hills, the prairies glistening in the sun, the wide and rising plains, the great mountains, and the sea. He means that he loves an inner air, an inner light in which freedom lives and in which a man can draw the breath of self-respect.

Speech, New York City, August 27, 1952

Let us present once more the true face of America—warm and modest and friendly, dedicated to the welfare of all mankind, and demanding nothing except a chance for all to live and let live, to grow and govern as they wish, free from interference, free from intimidation, free from fear.

Speech, 1955

Government [in a democracy] cannot be stronger or more tough-minded than its people. It cannot be more inflexibly committed to the task than they. It cannot be wiser than the people.

Speech, Chicago, September 29, 1952

The art of government has grown from its seeds in the tiny city-states of Greece to become the political mode of half the world. So let us dream of a world in which all states, great and small, work together for the peaceful flowering of the republic of man.

Speech, Harvard University, June 17, 1965

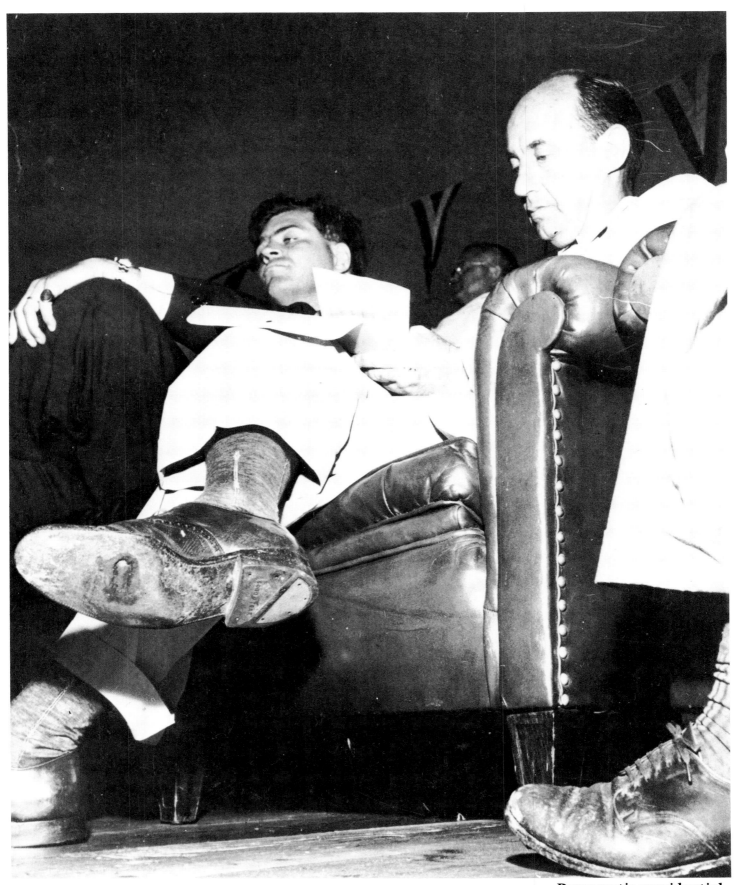

Democratic presidential candidate Adlai Stevenson bares a worn shoe sole to his Labor Day audience in Flint, Michigan, during the 1952 campaign. The picture helped endear Stevenson to millions.

68. How Shall We Use Our Power?: Eisenhower

Almost 34 million Americans voted for Dwight David Eisenhower when he ran for the presidency on the Republican ticket in 1952. It was the greatest vote ever cast for a presidential candidate in history, and it was an expression of the nation's admiration and gratitude for his efforts in World War II. For the first time in seventy-six years, a soldier President occupied the White House.

Without any political experience, Eisenhower, elected on a surge of personal popularity, brought a feeling of stability and confidence to the presidency. He favored strong national defense and aid to America's allies.

Near the end of his second term in office, President Eisenhower delivered a warning to the American people. In the growing advances of technology, combined with the growing defense requirements, the President foresaw a chance that the so-called military establishment might "exert an improper influence on the formation and conduct of national policy." It was significant since Eisenhower himself had emerged from the military.

Dwight D. Eisenhower: Farewell Address (January 17, 1961)

My Fellow Americans:

Three days from now, after half a century in the service of our country, I shall lay down the responsibilities of office as, in traditional and solemn ceremony, the authority of the Presidency is vested in my successor. . . .

We now stand ten years past the midpoint of a century that has witnessed four major wars among great nations. Three of them involved our own country. Despite these holocausts America is today the strongest, the most influential and most productive nation in the world. Understandably proud of this preeminence we realize that America's leadership and prestige depend, not merely upon our unmatched material progress, riches and military strength, but on how we use our power in the interests of world peace and human betterment.

Throughout America's adventure in free government, our basic purposes have been to keep the peace; to foster progress in human achievement, and to enhance liberty, dignity and integrity among people and among nations. To strive for less would be unworthy of a free and religious people. Any failure traceable to arrogance, or our lack of comprehension or readiness to sacrifice would inflict upon us grievous hurt both at home and abroad.

Progress toward these noble goals is persistently threatened by the conflict now engulfing the world. It commands our whole attention, absorbs our very beings. We face a hostile ideology—global in scope, atheistic in character, ruthless in purpose, and insidious in method. Unhappily the danger it poses promises to be of indefinite duration. To meet it successfully, there is called for, not so much the emotional and transitory sacrifices of crisis, but rather those which enable us to carry forward steadily, surely, and without complaint the burdens of a prolonged and complex struggle—with liberty the stake. Only thus shall we remain, despite every provocation, on our charted course toward permanent peace and human betterment. . . .

A vital element in keeping the peace is our military establishment. Our arms must be might, ready for instant action, so that no potential aggressor may be tempted to risk his own destruction.

**Dwight David
Eisenhower**

Our military organization today bears little relation to that known by any of my predecessors in peacetime, or indeed by the fighting men of World War II or Korea.

Until the latest of our world conflicts, the United States had no armaments industry. American makers of plowshares could, with time and as required, make swords as well. But now we can no longer risk emergency improvisation of national defense; we have been compelled to create a permanent armaments industry of vast proportions. Added to this, three and a half million men and women are directly engaged in the defense establishment. We annually spend on military security more than the net income of all United States corporations.

This conjunction of an immense military establishment and a large arms industry is new in the American experience. The total influence—economic, political, even spiritual—is felt in every city, every statehouse, every office of the federal government. We recognize the imperative need for this development. Yet we must not fail to comprehend its grave implications. Our toil, resources, and livelihood are all involved; so is the very structure of our society.

In the councils of government, we must guard against the acquisition of unwarranted influence, whether sought or unsought, by the military-industrial complex. The potential for the disastrous rise of misplaced power exists and will persist.

We must never let the weight of this combination endanger our liberties or democratic processes. We should take nothing for granted. Only an alert and knowledgeable citizenry can couple the proper meshing of the huge industrial and military machinery of defense with our peaceful methods and goals, so that security and liberty may prosper together.

Akin to, and largely responsible for the sweeping changes in our industrial-military posture, has been the technological revolution during recent decades.

In this revolution, research has become central; it also becomes more formalized, complex, and costly. A steadily increasing share is conducted for, by, or at the direction of, the federal government. . . .

The prospect of domination of the nation's scholars by federal employment, project allocations, and the power of money is ever present—and is gravely to be regarded.

Yet, in holding scientific research and discovery in respect, as we should, we must also be alert to the equal and opposite danger that public policy could itself become the captive of a scientific-technological elite.

It is the task of statesmanship to mold, to balance, and to integrate these and other forces, new and old, within the principles of our democratic system— ever aiming toward the supreme goals of our free society.

Another factor in maintaining balance involves the element of time. As we peer into society's future, we—you and I, and our government—must avoid the impulse to live only for today, plundering, for our own ease and convenience, the precious resources of tomorrow. We cannot mortgage the material assets of our grandchildren without risking the loss also of their political and spiritual heritage. We want democracy to survive for all generations to come, not to become the insolvent phantom of tomorrow.

Down the long lane of the history yet to be written, America knows that this world of ours, ever growing smaller, must avoid becoming a community of dreadful fear and hate, and be, instead, a proud confederation of mutual trust and respect.

Such a confederation must be one of equals. The weakest must come to the conference table with the same confidence as do we, protected as we are by our moral, economic, and military strength. That table, though scarred by many past frustrations, cannot be abandoned for the certain agony of the battlefield.

Disarmament, with mutual honor and confidence, is a continuing imperative. Together we must learn how to compose differences, not with arms, but with intellect and decent purpose. Because this need is so sharp and apparent I confess that I lay down my official responsibilities in this field with a definite sense of disappointment. As one who has witnessed the horror and the lingering sadness of war—as one who knows that another war could utterly destroy this civilization which has been so slowly and painfully built over thousands of years—I wish I could say tonight that a lasting peace is in sight.

Happily, I can say that war has been avoided. Steady progress toward our ultimate goal has been made. But, so much remains to be done. As a private citizen, I shall never cease to do what little I can to help the world advance along that road. . . .

69. The Thousand Days of JFK

The brief presidency of John Fitzgerald Kennedy was still long enough to provide America with renewed faith and to lift American heads a bit higher.

Not since Abraham Lincoln in the dark years of the Civil War had the language of the presidency been instilled with such vision.

President Kennedy once said of Britain's wartime leader, Winston Churchill: "He mobilized the English language and sent it into battle." It was thus with John Kennedy. With his flair for words, he mustered the forces of language to bring the American spirit back into our lives.

Kennedy approached language as an ally; he knew instinctively how to make it work for him and for the country. There was grace and elegance, and force, too, as he molded language into a banner for patriotism. American idealism rose to a new peak.

Kennedy, the youngest man ever to occupy the Oval Office, did not shed his youth and vigor when he sat in the chair of the chief executive. There was candor and wit in him, and he used it effectively in his press conferences and in generating enthusiasm with his public utterances.

In his inaugural masterpiece he declared: "Let the word go forth from this time and place, to friend and foe alike, that the torch has been passed to a new generation of Americans, born in this century, tempered by war, disciplined by

John F. Kennedy is inaugurated as the thirty-fifth President of the United States on January 20, 1961.

a hard and bitter peace, proud of our heritage, and unwilling to witness the slow undoing of those human rights to which this nation has always been committed and to which we are committed today, at home and around the world."

In dedicating the National Wildlife Federation Building in Washington on March 3, 1961, he charged: "It is our task in our time and in our generation to hand down undiminished to those who come after us, as was handed down to us by those who went before, the natural wealth and beauty which is ours."

At the United Nations, on September 25, 1961, he warned: "Unconditional war can no longer lead to unconditional victory. It can no longer serve to settle disputes. It can no longer be of concern to great powers alone. For a nuclear disaster, spread by winds and waters and fear, could well engulf the great and the small, the rich and the poor, the committed and the uncommitted alike. Mankind must put an end to war or war will put an end to mankind."

In a television address on June 12, 1963, he asserted: "Every American ought to have the right to be treated as he would wish to be treated, as one would wish his children to be treated."

At Amherst College on October 26, 1963, President Kennedy said: "I look forward to a great future for America, a future in which our country will match its military strength with our moral restraint, its wealth with our wisdom, its power with our purpose. I look forward to an America which will not be afraid of grace and beauty. . . ."

Kennedy pushed his programs for tax reform, aid to education, medicare, and civil rights. On the foreign front he came to a showdown with the Soviet Union on Cuban missile sites and forced the Russians to back down and dismantle the operation and he resisted Russian efforts to force the Allies out of Berlin.

The day before he was murdered in Dallas, President Kennedy declared: "This is a dangerous and uncertain world . . . no one expects our lives to be easy, not in this decade, not in this century."

In his all too brief hour in the White House, John Kennedy brought us a new respect for ourselves and a fresh appreciation of the American dream.

Ask not what your country can do for you—ask what you can do for your country.

JOHN F. KENNEDY,
Inaugural Address, 1961

John F. Kennedy: Inaugural Address (1961)

Vice-President Johnson, Mr. Speaker, Mr. Chief Justice, President Eisenhower, Vice-President Nixon, President Truman, Reverend Clergy, Fellow Citizens:

We observe today not a victory of a party but a celebration of freedom—symbolizing an end as well as a beginning—signifying renewal as well as change. For I have sworn before you and Almighty God the same solemn oath our forebears prescribed nearly a century and three quarters ago.

The world is very different now. For man holds in his mortal hands the power to abolish all forms of human poverty and all forms of human life. And yet the same revolutionary beliefs for which our forebears fought are still at issue around the globe—the belief that the rights of man come not from the generosity of the state but from the hand of God.

We dare not forget today that we are the heirs of that first revolution. Let the word go forth from this time and place, to friend and foe alike, that the torch has been passed to a new generation of Americans—born in this century, tempered by war, disciplined by a hard and bitter peace, proud of our ancient heritage—and unwilling to witness or permit the slow undoing of those human rights to which this Nation has always been committed, and to which we are committed today at home and around the world.

Let every nation know, whether it wishes us well or ill, that we shall pay any price, bear any burden, meet any hardship, support any friend, oppose any foe to assure the survival and success of liberty.

This much we pledge—and more.

To those old allies whose cultural and spiritual origins we share, we pledge the loyalty of faithful friends. United, there is little we cannot do in a host of cooperative ventures. Divided, there is little we can do—for we dare not meet a powerful challenge at odds and split asunder.

To those new states whom we welcome to the ranks of the free, we pledge our word that one form of colonial control shall not have passed away merely to be replaced by a far more iron tyranny. We shall not always expect to find them supporting our view. But we shall always hope to find them strongly supporting their own freedom—and to remember that, in the past, those who foolishly sought power by riding the back of the tiger ended up inside.

To those peoples in the huts and villages of half the globe struggling to break the bonds of mass misery, we pledge our best efforts to help them help themselves, for whatever period is required—not because the Communists may be doing it, not because we seek their votes, but because it is right. If a free society cannot help the many who are poor, it cannot save the few who are rich.

To our sister republics south of our border, we offer a special pledge—to convert our good words into good deeds—in a new alliance for progress—to assist free men and free governments in casting off the chains of poverty. But this peaceful revolution of hope cannot become the prey of hostile powers. Let all our neighbors know that we shall join with them to oppose aggression or subversion anywhere in the Americas. And let every other power know that this hemisphere intends to remain the master of its own house.

To that world assembly of sovereign states, the United Nations, our last best hope in an age where the instruments of war have far outpaced the instruments of peace, we renew our pledge of support—to prevent it from becoming merely a forum for invective—to strengthen its shield of the new and the weak—and to enlarge the area in which its writ may run.

Finally, to those nations who would make themselves our adversary, we offer not a pledge but a request: that both sides begin anew the quest for peace, before the dark powers of destruction unleashed by science engulf all humanity in planned or accidental self-destruction.

We dare not tempt them with weakness. For only when our arms are sufficient beyond doubt can we be certain beyond doubt that they will never be employed.

But neither can two great and powerful groups of nations take comfort from our present course—both sides overburdened by the cost of modern weapons, both rightly alarmed by the steady spread of the deadly atom, yet both racing to alter that uncertain balance of terror that stays the hand of mankind's final war.

So let us begin anew—remembering on both sides that civility is not a sign of weakness, and sincerity is always subject to proof. Let us never negotiate out of fear. But let us never fear to negotiate.

Let both sides explore what problems unite us instead of belaboring those problems which divide us. Let both sides, for the first time, formulate serious and precise proposals for the inspection and control of arms—and bring the absolute power to destroy other nations under the absolute control of all nations.

Let both sides seek to invoke the wonders of science instead of its terrors. Together let us explore the stars, conquer the deserts, eradicate disease, tap the ocean depths and encourage the arts and commerce.

Let both sides unite to heed in all corners of the earth the command of Isaiah—to "undo the heavy burdens and to let the oppressed go free."

And if a beach-head of cooperation may push back the jungle of suspicion, let both sides join in a new endeavor; not a new balance of power, but a new world of law, where the strong are just and the weak secure and the peace preserved.

All this will not be finished in the first one hundred days. Nor will it be finished in the first one thousand days, nor in the life of this Administration, nor even perhaps in our lifetime on this planet. But let us begin.

In your hands, my fellow citizens, more than mine, will rest the final success or failure of our course. Since this country was founded, each generation of Americans has been summoned to give testimony to its national loyalty. The graves of young Americans who answered the call to service surround the globe.

Now the trumpet summons us again—not as a call to bear arms, though arms we need—not as a call to battle, though embattled we are—but a call to bear the burden of a long twilight struggle, year in and year out, "rejoicing in hope, patient in tribulation"—a struggle against the common enemies of man: tyranny, poverty, disease and war itself.

Can we forge against these enemies a grand and global alliance, North and South, East and West, that can assure a more fruitful life for all mankind? Will you join in that historic effort?

In the long history of the world, only a few generations have been granted the role of defending freedom in its hour of maximum danger. I do not shrink from this responsibility—I welcome it. I do not believe that any of us would exchange places with any other people or any other generation. The energy, the faith, the devotion which we bring to this endeavor will light our country and all who serve it—and the glow from that fire can truly light the world.

And so, my fellow Americans: Ask not what your country can do for you—ask what you can do for your country.

My fellow citizens of the world: Ask not what America will do for you, but what together we can do for the freedom of man.

Finally, whether you are citizens of America or citizens of the world, ask of us here the same high standards of strength and sacrifice which we ask of you. With a good conscience our only sure reward, with history the final judge of our deeds, let us go forth to lead the land we love, asking His blessing and His help, but knowing that here on earth God's work must truly be our own.

In Dallas, a Chapter Ends

President Kennedy's tenure came to a sudden tragic close on Friday, November 22, 1963, when he was assassinated while riding in a motorcade in Dallas, Texas, where he was scheduled to make a speech. The assassin, Lee Harvey Oswald, was a "loner," who, two days later, was shot and killed by a nightclub owner, Jack Ruby. The events of those three days brought the nation together in a great tide of mourning and left America with a deep sense of grief. The President's young son, John, was photographed while saluting his father during the funeral ceremonies in Washington. America's glimpse of Camelot had lasted for just a thousand days.

John-John Kennedy saluting at his father's funeral.

70. From Disillusion to a New Patriotism

Left: **Operation Oregon,** a search and destroy mission conducted by an infantry platoon moving out in search of a suspected enemy outpost in April 1967.

Right: **Operation Baker,** a search and destroy operation approximately 7 kilometers north of Duc Pho to clear an area east of the highway. The action took place in June 1967.

It was, at best, an era of doubt. The years of the fifties, sixties, and seventies passed with a series of crises that beset a nation seeking to confirm its identity. Sometimes the questions, challenges, and controversies spilled into the streets. The conflict in Korea and the experience in Vietnam generated divisive bitterness. Would there be ever again the unity we had once known?

The Kennedy years brought us unity particularly in the face of the Cuban and Berlin crises. He contributed a sense of elan to the country. The events in Dallas on a grim November afternoon seemed to drain something from our dignity as a nation.

During the years of dissent, the flag, our cherished symbol, was desecrated in a hundred ways. The nation's campuses saw riots, marches, and demonstrations as a segment of the country's youth screamed dissent and anger against war-related policies. The nation was bewildered, splintered by discord.

Vietnam weakened our belief in ourselves and our purpose took the form of demonstrations and protests, sometimes violent ones, in a genuine crisis of the American spirit.

A remote jungle war that seared the American soul, Vietnam raised questions not easily answered: To what end did we lose 47,000 men in battle? Were we being told the whole truth? Were we finding ourselves in the role of imperialists? Was it indeed our fight?

Then the dissent seemed to burn itself out. The campuses turned quiet. The flag was restored to its place of respect. The songs and cheers of patriotism gathered new strength.

The celebrations for the Bicentennial gave us a moment of pause to reassess ourselves. What we saw was as inspiring as ever. We could indeed hold our heads high. Martin Luther King, Jr., had given many Americans, black and white, a share of his dream.

Operation Sail. On July 4, 1976, the United States of America celebrated its two-hundredth birthday. It was a memorable bicentennial holiday, and the national observance included parades, fireworks, speeches, and sporting events. Among the special displays was "Op-Sail," a gathering of tall-masted ships in the harbor at New York City. These old sailing vessels, carrying with them all the feelings associated with our historic past, comprised a fresh expression of love of country. A massing of the tall ships became a national patriotic symbol.

225

The moon landing on July 16, 1969, marked a significant milestone in the conquest of space. Three American astronauts—Neil A. Armstrong, Edwin E. Aldrin, Jr., and Michael Collins—traveling in the spacecraft *Apollo XI*, reached the moon. Armstrong and Aldrin, in a lunar module, landed on the Sea of Tranquility and remained on the moon for 21 hours and 36 minutes, during which they raised a flag and collected soil and rocks. It was a brief visit, but it marked a moment of great national pride.

In space, the United States took the unchallenged lead. In July 1969 we had been able to send a team of astronauts to the moon, a moment that symbolized the great strides of American science. This was followed by many more manned flights, unmanned landings on Mars, and a series of flybys of Jupiter and Saturn that produced some of the most spectacular astronomical photographs ever made. In the early 1980s began a series of space shuttle flights that emphasized our vision of future travel, and the progress of space science.

A memorable Olympic hockey victory at Lake Placid in 1980 was more than a sports triumph. It triggered a fervent expression of patriotism. And the same was true when fifty-two American citizens held hostage in the U.S. Embassy in Teheran, Iran, for 444 days, were released in January 1981 and came home to an emotional welcome.

Once more the flag was flown high, and the songs were sung fervently, and American patriotism had reemerged stronger than ever.

At Hermitage, Pennsylvania, a new American flag was raised to mark each day the Americans were held captive in Iran. The 444-day captivity of fifty-two American citizens in the United States Embassy in Teheran was looked upon as a national humiliation. An abortive attempt at rescue by helicopters only added to the sense of shame. Then, following many weeks of negotiations, on January 20, 1981, as the nation installed a new President, the hostages were released and returned home to a series of welcoming parades.

Sports have always provided springboards for patriotic fervor, but never so much as on that day in February 1980 when **the hockey team of the United States, in the Olympic winter games at Lake Placid, New York,** beat the Soviet team by the score of 4–3 and broke the Russian domination of that sport. With the nation watching on television, the breaking out of flags and the joyous singing of our national anthem lifted American hearts in every corner of the country.

227

More than one hundred tons of American technological know-how compressed into this most daring of flying machines, a space shuttle called the *Columbia,* brought the United States a fresh sense of strength and a fresh grip on the future.

As it rocketed into the skies from its Florida base and roared through space on its many orbits, and then, as millions watched on television, settled neatly "on the money" into its California landing strip, *Columbia* brought a new thrill to an America that had not forgotten the questions raised by Vietnam and Iran. No capsules or parachutes, no splashdowns at sea. We were at the controls all the way in space, and that meant the future. We were the leader.

Despite some initial setbacks the space shuttle program went forward, proving these man-made airships could be used and reused, and foreshadowing commuter runs into the cosmos.

The *Columbia* was moving in the paths opened by Wilbur and Orville Wright and Charles Lindbergh. Americans raised a cheer for the new pioneers.

Amid the roar of the rockets and the blast of steam the ***Columbia* space shuttle takes off** from its home base in Florida.

The *Columbia* space shuttle returns after its orbiting mission and glides to earth right "on the money" in the California desert.

The seal of the President of the United States, and that of the
Vice-President, are both adaptations of the Great Seal of the United States
approved by the Continental Congress in 1776 on the recommendation of
Benjamin Franklin, John Adams, and Thomas Jefferson. It was adopted as
the official seal six years later.

The American bald eagle, the central element in the seal, bears a striped
shield across its breast and carries in its beak a pennant emblazoned with
the slogan *"E Pluribus Unum,"* meaning "one made out of many." The bird
is surrounded by a ring of stars, one for each state, and a group of thirteen
separate stars recalling the thirteen original colonies. In one of the talons
the eagle bears an olive branch and in the other a group of arrows.

71. The Presidents of the United States

The presidency is a flexible set of duties that can expand or contract to fit the measure of the person who occupies the office. Of our forty Presidents, in the course of nearly two centuries, some have viewed the office innovatively and creatively and have added new dimensions to it. Others have appraised it more narrowly and have pulled in the reins. There have been men big enough to fill the desk chair in the Oval Office, others who did not measure up. Yet, not one of the chosen forty, no matter how inadequate or even self-destructive, has ever diminished the office itself.

The aura of the presidency seems to cover the land in subtle ways and to touch the consciousness of all Americans. The presidency is our great symbol of national unity; it is the focus of our patriotic faith.

The Oval Office, the seat of presidential power.

George Washington (1732–99)

George Washington,
by Gilbert Stuart

George Washington, who received a unanimous electoral vote for each of his two terms, was highly sensitive to his role as a precedent setter for the new republic he headed and for the office he filled.

The first President deplored politics, and in his position as chief executive sought to counter the factionalism that swirled around him. An honest, decisive, and courageous man, he conferred a basic dignity on his office and used his popularity as a force for cohesive government.

Washington stood six feet three inches tall but never weighed over two hundred pounds. He enjoyed the theater, loved to dance, and was meticulous about his office routine. But his great passion was for his farm at Mount Vernon, to which he retired at the end of his second term.

John Adams (1735–1826)

John Adams,
by Edgar Parker

John Adams, who served two terms as George Washington's Vice-President, came to the presidency with a background in diplomacy. Most notable had been his handling of the fragile relations between the new country and the French.

A Harvard-educated lawyer, Adams was a man of intelligence and learning who stood a bit aloof from his contemporaries. His term of office was marked by strains within his cabinet. Of the presidency, Adams wrote to his witty and attractive wife, Abigail: "May none but the honest and wise ever rule under this roof."

Short, chubby, and usually a bit irritable, John Adams liked to dress in plain clothes. He outlived his wife by eight years, saw his son, John Quincy Adams, elected to the White House, and died in 1826 in his ninety-first year.

Thomas Jefferson (1743–1826)

Thomas Jefferson, tall, sharp-featured, auburn-haired, was an aristocrat to his fingertips. Multitalented, he was a musician, architect, inventor, and a brilliant writer. He was only thirty-three when he wrote the Declaration of Independence.

A tireless advocate of civil liberties, a champion of states' rights, and a strict constructionist on the Constitution, Jefferson also favored the agricultural view of America's future. One of his greatest achievements as President was the purchase in 1803 of the Louisiana Territory from Napoleon. It represented an enormous step in shaping the nation.

Thomas Jefferson was the man who wrote: "I have sworn on the altar of God eternal hostility toward every form of tyranny over the mind of man."

Thomas Jefferson,
by Rembrandt Peale

James Madison (1751–1836)

James Madison was the smallest of our Presidents, measuring five feet four inches and weighing about one hundred pounds. His wife, Dolley, who became one of the memorable personalities of White House history, referred to him as "my darling little husband."

In office Madison found he had to go back to war with the British when they persisted in impressing American seamen and seizing American cargoes. The British carried the war right into Washington, and on August 24, 1814, the White House was burned. Andrew Jackson helped to even the score by whipping the British in the Battle of New Orleans.

In keeping with his diminutive stature, Madison was equipped with a small, almost inaudible voice. He was a gentle and scholarly man.

James Madison,
by John Vanderlyn

233

James Monroe (1758–1831)

James Monroe,
by Samuel F. B. Morse

James Monroe was the last of that distinguished group of Virginians who led the Republic in its earliest years. It was he who, as President, made it clear that the Western Hemisphere was closed to further European colonization.

His doctrine, a keystone of U.S. foreign policy for many decades, stated: "The American continents by the free and independent position which they have assumed and maintained, are henceforth not to be considered as subjects for future colonization by any European power."

"Good feeling" marked the Monroe period in the White House. The Democrat-Republicans were the only party, industry was being developed, the West was being settled, and there was the sense of prosperity through the country. By traveling extensively, Monroe determined for himself the temper of the nation.

James Monroe was quiet, dignified, blue-eyed, and tall. He was the last of the American Presidents to wear knee breeches.

John Quincy Adams (1767–1848)

John Quincy Adams,
by G.P.A. Healy

John Quincy Adams was the only U.S. President who was the son of a President. An accomplished linguist and diarist, he came to the highest office after having served as secretary of state.

Chubby and bald like his father, John Adams, he led a rigorous life as the resident of the White House. He loved to play billiards and to swim in the Potomac.

Adams wanted the government to sponsor development in the arts and sciences and urged the establishment of a national university and observatory. After he left the presidency he returned to Washington to serve in the House for seventeen years.

Andrew Jackson (1767–1845)

Andrew Jackson was the first President born in a log cabin and thereby became known as the first of the frontier Presidents. A military hero in the War of 1812, he was elected President in 1829. His inaugural party became one of the most hectic episodes in White House history when he invited the general public to the residence. The food and furnishings took a memorable beating, and the new President finally had to escape through a window.

Jackson believed firmly in rule by the people. He gave jobs to his friends in the party and had little use for the "experts." An audacious and skillful politician, he knew his way in the halls of government. Tall, courtly, dignified, and well mannered, Jackson, nicknamed "Old Hickory," was an expert horseman.

Andrew Jackson,
by John Wesley Jarvis

Martin Van Buren (1782–1862)

Martin Van Buren, who came to the White House in 1837 having already served as U.S. senator and governor of New York, was the first chief executive born under the flag of the United States.

After hardly a month in office, Van Buren was faced with a major financial crisis in the nation as the banks closed and the country experienced its first great depression. Opposed to federal activism, Van Buren failed to do much about the crisis other than tighten expenditures so much that the government had to sell off the tools it had acquired for public works projects.

Martin Van Buren, a smallish man, was a fastidious dresser and favored orange cravats. He carried the nickname of "Little Magician," but his opponents spoke of him as "Little Van, the used up man."

Martin Van Buren,
by G.P.A. Healy

William Henry Harrison (1773–1841)

William Henry Harrison,
by E. F. Andrews

William Henry Harrison came from a line of Virginia planters. His father was a signer of the Declaration of Independence, but Harrison's well-deserved image was that of a frontier Indian fighter. He had been studying medicine in Philadelphia when he received an appointment into the Army that led to his being named territorial governor of Indiana. In November 1811 at Tippecanoe on the Wabash he defeated the Indians under Tecumseh and emerged a national hero. He added to his military distinction in the War of 1812.

Tall, slim, and impressive in the saddle, Harrison was also a capable vote getter, and the slogan "Tippecanoe and Tyler Too" and the log cabin–hard cider image were strong weapons of political propaganda in the campaign of 1840. Just a month after his inauguration, "Tippecanoe" contracted pneumonia and became the first President to die in office.

John Tyler (1790–1862)

John Tyler,
by G.P.A. Healy

John Tyler, another son of the Virginia aristocracy, was the first Vice-President to come to the highest office through the death of a President. When he acceded to the presidency Tyler insisted on full recognition of his powers; he was no "acting" President.

Tyler proved himself a capable administrator, though he was constantly in a state of deadlock, whether with his own party or with the Congress. The issue of the national bank was still a controversial one, and Tyler was against its reestablishment. He did manage to maneuver the annexation of Texas.

Tall, kindly, a thin man with sharp blue eyes, he was an adamant states' righter and advocated Secession in the final months before the Civil War started.

James Knox Polk (1795–1849)

Eleventh President: 1845–49

James Knox Polk, whose father had fought in the Revolution, stretched the nation's western border to the shores of the Pacific. Some saw him as a patriot, others as an imperialist. Charging Mexico with aggression and unpaid claims, Polk led the U.S. into war, resulting in the addition of California and New Mexico to U.S. territory. He also made an agreement with England, setting the northern border of the Oregon region at the 49th parallel, even though his 1844 presidential campaign had called for "54-40 or fight."

Polk's flair as an orator served him well in his political career, which included a term as governor of Tennessee and seven terms in the Congress. In the presidency James Polk was a diligent worker. As a politician he was contemptuous of the spoils system. Small of build, gray-eyed, reticent, and serious, Polk displayed an air of composure that was hardly the image of the frontiersman the country had come to expect.

James K. Polk,
by G.P.A. Healy

Zachary Taylor (1784–1850)

Twelfth President: 1849–50

Zachary Taylor, from Virginia by way of Kentucky, had spent forty years in Army uniform before he became President of the United States.

Taylor had little schooling, and knew very little of politics, but his military achievements, especially in the Mexican war, gave him national recognition and the nickname "Old Rough and Ready." He was the first regular army man to be elected President.

From the start of his brief tenure he was caught up in the political whirlpool that marked the slavery issue, and he tried, however briefly, to bring about reconciliation and heal the widening gap between North and South.

Taylor was short and on the chubby side, enjoyed his chewing tobacco, and was not too careful in his dress. His manners were seen as crude, but he was regarded as a good man. He died on July 9, 1850, of what appeared to be cholera.

Zachary Taylor,
by Joseph H. Bush

237

Millard Fillmore (1800–74)

Millard Fillmore,
by G.P.A. Healy

Millard Fillmore was an upstate New York lawyer who at one time owned the largest mansion in the city of Buffalo. He was active in New York state politics and served four terms in the U.S. Congress.

As Vice-President to Zachary Taylor he succeeded to the presidency in 1850 and continued, with little success, to push for some kind of compromise on slavery.

Fillmore was a six-footer, very erect of carriage, and fond of wearing suits that were a bit too large for him. He never smoked or drank or gambled, and always stayed at a temperance hotel. His wife, Abigail Powers Fillmore, established a library for White House use and installed the first bathtub.

Franklin Pierce (1804–69)

Franklin Pierce,
by G.P.A. Healy

Franklin Pierce, a Democrat from New Hampshire, served his state in both the House and Senate, but he had little ambition for the presidency. He was a true dark horse, finally nominated on the forty-ninth ballot, and although he carried every state but four, he won by less than a fifty-thousand-vote plurality.

A reasonable man with a bright personality, Pierce strove for harmony during his administration. Unfortunately, he was more a follower than a leader. Pierce envisioned a major place for the United States in the world picture. He unsuccessfully negotiated for the purchase of both Hawaii and Alaska, but he did manage to open Japan to trade.

James Buchanan (1791–1868)

James Buchanan, a wealthy farmer from Pennsylvania, was our only bachelor President. He had served in the House and Senate and as U.S. Minister to Russia and England.

Buchanan strove to maintain the "sacred balance" between the North and South but was unable to stop the trend to Secession.

Tall and blue-eyed, Buchanan carried his head to one side because of impaired vision. He provided the official residence with its first furnace, but during the summer he left the White House because of the danger of malaria.

Buchanan seemed unable to grasp the full import of the politics of his day. He left the office with the nation on the brink of civil war.

James Buchanan,
by William M. Chase

Abraham Lincoln (1809–65)

Abraham Lincoln grew up on the Kentucky-Indiana frontier. A large-boned youth, he stood six feet four inches, weighed about 180 pounds, and had black hair and gray eyes. Largely self-taught, in his youth he ran a grocery store and served as a postmaster in his Illinois village.

He served in the U.S. House of Representatives and ran twice for the U.S. Senate. He was defeated both times, but his participation in the debates against his opponent Stephen A. Douglas brought him national attention.

Lincoln was elected President in 1860. His conduct of the Civil War was bold and assertive, as he put preservation of the Union above all other considerations. He was assassinated on April 15, 1865, shortly after his second inauguration and only six days after the South had surrendered.

Abraham Lincoln,
by G.P.A. Healy

239

Andrew Johnson (1808–75)

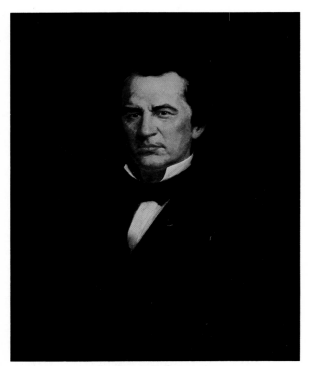

Andrew Johnson,
by E. F. Andrews

Andrew Johnson was the only President of the United States who never had a formal education. He had been a tailor's apprentice, and his wife had taught him to read and write. Johnson showed a talent for stump speeches and was elected governor of Tennessee and then senator from that state.

When he became President, following Abraham Lincoln's assassination, Johnson quickly found himself locked in a bitter political struggle with the so-called Radical Republicans in the Congress over the issues raised by Reconstruction. Though lacking in the political wisdom and tact the times demanded, Johnson was a grim and determined fighter. He carried his struggle in speeches to the people, but it was not a productive maneuver. The conflict culminated in Johnson's impeachment by the House. He was acquitted by one vote in the Senate.

Despite the humiliation of his White House career, Johnson came back to the Senate in 1874, serving there briefly.

Ulysses Simpson Grant (1822–85)

Ulysses S. Grant,
by Henry Ulke

He was born Hiram Ulysses Grant, but those initials spelled "H.U.G." so he changed his name to Ulysses Simpson Grant. The initials "U" and "S" came to stand for "Unconditional Surrender" Grant. One of the great generals in the Civil War, it was he who accepted the surrender of Robert E. Lee at Appomattox Court House.

The two terms of his administration were marked by scandal and fiscal maneuvering, as the presidency came under the influence of market manipulators. Grant, who had no taste for politics, was not involved himself, but he was a poor judge of character and his early appointments were weak ones.

Ulysses Grant was a shy man who hated war and never cursed. He loved good horses and had new stables built around the White House. It fell on his shoulders to see the country through the bitter aftermath of the Johnson administration turmoil. His memoirs, written during his last years, are among the classics of military history.

Rutherford Birchard Hayes (1822–93)

Rutherford B. Hayes had served as an officer in the Civil War and as governor of Ohio before he reached the White House. Though Samuel J. Tilden of New York had two hundred thousand more popular votes, it was Hayes who achieved victory in the electoral vote, 185 to 184, as the result of a decision of a special commission that debated 19 controversial electoral ballots.

Hayes proved to be a serious, independent, efficient, conservative chief executive. He adhered to a "hard money" policy, paying the public debt in gold when the pressure from farmers and workingmen was for paper currency.

Hayes's wife, Lucy, refused to serve hard liquor in the White House and became known as "Lemonade Lucy." She also introduced the custom of Easter egg–rolling on the White House lawn.

Rutherford B. Hayes,
by Daniel Huntington

James Abram Garfield (1831–81)

James A. Garfield was a farmer, carpenter, and bargeman in his youth, later taught classics, was a college president, and served seventeen years as a member of the U.S. House of Representatives.

Blue-eyed, with yellow beard and hair, Garfield was a first-rate orator, a lover of poetry and the classics, and fluent in both Latin and Greek. He was nominated as a dark-horse candidate by the Republicans in 1880 and elected by a narrow margin. As President he resisted the tight patronage system of his time and eliminated fraud he found in the postal system.

On July 2, 1881, four months after his inauguration, President Garfield was shot in a Washington railroad station by a disappointed office seeker named Charles J. Guiteau. Garfield died in September of that year.

James A. Garfield,
by Calvin Curtis

241

Chester Alan Arthur (1830–86)

Chester A. Arthur,
by Daniel Huntington

Chester A. Arthur was a schoolteacher and a lawyer before he turned to politics. He was active in the New York state political organization and held the federal post of customs collector for the port of New York City.

Arthur stood over six feet and was always stylishly dressed. His manner carried a certain dignity, and contemporaries said he looked the way a President should look.

Chester Arthur led the nation at a time of growing prosperity, and though he was a member of the so-called Republican stalwarts, he was also regarded as an honest and efficient executive.

His views leaned toward high tariff, hard money, and civil service reform, particularly a system in which certain government jobs would be available only through competitive written examinations.

Grover Cleveland (1837–1908)

Twenty-second and Twenty-fourth President: 1885–89 and 1893–97

Grover Cleveland,
by Eastman Johnson

Stephen Grover Cleveland was a descendant of Moses Cleveland, who founded the city of Cleveland, Ohio. He was the first Democrat to win the White House after the Civil War. A former schoolteacher, he had served as mayor of Buffalo, New York, and governor of New York.

Once in the White House, the amiable Cleveland, a bulky man who weighed 260 pounds, proved to be a hardworking executive who remained at his desk until 2:00 or 3:00 A.M., occupied with problems on the labor and economic fronts. He broke a railroad strike with troops to move the mail and resolved a monetary crisis brought on by heavy government purchases of silver.

Cleveland, independent, stubborn, and honest, was known as "Grover the Good." He observed that "Public office is a public trust." Cleveland was the first and only President to be married in the White House.

Grover Cleveland regained the presidency in 1892. Never before had a once-defeated President done that.

Benjamin Harrison (1833–1901)

Twenty-third President: 1889–93

Benjamin Harrison,
by Eastman Johnson

Benjamin Harrison's great-grandfather had been a signer of the Declaration of Independence, his grandfather was William Henry ("Tippecanoe") Harrison, the ninth President, and his father had served in the Congress. He himself had served in the U.S. Senate and was elected President in 1888, following a widely publicized "front-porch" campaign, in which he did his speechmaking from his own steps.

Aloof, dignified, fastidious, Harrison was a cautious President who prided himself on his assertive foreign policy, especially his friendship with Latin American nations. Six new states were brought into the federal Union during his time in office. Harrison introduced a rigid daily office routine into the presidency. Under his administration the federal government for the first time became a billion-dollar operation.

William McKinley (1843–1901)

Twenty-fifth President: 1897–1901

William McKinley, the last Civil War veteran to serve his country as President, served in the U.S. House of Representatives and for two terms as governor of the state of Ohio. In his 1896 campaign against William Jennings Bryan, McKinley, arguing for high tariffs and the gold standard, stayed home and spoke from his front porch in Canton, Ohio, while Bryan toured the country four times and made more than six hundred speeches. McKinley won by a landslide.

During McKinley's administration the U.S. went to war against Spain. This hundred-day, one-sided conflict marked the emergence of the United States as a world power. At home the President's "full dinner pail" slogan carried strong appeal.

On September 6, 1901, while McKinley was visiting the Pan American exposition in Buffalo, New York, he was shot by a young anarchist named Leon Czolgosz. He died eight days later.

William McKinley,
by Harriet Murphy

Theodore Roosevelt (1858–1919)

Theodore Roosevelt,
by John Singer Sargent

Theodore Roosevelt, scholar, soldier, ranchman, politician, brought a special personal flair to the office of the presidency. In succeeding McKinley at the age of forty-two, Roosevelt became the youngest President in the history of the United States.

Teddy Roosevelt had such wide appeal, he even had a stuffed toy named after him. Following a sickly childhood, he became an avid outdoorsman and physical-fitness devotee, exuding energy in everything he did. He was short, walked with an awkward carriage, and punctuated his speeches with nervous gestures.

As President, Roosevelt fought the trusts and the political spoils system, campaigned for pure food and drug laws, and promoted conservation. He considered the Oval Office, a "bully pulpit" and saw his methods as a way to "speak softly and carry a big stick."

William Howard Taft (1857–1930)

William H. Taft,
by Anders L. Zorn

William Howard Taft, whose father had served in President Grant's cabinet, was the only man in our history to hold the nation's two highest offices: President and Chief Justice of the Supreme Court.

Good-natured and jovial, Taft was a giant of a man, weighing over three hundred pounds. People often compared him to a bison. As President he seemed to lack some qualities of executive force, but he was able to establish a budget system for the government, pursue the battle against the trusts, especially in oil and tobacco, and start a federal Department of Labor.

Taft saw the presidency as a lonesome place. He is said to have commented, "I don't remember that I was ever President." In 1921 President Harding named him Chief Justice of the U.S. Supreme Court, thus allowing him to fulfill a lifelong ambition.

Woodrow Wilson (1856–1924)

Woodrow Wilson belonged to the distinguished line of Virginia-born Presidents. A respected historian and later president of Princeton University, he had the air of the schoolmaster about him. After going into politics, he became governor of New Jersey and then, in 1912, the Democratic nominee for the presidency. A split in the Republican ranks, brought on by Theodore Roosevelt's third-party Bull Moose candidacy, brought him a substantial victory.

As chief executive he was regarded as somewhat aloof and self-righteous, but he was seen as a champion of the underdog. In his presidency, Wilson lowered the tariff, set up a federal income tax, established a federal trade commission, and added laws to bar child labor. Wilson is best remembered as the nation's leader during World War I, when this country reacted to German submarine activity against U.S. shipping. He was deeply disappointed after the war when Congress rejected U.S. participation in the League of Nations.

Woodrow Wilson,
by F. Graham Cootes

Warren Gamaliel Harding (1865–1923)

Warren G. Harding, who, it was said, "looked like a President," was a handsome man with large eyes and a pleasant, vibrant voice. An Ohio senator, he received his party's presidential nomination to dissolve a convention deadlock. He stressed the need to return to "normalcy" after World War I, offering the campaign message of "Less government in business and more business in government." In the Harding years immigration was restricted, tariffs were raised, and antistrike legislation was voted.

An affable, easygoing gentleman, who, it was said, never learned to say no, Warren Harding was a poor judge of character. He put cronies into office and they betrayed him. The end of his administration was marred by the Teapot Dome scandals involving Navy oil reserves. Harding died in office, on August 2, 1923, while he was on a Western trip.

Warren G. Harding,
by E. Hodgson Smart

245

Calvin Coolidge (1872–1933)

Calvin Coolidge,
by Charles S. Hopkinson

By lantern light at 2:30 A.M. on August 3, 1923, Calvin Coolidge was sworn in as President by his father, who was a justice of the peace.

Coolidge first attracted national attention in 1919, when he was governor of Massachusetts. Calling out the state guard during a Boston police strike, he had said, "There is no right to strike against the public safety by anyone, anywhere, anytime." In 1920 he became Warren Harding's running mate.

A taciturn individual, he was somewhat shy and remote, but he had a flair for wit. Once asked to name his hobby, he answered: "Holding office." Actually, he enjoyed fishing and taking walks.

The theme of his administration was "the business of America is business." On the international front he sought to outlaw war through the Kellogg-Briand pact. While on vacation in August 1927 he issued his famous statement: "I do not choose to run for President in 1928."

Herbert Hoover (1874–1964)

Herbert Hoover,
by Elmer W. Greene

Herbert Hoover was a successful mining engineer and a multimillionare. Even before he went into government he became well known for his able administration of food relief programs. Later he served as secretary of commerce in the Coolidge administration.

Shortly after he took office in 1929 the stock market crashed and there was a rapid erosion of confidence in the nation's economy.

Hoover was a skillful administrator and tried to help agriculture by encouraging farm cooperatives, promoting federal conservation, and launching highway construction programs, but he seemed unable to grasp fully the human problems arising from the nation's worst depression, and he became, inevitably, the symbol of the Great Depression and the scapegoat for the nation's misery.

When Hoover ran for reelection in 1932, he could gather only 59 electoral votes; his opponent, Franklin D. Roosevelt, won 472.

Franklin Delano Roosevelt (1882–1945)

Franklin Delano Roosevelt was the first President to serve more than two terms—he was elected four times—through the nation's greatest depression and its greatest war.

Roosevelt entered politics early, serving in a variety of offices. When he was thirty-nine, he was stricken with poliomyelitis. From then on he required a wheelchair or crutches, but this did not impede his political rise, to the governorship of New York in 1928, to the U.S. presidency in 1932.

Roosevelt, noting in his first inaugural that "the only thing we have to fear is fear itself," faced massive domestic problems when he entered the Oval Office. He met them with speedy action and daring initiative, attacking a broad front with his "New Deal" economic program. Meanwhile, Europe was headed into a new war and, at first avoiding war, Roosevelt threw American industrial and military strength against the Axis powers.

After Pearl Harbor the challenge was clear. For four years Roosevelt worked with other Allied leaders to shape the victory. Exhausted and sick, he died in Warm Springs, Georgia, on April 12, 1945.

Franklin D. Roosevelt,
by Frank O. Salisbury

Harry S Truman (1884–1972)

Less than three months after he had been sworn in as Roosevelt's Vice-President, Harry S Truman became the seventh "accidental" chief executive. He later remarked, "I felt like the moon, the stars, and all the planets had fallen on me."

What had fallen on Truman was responsibility for an avalanche of vital decisions: use of the atomic bombs against Japan, participation in the formation of the United Nations and the North Atlantic Treaty Organization, implementation of the Marshall Plan and the Truman Doctrine, the containment of Russian communism. In 1948 Truman countered the Soviet blockade of Berlin with a massive airlift; in 1950 he called for a United Nations police action to meet North Korean aggression against South Korea.

Truman had a limited background for the Oval Office, but he had served as a U.S. senator since 1934 and was endowed with an ability to view the issues clearly. In the 1948 campaign he traveled 31,000 miles and made 350 speeches to defeat Republican Thomas Dewey in an historic upset. It was said of Truman that he reflected an image of the common man.

Harry S Truman,
by Martha G. Kempton

Dwight David Eisenhower (1890–1969)   *Thirty-fourth President: 1953–1961*

Dwight D. Eisenhower,
by J. Anthony Wills

Dwight D. Eisenhower, Texas-born and Kansas-bred, graduated from West Point in 1915. He was supreme commander for the invasion of France in June 1944 and in that important post exhibited great tact and administrative ability.

At the end of World War II Eisenhower was named president of Columbia University. He then ran for the presidency successfully in 1952 and was reelected in 1956.

Eisenhower, or "Ike," as he came to be called, was an affable, good-natured person. As President, accustomed to an army staff system, he came to depend on his cabinet. Internationally, he tried to ease world tension and promoted foreign aid. He was able to guide the conflict in Korea to a conclusion. Domestically, he pursued desegregation of the public school system, expanded Social Security, enlarged highway building, and warned against the power of the American military-industrial complex.

John Fitzgerald Kennedy (1917–63)   *Thirty-fifth President: 1961–63*

John F. Kennedy,
by Aaron Shikler

In his memorable inauguration speech in 1961, President John Fitzgerald Kennedy spoke these words: "Ask not what your country can do for you—ask what you can do for your country." At forty-three, he was the youngest man and the first Roman Catholic to be elected President.

John F. Kennedy came of a politically oriented Massachusetts family. A PT boat commander during World War II, Kennedy later served in both the U.S. House and Senate and won a Pulitzer Prize for his book, *Profiles in Courage.* To the Oval Office he brought a certain wit and intelligence, as well as a group of bright young aides. Much of his proposed legislation was blocked by a conservative coalition. In October 1962 he held his ground in a confrontation with Russia over missiles in Cuba. The Soviets dismantled the weapons.

Kennedy was slain by an assassin's bullet when he was visiting Dallas in November 1963. He was the youngest President to die in office.

Lyndon Baines Johnson (1908–73)

Lyndon Baines Johnson was sworn in as President in the aircraft that was to take John F. Kennedy's body from Dallas back to Washington.

Johnson had taught school in his native Texas, served six terms in the House, and in 1948 moved to the Senate, where he was regarded as an energetic and forceful legislator with a special genius for political persuasion. As chief executive, he operated with skill and determination. On the domestic scene he envisioned what he called a "Great Society," working for civil rights, aid to education, housing, and medical aid for the aged, developing programs against poverty and pollution, and promoting new tax laws. On the foreign front, the Johnson presidency was dominated by the ongoing war in Vietnam, which seriously divided the nation.

In 1964 Johnson ran against the Republican Barry Goldwater and won with the greatest popular margin in political history.

Lyndon B. Johnson,
by Elizabeth Shoumatoff

Richard Milhous Nixon (1913–   )

Richard M. Nixon, who had served in the U.S. House and Senate, and as Vice-President under Dwight Eisenhower, worked long and hard to reach the Oval Office. After being defeated for the presidency in 1960 and the California governorship in 1962, he staged a comeback. With the help of a "Southern strategy," he defeated Democrat Hubert Humphrey in 1968 and was reelected in 1972 with a near-record landslide over Democrat George McGovern.

An ardent anti-Communist during his early years, Nixon nonetheless visited China and Russia during his presidency to meet with leaders of those countries, and he was able to reopen America's long-ruptured diplomatic relations with China. He also reached a peace accord with North Vietnam. The fighting ended in 1975 with a cost to the United States of 56,000 deaths and $150 billion.

Investigation of the break-in at the Democratic National Committee offices in the Watergate Hotel brought the President to the brink of impeachment, and on August 7, 1974, Richard Nixon became the only U.S. President to resign the office.

Richard M. Nixon,
by Robert S. Oakes

Gerald Rudolph Ford (1913–   )

Thirty-eighth President: 1974–77

Gerald R. Ford,
by Everett Raymond Kinstler

Gerald Ford arrived at the presidency having been elected neither as President nor as Vice-President. A member of the U.S. House of Representatives and House Republican leader, he had served on the Warren Commission to investigate the assassination of President Kennedy. On October 12, 1973, following the resignation of Vice-President Spiro Agnew in connection with a corruption scandal, Ford, under the stipulations of the Twenty-fifth Amendment, was named to the vice-presidency. Less than a year later, upon Richard Nixon's resignation, he became chief executive.

Gerald Ford was regarded as a moderate, conservative President. He cut business taxes and regulatory controls and, on the international scene, acted to maintain U.S. power in southeast Asia. President Ford ran as the Republican candidate in 1976 but was defeated by Jimmy Carter of Georgia.

Jimmy (James Earl) Carter (1924–   )

Thirty-ninth President: 1977–81

Jimmy Carter,
by Karl Schumacher

Jimmy Carter, of Plains, Georgia, was the first U.S. President from the Deep South since Zachary Taylor came out of Louisiana in 1848. Carter graduated from Annapolis and served in the nuclear submarine program. He was elected governor of Georgia in 1970. Following a lonely "antiestablishment" campaign for the Democratic nomination in 1976, he won his party's nod and defeated the Republican incumbent, Gerald Ford.

As President, Carter reorganized the federal executive structure, establishing a Department of Energy for the control and conservation of power sources, worked for civil service reform and higher minimum wages, and halted or blocked construction of big bombers and nuclear aircraft carriers. Carter's conduct of foreign affairs was marked by a strong moral flavor as he worked for human rights around the world, but he was unable to free fifty-two American hostages held by Iranian revolutionaries until Inauguration Day in 1981. Inflation was a large factor in eroding his popularity, and he was badly defeated for reelection by former Governor Ronald Reagan of California.

Ronald Wilson Reagan (1911–   )

Ronald Reagan, spokesman for the conservative wing of the Republican party, rode to the White House on the crest of a landslide victory over Jimmy Carter in the presidential election of 1980.

A sports announcer and a successful motion picture actor in his youth, Reagan had served as president of the Screen Actors Guild. Politically he had been a liberal Democrat but had switched to conservative Republican, and was elected governor of California in 1966 and reelected in 1970.

As President, his budget proposals called for cuts in taxes but increases in military expenditures. To restrain the increasing inflation in the national economy he sought heavy reduction in nonmilitary expenditures. He took an important new initiative by appointing the first woman, Sandra Day O'Connor, to the U.S. Supreme Court. On the international front, President Reagan approved the sale of AWACS planes to Saudi Arabia and endorsed the production of the neutron bomb.

On March 30, 1981, President Reagan survived an assassination attempt in Washington, D.C.

Ronald W. Reagan

72. Long May It Wave

On June 14, 1777, a date we still celebrate as Flag Day, the Second Continental Congress, on the suggestion of its Maritime Committee, adopted this resolution:

> Resolved that the flag of the United States be thirteen stripes, alternate red and white; that the union be thirteen stars, white in a blue field, representing a new constellation.

That was it, no further specifics, but it was the birth certificate for the American flag as we know it today. There had been state, regimental, and militia flags before, and there would be a variety afterward, but the main pattern was set, although it was not until 1783, when the war was over, that the new flag would be put into use.

There is some question as to just who produced the first flag. Philadelphia seamstress Betsy Ross, who did make some naval flags, has been generally credited, but historians are not ready to verify this.

For some years there was little consistency in the design of the flag. Sometimes the stars were blue on white, blue stripes might be mingled with red and white stripes, and in some flags the stripes were vertical. In 1818 Congress finally specified that the stripes be horizontal, but it was not until 1912 that the arrangement for the stars was formalized. Each new state was to be represented by a new star, with no particular star for any special state; revised flags were to be adopted on the July 4 following admission of any new state.

Here is a selection of flags, militia, regimental, and ornamental, that are part of the early history of the Stars and Stripes:

Among the flags illustrated on the following page, some are of particular historic interest.

Rhode Island (1772): The Rhode Islanders were strong advocates of the Revolutionary cause. As early as June 10, 1772, they showed their feelings in an act of defiance by capturing and burning the British cutter *Gaspée.* The anchor became a symbol for the Rhode Island state flag.

Bedford (April 19, 1775): The Minutemen, who came from Bedford, Massachusetts, to face the Redcoats, carried this flag, which had probably been in use in the middle of the seventeenth century. It was the first flag of the Colonies fired on by the British troops.

Washington's Cruisers (1775): This was the banner selected to identify the six schooners outfitted by General Washington himself for service along the East Coast. Massachusetts later made use of this style of flag.

The Green Mountains (May 10, 1775): This was the flag carried by Ethan Allen's men when he captured Fort Ticonderoga in May 1775. Allen demanded capitulation in the "name of the Great Jehovah and the Continental Congress."

FAMOUS FLAGS IN AMERICAN HISTORY

FLAGS OF DISCOVERY AND SETTLEMENT

SPANISH · FRENCH · ENGLISH · DUTCH

COLONIAL AND REVOLUTIONARY WAR FLAGS

SWEDISH · ANDROS · NEW ENGLAND · BEDFORD

HANOVER ASSOCIATORS · TAUNTON · CULPEPER · MARKOE · HOPKINS

FIRST NAVY JACK · WASHINGTON'S CRUISERS · FORT MOULTRIE · RHODE ISLAND · GREEN MOUNTAIN BOYS

FLAGS OF THE 1800'S

EUTAW · GUILFORD · RUSSIAN-AMERICAN CO. · OLIVER PERRY

ALAMO · TEXAS NAVY · CALIFORNIA REPUBLIC · BONNIE BLUE · CONFEDERATE BATTLE FLAG

EVOLUTION OF THE STARS AND STRIPES

CONTINENTAL COLORS · JUNE 14, 1777 · BENNINGTON · 3D MARYLAND REGIMENT · FORT McHENRY

JULY 4, 1818 · 1859 TO 1861 · 1908 TO 1912 · 1912 TO 1959 · 1959 TO 1960

Rattlesnake (1776): The naval forces of the Revolution used this flag aboard the *Alfred,* flagship of the fleet. The "Striped Rattlesnake Flag" with the warning "Don't Tread On Me," or a variation, was favored by American vessels during the Revolutionary years.

Grand Union (January 1, 1776): This might be called the first formal flag of the new nation, since Washington himself, in taking command on this date, accepted this standard "in compliment to the United Colonies." The British insignia in the canton seems to express a reluctance to break ties with the mother country.

Bennington (August 16, 1777): When the Colonial militia faced a British raiding force at Bennington, Vermont, on August 16, 1777, this was the flag carried by the Americans under General John Stark. They gained a victory over the British, and the boost to morale was so effective that victory was again gained at Saratoga two months later.

Cowpens (January 17, 1781): Originally the emblem of the Third Maryland regiment, this was the flag used by the Continental Line when, under the command of General Daniel Morgan, the Americans defeated the British at Cowpens, South Carolina, in a strategic victory.

Commodore Perry (September 10, 1813): In action against the British, Commodore Oliver Hazard Perry, leading an American squadron in the battle of Lake Erie on September 10, 1813, flew this flag on the mast of his flagship *Lawrence.* The vessel had been named after naval hero Captain James Lawrence, whose dying words were "Don't give up the ship."

Star-spangled Banner (September 13, 1814): This historic flag (with fifteen stars and fifteen stripes) was on the flagpole at Fort McHenry on the night of September 13, 1814, when Francis Scott Key witnessed the British bombardment and wrote "The Star-spangled Banner."

Confederate Battle (1861): On the battlefields of the Civil War there emerged several different Confederate banners. This thirteen-star flag represented the thirteen states that had joined the Confederacy.

When You Display the Flag

INDOORS

1. The flag should always be positioned to its own right. It should be placed to the right of the speaker, other flags to the left.

2. When state and other flags are grouped, the flag of the United States should be at the center and highest point of the group.

3. When another flag is used with the American flag and the staffs are crossed, the U.S. flag should be placed on its own right with its staff in front of the other flag.

4. When presenting the flag against a wall, either vertically or horizontally, the flag's union or stars should be at the top, or the flag's right.

OUTDOORS

1. If the flag is flown out of a window, building, or balcony, the stars should be at the peak of the staff. When flown from a pole with other flags, the U.S. flag must always be at the top. However, a church pennant may be flown above the flag during services by a Naval chaplain at sea.

2. When displayed over a street, the flag should be hung vertically, with the stars to the north or east.

3. When flown on separate poles in a group with other flags, the U.S. flag is always placed to the right. No other flag is ever placed above it, and it is the flag first raised and last lowered.

4. The flag should always be raised briskly and lowered slowly. Ordinarily, it is displayed only between sunrise and sunset. However, on special occasions it is displayed at night, and when so displayed it is considered desirable to illuminate the flag by floodlights.

FLAGS OF THE STATES

THE 50 STATES
AND THE DISTRICT
OF COLUMBIA

ALABAMA — ALASKA — ARIZONA
ARKANSAS — CALIFORNIA — COLORADO — CONNECTICUT
DELAWARE — DISTRICT of COLUMBIA — FLORIDA — GEORGIA
HAWAII — IDAHO — ILLINOIS — INDIANA
IOWA — KANSAS — KENTUCKY — LOUISIANA
MAINE — MARYLAND — MASSACHUSETTS — MICHIGAN
MINNESOTA — MISSISSIPPI — MISSOURI — MONTANA

FLAGS OF THE STATES (Continued)

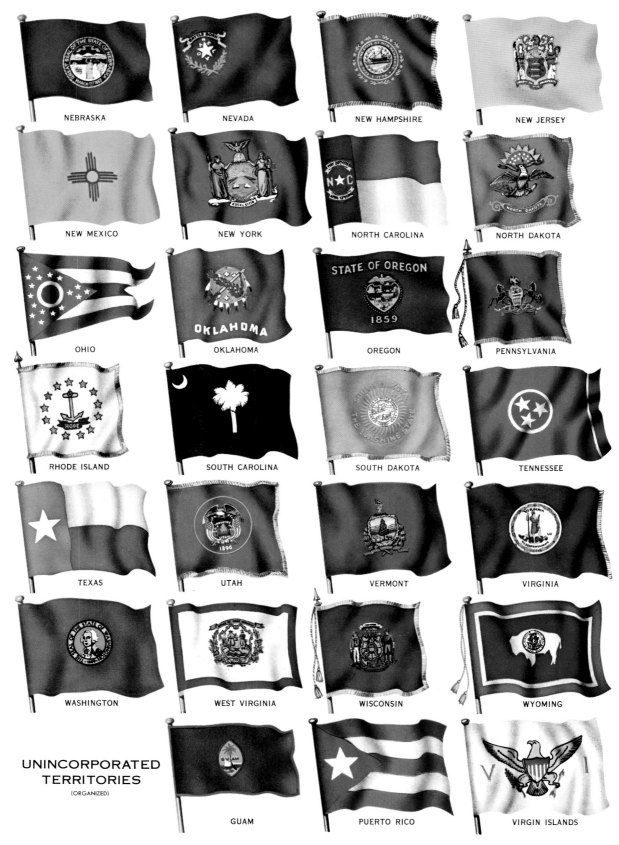

NEBRASKA	NEVADA	NEW HAMPSHIRE	NEW JERSEY
NEW MEXICO	NEW YORK	NORTH CAROLINA	NORTH DAKOTA
OHIO	OKLAHOMA	OREGON	PENNSYLVANIA
RHODE ISLAND	SOUTH CAROLINA	SOUTH DAKOTA	TENNESSEE
TEXAS	UTAH	VERMONT	VIRGINIA
WASHINGTON	WEST VIRGINIA	WISCONSIN	WYOMING

UNINCORPORATED
TERRITORIES
(ORGANIZED)

GUAM	PUERTO RICO	VIRGIN ISLANDS

73. Armed Forces Decorations and Awards

On August 7, 1782, George Washington ordered the country's first award for soldiers, the badge of Military Merit. A figure of a heart covered with purple cloth, it was the forerunner of the Purple Heart, which now goes to those wounded in action. It was to be given to officers or enlisted men for acts of special gallantry. Only three badges of Military Merit were issued during the Revolution.

After the Revolution the badge of Military Merit was discontinued, and the United States was without an official decoration until the Civil War. In 1862 the Medal of Honor, still the nation's highest military award, was authorized and approved by President Lincoln. The first medals went to a group of nineteen volunteers from the Union forces who, in April 1862, sabotaged an important rail line between Atlanta and Chattanooga.

The Congressional Medal of Honor

ARMED FORCES DECORATIONS AND AWARDS

Awarded to eligible personnel of all Services
unless otherwise specified in title or description

(Arrangement does not necessarily
follow order of precedence)

74. A Calendar for Americans

In the United States, each of the states has jurisdiction over its own holidays, which are designated either by legislative act or by executive order. However, most states do observe the federal legal public holidays; these include New Year's Day, Washington's Birthday, Memorial Day, Independence Day, Labor Day, Columbus Day, Veterans' Day, Thanksgiving, and Christmas. The President and Congress can legally designate holidays only for the District of Columbia and federal employees.

JANUARY

1	New Year's Day (observed in all states)
2	Ratification day in Georgia (1788)
3	Admission day in Alaska (1959)
4	Admission day in Utah (1896)
6	Admission day in New Mexico (1912)
8	Battle of New Orleans Day in Louisiana (1815)
9	Ratification day in Connecticut (1788)
15	Martin Luther King, Jr.'s, birthday (Connecticut, District of Columbia, Florida, Georgia, Illinois, Louisiana, Maryland, Massachusetts, Michigan, New Jersey, New York, Ohio, Pennsylvania, and South Carolina)
Third Monday	Robert E. Lee's birthday (Alabama, Arkansas, Florida, Georgia, Louisiana, Mississippi, North Carolina, South Carolina, Texas (Confederate Heroes Day), and Virginia (Lee-Jackson Day)
20	Inauguration Day (observed in the District of Columbia every fourth year)
26	Admission day in Michigan (1837)
	General Douglas MacArthur Day in Arkansas
29	Admission day in Kansas (1861)

FEBRUARY

1	National Freedom Day (to commemorate the signing of the Thirteenth Amendment, abolishing slavery, 1865)

3 Four Chaplains Memorial Day (in memory of the clergymen of four faiths who perished with their sinking ship in World War II)

6 Ratification day in Massachusetts (1788)

12 Lincoln's Birthday (Alaska, California, Connecticut, Florida, Illinois, Indiana, Kansas, Maryland, Missouri; Montana, New Mexico, New York, Utah, Vermont, Washington, and West Virginia. In Delaware and Oregon it is celebrated on February 1; in Arizona on February 8.)

Georgia Day in that state

14 Admission day in Arizona (1912) and Oregon (1859)

Third Monday George Washington's Birthday (observed in all states; called Lincoln-Washington Day in Ohio, South Dakota, Texas, Wisconsin, and Wyoming, and President's Day in Hawaii and Minnesota)

MARCH

1 Admission day in Nebraska (1867) and Ohio (1803)

2 Texas Independence Day

3 Admission day in Florida (1845)

4 Admission day in Vermont (1791)

First Tuesday Town Meeting day in Vermont

15 Andrew Jackson's birthday observed in Tennessee; admission day in Maine (1820)

17 Evacuation Day in Suffolk County, Massachusetts (British leaving Boston, 1776)

25 Maryland Day in that state

26 Kuhio Day in Hawaii (Honah Kuhio Kalanianole, delegate to U.S. Congress, 1902–22)

Last Monday Seward's Day in Alaska

APRIL

12 Anniversary of signing Halifax Resolves, in North Carolina

13 Thomas Jefferson's birthday, in Alabama

14 Pan American Day

19 Patriots Day, in Massachusetts and Maine

21 San Jacinto Day in Texas (Sam Houston–Santa Anna battle on the banks of the San Jacinto River, 1836)

22 Ratification day in Oklahoma (1907)

Last Monday Confederate Memorial Day (Florida, Georgia, and Mississippi)

23 Confederate Memorial Day in Alabama

28 Ratification day in Maryland (1788)

30 Admission day in Louisiana (1812)

MAY

1 Law Day

4 Independence Day for Rhode Island

7 VE Day (Victory in Europe)

8 Harry Truman's birthday, observed in Missouri

10 Confederate Memorial Day in North and South Carolina

11 Admission day in Minnesota (1858)

18 Primary Election day in Pennsylvania

Third Saturday Armed Forces Day (replaces Army, Navy, and Air Force Days)

22 National Maritime Day

23 Ratification day for South Carolina (1788)

28 Confederate Memorial Day in Virginia

29 Admission day in Wisconsin (1848); ratification day for Rhode Island (1790)

Last Monday Memorial Day (observed in all states except Mississippi and South Carolina)

JUNE

1 Admission day in Kentucky (1792) and Tennessee (1796)

3 Confederate Memorial Day in Louisiana; Jefferson Davis's Birthday in Florida and Georgia (celebrated in Mississippi on the first Monday in June)

11 Kamehameha I Day in Hawaii (Kamehameha the Great, ruler of all the Hawaiian islands, 1810)

14	Flag Day (observed in all states; a legal holiday in Pennsylvania)
15	Admission day in Arkansas (1836)
17	Bunker Hill Day in Suffolk County, Massachusetts
20	Admission day in West Virginia (1863)
21	Ratification day in New Hampshire (1788)
25	Ratification day in Virginia (1788)

JULY

3	Admission day in Idaho (1890)
4	Independence Day (observed in all states)
10	Admission day in Wyoming (1890)
24	Pioneer Day in Utah
25	Commonwealth Day in Puerto Rico (1952)
26	Ratification day in New York (1788)

AUGUST

First Monday	Colorado Day (admitted 1876)
Second Monday	VJ Day (Victory in Japan)
10	Admission day in Missouri (1821)
14	World War II Memorial Day
16	Bennington Battle Day in Vermont
Third Friday	Admission day in Hawaii (1959)
19	National Aviation Day
27	Lyndon B. Johnson's birthday, observed in Texas
30	Huey Long's birthday, observed in Louisiana

SEPTEMBER

First Monday	Labor Day (all states)
9	Admission day in California (1850)
13	Defenders' Day in Maryland

14	Primary Election day in Wisconsin
17	Citizenship Day (replaces I Am an American Day and Constitution Day)
Fourth Friday	American Indian Day

OCTOBER

Second Monday	Pioneers Day in South Dakota
Second Monday	Columbus Day (Arizona, California, Connecticut, District of Columbia, Florida, Georgia, Hawaii, Idaho, Illinois, Indiana, Kansas, Maine, Massachusetts, Minnesota, Missouri, Montana, Nevada, New Hampshire, New Jersey, New Mexico, New York, North Carolina, Ohio, Pennsylvania, Rhode Island, South Dakota, Tennessee, Texas, Vermont, Virginia, West Virginia, Wisconsin, Wyoming, Puerto Rico. Observed on October 12 in Maryland and Ohio. Referred to as Discover's Day in Hawaii and Landing Day in Wisconsin.)
11	General Pulaski, Memorial Day in Indiana
18	Alaska Day in that state
24	United Nations Day
31	Nevada Day in that state (admitted 1864)

NOVEMBER

First Tuesday after First Monday	General Election Day (Delaware, Florida, Georgia, Hawaii, Illinois, Indiana, Louisiana, Maryland, Missouri, Montana, New Hampshire, New Jersey, New York, North Dakota, Pennsylvania, Tennessee, Virginia, Wisconsin, and Wyoming)
2	Admission day in North Dakota (1889) and South Dakota (1889)
8	Admission day in Montana (1889)
11	Veterans' Day (Armistice Day), all states; admission day in Washington (1889)
12	Elizabeth Cady Stanton Day
16	Admission day in Oklahoma (1907)
21	Ratification day in North Carolina (1789)
25	John F. Kennedy Day in Massachusetts
Fourth Thursday	Thanksgiving Day, all states

DECEMBER

3 Admission day in Illinois (1818)

7 Pearl Harbor Day; ratification day in Delaware (1787)

10 Admission day in Mississippi (1817); Wyoming Day in that state

11 Admission day in Indiana (1816)

12 Ratification day in Pennsylvania (1787)

14 Admission day in Alabama (1819)

15 Bill of Rights Day

18 Ratification day in New Jersey (1787)

21 Forefathers' Day (Landing on Plymouth Rock in 1620)

25 Christmas Day (all states)

28 Admission day in Iowa (1846)

29 Admission day in Texas (1845)

Index

Abigail Adams (Stuart) (painting), 32
Adams, Abigail, 32–33
Adams, John, 13, 14, 22, 28, 29,
    32–33, 232
  defense of Redcoats by, 12
Adams, John Quincy, 234
Adams, Samuel, 14, 16
Agricultural Administration, 186
Air Force, U.S., 207
Alamo, battle of, 86
Aldrin, Edwin E., 226
Alexander Hamilton (Trumbull)
    (painting), 52
Allen, Ethan, 14, 254
"America" (Smith), 88
"America, the Beautiful" (Bates), 153
"American Creed, The" (Page), 170
American Expeditionary Forces, 166,
    172
Andrew Hamilton (Cogswell)
    (painting), 9
Andrew Jackson (Fowler), (painting),
    85
Anthony, Susan B., 140
Antietam, battle of, 112
Apotheosis of Washington (Brumid),
    xxi
Appomattox, surrender at, 121–122
Armed Freedom, xxi
Armstrong, Neil A., 226
Army Air Corps, U.S., 207
Arnold, Henry Harley "Hap," 198
Arthur, Chester Alan, 242
Attucks, Crispus, 12
Awards and decorations, 258–259

"Barbara Frietchie" (Whittier), 102,
    103
Barbara Frietchie (Wyeth) (painting),
    102
Barbary States, American war against,
    75, 76
Barrett, James, 20
Bartholdi, Frédéric Auguste, 147–148
Bassett, Richard, 56
Bates, Katherine Lee, 153
"Battle Cry of Freedom" (Root), 111
"Battle Hymn of the Republic"
    (Howe), 111
Battle of Lexington, The (Tiebout),
    19
Beanes, William, 77
Bedford flag, 252
Beecher, Henry Ward, 108, 109
Bell, Alexander Graham, 140
Benjamin Franklin (Martin)
    (painting), 50
Bennett, Henry Holcomb, 137
Bennington flag, 254
Benton, Thomas Hart, 82
Bicknell, Francis, 113
Bingham, George Caleb, 80
Birth of Our Nation's Flag, The
    (Weisgerber), 42
Bixby, Mrs., Lincoln's letter to, 117
Black Friday, 11
Black Thursday, 180
Blount, William, 57
"Blue and the Gray, The" (Finch),
    118
Boone, Daniel, 80
Booth, John Wilkes, 127
Boston, Revolutionary War in, 12–14
Boston Massacre, 12
"Boston Massacre," The (Revere), 12
Boston Navy Yard, 74
Boston Tea Party, 13, 35
Bowie, Jim, 86
Boy Lincoln, The (Johnson), 91
Braddock, Thomas, 22–24
Bradley, Omar Nelson, 198
Brady, Mathew, 105, 130

Brandywine, battle of, 41, 43
Brave Men (Pyle), 203
Brearley, David, 54
Breed's Hill, fight at, 16, 252
Brown, John, 100–101
Brumid, Constantino, xxi
Buchanan, James, 239
Buffalo Bill, 143, 162–163
"Building of the Ship, The"
    (Longfellow), 108
Buntline, Ned, 163
Burr, Aaron, 52, 72
Butler, Pierce, 57
Butterfield Overland Trail, 78
Byrd, Richard E., 178

Calendar for Americans, 260–265
California, acquisition of, 78
Capitol, U.S., xxi
  Statuary Hall of, xxi
Captain Nathan Hale (Pratt) (statue)
    40
Carmichael, William, 73
Carrington, Edward, 73
Carter, Jimmy (James Earl), 250
Centennial Exposition (Philadelphia),
    37, 140, 147
  Grant's speech at, 143–145
Chappel, Alonzo, 7, 15, 75
Chesapeake Bay, battle of, 77
Chicago World's Fair (1893),
    142–143, 163
  postage stamps issued for, 5
Christopher Columbus (Piombo)
    (painting), 2
Christy, Howard Chandler, 53
Churchill, Winston, 219
Civilian Conservation Corps, 186
Civil War, 78
  Appomattox surrender in, 121–122
  battles of, 112, 114
  Confederate defeat in, 104, 119,
    123
  heroes in, 100–103
  secessionist movement before, 96
  slavery question in, 92
  songs about, 110–111, 124
  Union generals in, 106–107
Clark, William, 78
Cleveland, Grover, 148, 242
Clipper ships, 89
Coates, F. Graham, 168
Cody, William Frederick, 143,
    162–163
Cogswell, William, 9
Cohan, George M., 175
Collins, Michael, 226
Colonial period, 11–13
Columbian exposition, 142–143, 163
  postage stamps issued for, 5
Columbia space shuttle, 228–229
Columbus, Christopher, 2–4
  commemoration of, 5
"Columbus" (Miller), 4
Commodore Dewey on the Bridge of
    the Flagship Olympia at the
    Battle of Manila Bay (Zogbaum),
    150
Commodore Perry (Meyer) (painting),
    75
Common Sense (Paine), 44, 45
Composition (Davis), 187
Concord, battle of, 14, 19–20
"Concord Hymn" (Emerson), 20
Confederate Battle flag, 255
Confederate States of America, 123
Congress, First Continental, 13, 14, 29
Congress, Second Continental, 28, 34,
    42, 252, 254
Congress, U.S., 34
Constitution, U.S., xix, 34, 51, 52, 58
  amendments to, 58–59, 112, 114, 179

framers of, 54–57
  text of, 54–57
  writing of, 53
Constitution, USS (Old Ironsides),
    74, 76
Constitutional Convention, 53
Continental Army, 22, 34, 48
Coolidge, Calvin, 176, 246
Cooper, Washington B., 86
Copley, John Singleton, 29, 33
Corliss steam engine, 140, 144, 145
Cornwallis, Lord, 47–48
Cosby, William, 8
Cowboys, history of, 161
Cowpens flag, 254
Cowpuncher, The (Remington), 160
Crawford, Robert McArthur, 207
Crisis, The (Paine), 44, 45–46
Crockett, Davy, 86
Cumberland Gap, trail over, 80
Currier, N., 13
Currier and Ives, 134

Daniel Boone Escorting Settlers
    through the Cumberland Gap
    (Bingham), 80–81
Daniel Webster (unknown)
    (painting), 88
Davis, Jefferson, xxi, 124, 125
  last message of, 123–124
Davis, Stuart, 187
Davy Crockett (Osgood) (painting),
    86
Dawes, William, 14, 16
Decatur, Stephen, 75
Declaration of Independence, 28, 34,
    35, 69, 73
  signers of, 30
  text of, 28–31
  writing of, 28, 69
Decorations and awards, 258–259
"Defense of Fort McHenry, The"
    (Key), 77
De Laboulaye, Edouard, 147
DeLand, Clyde O., 6
Delaware River, Washington's
    crossing of, 37–39
Dempsey, Jack, 178, 179
Destruction of Tea at Boston Harbor,
    The (Currier), 13
de Triana, Rodrigo, 3
Dewey, George, 150, 151
Dickinson, John, 56
"Dixie" (Emmett), 124
Douglas, Stephen, 92, 93
Drayton, Jonathan, 53

East India Company, 13
Eiffel, Gustave, 147
Eisenhower, Dwight David:
  as general, 195
  as president, 216, 248
  presidential farewell address of,
    216–218
"El Capitan" (Sousa), 136, 137
Ellis Island, 131
Emancipation Proclamation (Lincoln),
    112–113
Emerson, Ralph Waldo, 20, 135, 164
Emmett, Daniel Decatur, 124
Evans, Rudulph, 71
Explorers Meriwether Lewis and
    William Clark (Remington)
    (painting), 79

Federalist Papers, 52
Federal Theatre, 187
Ferris, Jean L. G., 91
Few, William, 57
Fillmore, Millard, 238

Finch, Francis Miles, 118
Flag, U.S., 252
  largest, 138–139
  rules for display of, 255
"Flag Goes By, The" (Bennett), 137
Flags:
  historical, 252–255
  state, 256–257
Florida, territory of, 78
Flying Cloud (Sheppard), 89
Ford, Gerald Rudolph, 250
Ford's Theater, 127
Forgy, Howell M., 207
Fort McHenry, 77, 255
Fort Sumter, attack on, 96
Fort Ticonderoga, capture of, 14, 254
Fourth of July (Moses), 164
Fowler, Trevor Thomas, 85
Franco-American Union, 147
Franklin, Benjamin, 28, 29, 41, 44,
    53, 74, 140
  Constitutional Convention speech
    of, 50–51
Fraunces Tavern, 48
Freedom from Fear (Rockwell), 191
Freedom from Want (Rockwell), 191
Freedom of Speech (Rockwell), 190
Freedom of Worship (Rockwell), 190
French, Daniel Chester, 20, 127,
    134–135
French and Indian War, 11, 14, 47
Frietchie, Barbara, 102–103

Gadsden Strip, acquisition of, 78
Gage, Thomas, 14, 16
Gall, Gilbert, 40
Garfield, James Abram, 241
General George Washington resigning
    his commission as commander in
    chief (Trumbull) (painting), 48
General Pershing (Volk) (painting),
    172
George III, King of England, 13, 28
George Washington (Stuart)
    (painting), 27
George Washington takes the
    Presidential oath (unknown)
    (painting), 60
Germantown, battle of, 41, 43
Gettysburg, battle of, 114
Gettysburg Address (Lincoln),
    116–117, 127
Gounod, Charles, 147
Grand Canyon, The (Moran)
    (painting), 154–155
Grandma Moses Going to the Big
    City (Moses), 165
Grand Union flag, 42, 254
Grant, Ulysses Simpson, 107, 140,
    240
  Lee's surrender to, 121–122
  Philadelphia Centennial speech of,
    143–145
Grasse, François de, 47, 74
Great Britain:
  Revolutionary War against, 11–49
  in War of 1812, 76, 77
Great Depression, 180
  Roosevelt's administration in,
    180–187
Green Mountains flag, 254
Guerin, Jules, 127
Guillaume, Louis M. D., 121
Guthrie, Woody, 187

Hale, Nathan, 40
Halsey, William Frederick, 196
Hamilton, Alexander, 52, 53, 63
Hamilton, Andrew, 8
  Zenger defense speech by, 8–10
Hancock, John, 14, 16, 29

266

Harding, Warren Gamaliel, 176, 245
Harlem Heights, Washington's
    encampment at, 40
Harpers Ferry, fight at, 100
Harrison, Benjamin, 243
Harrison, William Henry, 75, 236
Hayes, Rutherford Birchard, 241
Hayne, Robert, 87
Henry, Patrick, 14
    Virginia House of Burgesses speech,
    15–16
Hessians, 36, 37
Historical events, calendar of,
    260–265
Hitler, Adolf, 188
Holmes, Oliver Wendell, 74, 76
Homecoming G.I., The (Rockwell)
    (painting), 206
"Home on the Range," 161
Homer, Winston, 110
Hoover, Herbert, 77, 176, 181, 246
Hostages, held by Iran, 226, 227
Houston, Sam, 86
Hovenden, Thomas, 100
Howe, Julia Ward, 111
Howe, William, 36
Hunt, Richard, 148

"I Am an American" (Lieberman),
    171
"I Hear America Singing"
    (Whitman), 135
Immigration to America, 131–133
Independence and the Opening of
    the West (Benton), 82
Independence Hall, 34, 35, 141, 255
Independence National Park, 35
Indiana, settlement of, 79
Ingersoll, Jared, 55
Isabella, Queen of Spain, 3
Iwo Jima, flag raising at, 202

Jackson, Andrew, 85, 235
Jarvis, John W., 75
Jefferson, Thomas, 29, 52, 63, 69, 83,
    233
    Declaration of Independence
    drafted by, 28
    election of, 73
    inaugural address of, 69–73
Jefferson Davis (Sartain) (painting),
    125
Jefferson Memorial, 71, 72
John Adams (Copley) (painting), 33
John Hancock (Copley) (painting), 29
John Paul Jones aboard the
    Bonhomme Richard (Stahl)
    (painting), 74
Johnson, Andrew, 240
Johnson, Eastman, 91
Johnson, Lyndon Baines, 249
Johnson, Thomas, 22
Jones, John Paul, 74, 254

Keene, Laura, 127
Kennedy, John Fitzgerald, 219–220,
    248
    assassination of, 223
    inaugural address of, 220–223
Key, Francis Scott, 77, 255
King, Ernest Joseph, 197
King, Martin Luther, Jr., 223
King, Rufus, 54
Knox, Henry, 48
Korean War, 208
Kosciusko, Thaddeus, 41

Lafayette, Marquis de, 41, 48
Lafayette (Peale) (painting), 41
Lake Placid Olympic Games, 226, 227
Landing of Roger Williams
    (Chappel), 7
Langdon, John, 54
Last Moments of John Brown, The
    (Hovenden), 101
Lazarus, Emma, 149
Leaves of Grass (Whitman), 135
Lee, Henry, 63
Lee, Robert E., 100, 114, 122
    farewell speech to army of, 122

surrender to Grant of, 121–122
Lee Surrendering to Grant
    (Guillaume) (painting), 121
Lend-lease bill, 188
Leutze, Emanuel, 37, 39
Lewis, Meriwether, 78
Lexington, battle of, 14, 16, 19–20
Liberty bell, 1, 35
Liberty Pole, 11
Lieberman, Elias, 171
Lincoln, Abraham, xxi, 90–99, 119,
    239, 255, 258
    assassination of, 127
    first inaugural address of, 96–99
    Gettysburg Address of, 116–117,
    127
    letter to Mrs. Bixby of, 117
    second inaugural address of, 120,
    127
    slavery speech of, 92–95
    Springfield, Illinois farewell speech
    of, 95
Lincoln and his generals (Brady)
    (photograph), 105
Lincoln Memorial, 126, 127–129
Lindbergh, Charles A., 179
Lister, Thomas, 35
Livingstone, Robert R., 28, 29, 62
Loesser, Frank, 207
Longfellow, Henry Wadsworth, 18,
    108
Long Island, battle of, 36, 40
Louisiana Purchase, 62, 73, 78, 83
Louisiana Purchase Exposition, 143,
    145
Lusitania, sinking of, 166

MacArthur, Douglas, 196, 208–209
    Truman's dismissal of, 208
    West Point speech of, 209–213
McCauley, Mary, 40
McClellan, George B., 106, 119
McHenry, James, 56
McKinley, William, 143, 151, 243
Madison, Dolley, 77
Madison, James, 56, 77, 233
Maine, U.S. battleship, 150, 151
"Marines' Hymn," 174
Marshall, George Catlett, 198, 199
Marshall, John, 35
Martha Washington (Stuart)
    (painting), 26
Martin, David, 50
Massachusetts, Puritan settlements in,
    6, 7
Matteson, Tompkins Harrison, 6
Mayflower Compact, 6
Meade, George Gordon, 107, 114
Medal of Honor, Congressional, 258
Mexican War, 78, 86
Meyer, Henry, 75
Midnight Ride of Paul Revere
    (Wood), 17
Mifflin, Thomas, 55
Miller, Joaquin, 4
Mills, Robert, 67
Minute Man of Concord (French), 20,
    127
Minutemen, 14, 16, 19–20, 252
Molly Pitcher at Monmouth (Gall),
    40
Monmouth, N.J., battle at, 40
Monroe, James, 44, 83–85, 234
Monroe Doctrine, 83–85
Monticello, 70
Moon landing, 226
Moran, Thomas, 155
Morgan, Daniel, 254
Mormon Trail, 78
Morse, Samuel F. B., 157
Moses, Anna Mary Robertson
    ("Grandma"), 164–165
Mosher, Hugh, 37
Mount Vernon, 60, 64
Mount Vernon Ladies Association, 64
"My Country, 'tis of Thee" (Smith),
    88

"National Flag, The" (Beecher),
    108–109
National Recovery Administration,
    186

National Women's Party, 177
Navigation Acts, 11
Navy, Continental, 74
"New Colossus, The" (Lazarus), 149
New Deal, 186–187
New York, Revolutionary War in, 11,
    47, 48
New-York Weekly Journal, 8
New York World, 148
New York World's Fair (1940), 143
New York World's Fair (1964–65),
    143
Niagara, 75
Niagara Falls (Morse) (painting),
    156–157
Nimitz, Chester William, 197
Nina, 3
Nineteenth Amendment, 177
Nixon, Richard Milhous, 249
North Church, 16
Northwest Ordinance, 78

Oakley, Annie, 163
"O Captain! My Captain!"
    (Whitman), 102, 130
"Off We Go into the Wild Blue
    Yonder" (Crawford), 207
O'Hara, Charles, 48
Ohio, settlement of, 79
"Old Ironsides" (Holmes), 76
Old Ironsides (USS Constitution), 74,
    76
Olympia, USS, 151
One Third of a Nation, 187
Operation Sail, 225
Oregon Trail, 78
Osgood, S. S., 86
Otis, Sam, 14
Our American Cousin, 127
"Over There" (Cohan), 175

Page, William Tyler, 170
Paine, Thomas, 44
    Common Sense, 44, 45
    The Crisis, 44, 45–46
Pan American Exposition, 143
Paris, Treaty of (1783), 78
Pass and Stow foundry, 35
Patrick Henry (Chappel) (painting),
    15
Patton, George Smith, 196
"Paul Revere's Ride" (Longfellow),
    17–18
Peale, Charles Wilson, 23, 24, 41
Pearl Harbor, attack on, 192, 195, 207
Pennsylvania, Revolutionary War in,
    22, 28, 34, 35, 43
Pennsylvania, University of, 51
Pennsylvania Gazette, 50
Pennsylvania Historical Society, 42
Perry, Oliver Hazard, 75
    flag used by, 255
Pershing, John Joseph, 166, 172–173
Philadelphia, Revolutionary War in,
    22, 28, 34, 35
Philip, John W., 151
Pickett, George E., 114
Pierce, Franklin, xxi, 238
Pilgrims at Plymouth (DeLand), 6
Pinta, 3
Pitcairn, John, 19
Pitcher, Molly, 40
Polk, James Knox, 237
Poor Richard's Almanack, 50
Postage stamps, issued for Columbian
    Exposition, 5
"Praise the Lord and Pass the
    Ammunition!" (Loesser), 207
Pratt, Bela Lyon, 40
Prescott, Samuel, 14, 16
President, office of U.S., 231
Presidential seal, 230
President Lincoln reading the first
    draft of the Emancipation
    Proclamation to his Cabinet
    (Bicknell) (painting), 113
Presidents, list of, 232–251
Press freedom, 8–10
Prohibition, 177
Promontory, Utah, joining of railroads
    at, 78
Providence, colony of, 7

Pulaski, Count, 41
Pulitzer, Joseph, 148
Puritans, 7
Pyle, Ernie, 203

Quartering Act, 11

Rattlesnake flag, 42, 254
Read, W. G., 152
Reagan, Ronald Wilson, 251
Redcoats, 11, 12, 14, 16, 19, 20, 36,
    252
Religious freedom, 7
Remington, Frederic, 77, 161
Revere, Paul, 12
    midnight ride of, 14, 16–18
Revolutionary War:
    battles in, 14, 16–20, 36, 40
    Declaration of Independence and,
    28–33
    heroes of, 40–41
    origins of, 11–13
    Treaty of Paris for, 78
    Valley Forge retreat during, 43
    Washington as general in, 22–28,
    48–49
    Yorktown surrender in, 47–48
Rhode Island, 53
    flag of, 252
    founding of, 7
Roaring Twenties, 176–179
Rockwell, Norman, 190, 204, 206
Roosevelt, Franklin Delano, 247
    declaration of war of, 193–194
    fireside chat of, 184–185
    Four Freedoms speech of, 188–191
    inaugural address of, 180–183
    New Deal program of, 186–187
Roosevelt, Theodore, 181, 244
    San Juan Hill charge of, 152
Root, George Frederick, 111
Rosie the Riveter (Rockwell)
    (painting), 204
Ross, Betsy, 42, 252, 254
Rough Riders' charge up San Juan
    Hill (Read) (painting), 152
Rush, Benjamin, 72
Ruth, George Herman (Babe), 179

Saint-Gaudens, Augustus, 134–135
Sam Houston (Cooper) (painting), 86
San Francisco World's Fair (1939),
    143
San Jacinto, battle of, 86
San Juan Hill, Roosevelt's charge up,
    152
San Salvador, 3
Santa Anna, Antonio de, 86
Santa Fe Trail, 78
Santa Maria, 3
Sartain, William, 125
Savannah, battle of, 41
Scene at the Signing of the
    Constitution of the United
    States (Christy), 53
Schuckburg, Richard, 21
Sebastiano del Piombo, 2
"Semper Fidelis" (Sousa), 136, 137
Serapis, 74
Sharpshooter of the Army of the
    Potomac, A (Homer) (painting),
    110
Sheppard, J. Warren, 89
Sherman, Roger, 28, 29, 54
Sherman, William Tecumseh, 106,
    140
Short, William, 73
Significance of the Frontier in
    American History, The (Turner),
    82
Signing of the Declaration
    (Trumbull), 29
Signing the Social Compact in the
    Cabin of the Mayflower
    (Matteson), 6
Sitting Bull, 163
Smith, John Stafford, 77
Smith, Samuel Francis, 88
Sons of Liberty, 11, 12, 14
Sousa, John Philip, 136–137
Southwest, acquisition of, 78

space program, American, 226, 228–229
Spaight, Richard Dobbs, 57
Spanish-American War, 150–152
Spirit of St. Louis, 179
Spirit of '76, The (Willard), 37
Spokane World's Fair (1974), 143
Stahl, Ben, 74
Stamp Act, 11, 14
Stark, John, 254
"Stars and Stripes Forever, The" (Sousa), 136
Star-spangled Banner flag, 255
"Star-spangled Banner, The" (Key), 77
Statuary Hall of Capitol, xxi
Statue of Liberty, 146–149
Stephen Decatur (Alonzo Chappel) (painting), 75
Steuben, Baron Friederich Wilhelm von, 41, 43
Stevenson, Adlai E., 214–215
Stock Market, crash of, 179
Stowe, Harriet Beecher, 109
Stuart, Gilbert, 25–27, 32
Sugar Act, 11
Supreme Court, U.S., xxii, 34
Surrender of Lord Cornwallis at Yorktown, The (Trumbull), 47

Taft, William Howard, xxii, 244
Taylor, Zachary, 237
Texas, Republic of, 78, 86
Thanksgiving Turkey (Moses), 165
Thirteenth Amendment, 112
"This Land Is Your Land" (Guthrie), 187
Thomas Jefferson (Evans) (painting), 71
Thorton, William, xxi
Tiebout, Cornelius, 19

Tilden, Bill, 178, 179
"To Anacreon in Heaven" (Smith), 77
Travis, William B., 86
Trenton, battle of, 37
Tripoli, American war against, 75
Truman, Harry S, 247
    MacArthur's dismissal by, 208
Trumbull, John, 29, 47, 48, 52
Tuckerman, Salisbury, 76
Turner, Frederick Jackson, 82
Tyler, John, 236

Underground Railway, 100
Union Pacific and Central Pacific railroads, joining of, 78
USS *Arizona* memorial, 194
USS Constitution (Tuckerman), 76

Valley Forge, 41, 43
Van Buren, Martin, 235
Vernon, Edward, 64
Vespucci, Amerigo, 3
Vicksburg, fall of, 114
Vietnam War, 224–225
Vietnam War Memorial, The, 225
Villa, Pancho, 172
Virginia, Revolutionary War in, 28, 47
Virginia, University of, 70, 72
Virginia House of Burgesses, 14
Volk, Douglas, 172
von Steuben, Baron Friederich Wilhelm, 41, 43

Wainwright, Jonathan Mayhew, 197
Walt Whitman (Brady) (photograph), 130
Ward, Samuel A., 153

War of 1812, 76, 77
Washington, George, 22–24, 53, 140, 143, 232
    battle of Long Island, site of, 36
    Crossing the Delaware, 37–39
    farewell address of, 63–68
    as general, 22–28, 40, 41, 43, 44, 47–49, 52, 254, 258
    inaugural address of, 61–62
    letter to Martha Washington of, 25
    Mount Vernon home of, 60, 64
    as president, 60–68
    resignation as general of, 48–49
    Stuart's portrait of, 27, 77
Washington, Lawrence, 64
Washington, Martha, 25
    Stuart's portrait of, 26
Washington (at forty by Peale) (painting), 24
Washington (full-length portrait by Peale) (painting), 23
Washington Crossing the Delaware (Leutze), 37–39
Washington Cruisers, flag of, 254
Washington Monument, 67
Waskow, Henry T., 203
Webster, Daniel, 87
    speech on the Union, 87–88
Weisgerber, Charles H., 42
West, American, 78–79
"When the Warrior Returns" (Keyes), 77
White House, xx
Whitman, Walt, 102, 130, 135
Whittier, John Greenleaf, 102, 103
"Wild Blue Yonder" (Crawford), 207
Wild West Show, 163
Willard, Archibald M., 37
Willard, Samuel, 37
Williams, Roger, 7
Wilson, James, 55
Wilson, Woodrow, 136, 173, 176, 245

declaration of war from, 166–168
Wood, Grant, 17
Woodrow Wilson (Coates) (painting), 168
Works Program, 186
World fairs, American, 140–146
World's Industrial and Cotton Centennial, 142
World War I:
    American involvement in, 166, 170
    heroes in, 172–173
    songs about, 174
    Wilson's declaration of war in, 166–169
World War II:
    American commanders in, 195–198
    American involvement in, 188, 199–203
    domestic war effort in, 204–205
    Pearl Harbor attack in, 192, 195, 207
    Roosevelt administration in, 188–194
    songs about, 207
Wyeth, N. C., 102

"Yankee Doodle," 21
"Yankee Doodle Boy, The" (Cohan), 175
"Yankee Doodle Dandy" (Cohan), 175
York, Alvin C., 173
Yorktown, surrender at, 21, 41, 47–48, 74
Young, Brigham, 78
Young Abraham Lincoln (Ferris) (painting), 91

Zenger, John Peter, 8–10
Zogbaum, Rufus, 150